OUTDOOR PASTIMES OF AN AMERICAN HUNTER

Theodore Roosevelt

OUTDOOR PASTIMES

OF AN

AMERICAN HUNTER

BY

THEODORE ROOSEVELT

ILLUSTRATED

STACKPOLE BOOKS
THE CLASSICS OF AMERICAN SPORT SERIES

Printed in the United States of America

10 9 8 7 6 5 4 3

Stackpole Books wishes to thank Wallace Finley Dailey for his help in identifying Roosevelt's children shown in the photographs in Chapter XI. Mr. Dailey is the curator for the Theodore Roosevelt Collection at the Houghton Library at Harvard University.

Cover design by Tracy Patterson
Cover illustration by Dan Andreasen

Library of Congress Cataloging-in-Publication Data

Roosevelt, Theodore, 1858–1919.
    Outdoor pastimes of an American hunter / by Theodore Roosevelt.
        p.   cm.
    Reprint. With new foreword.
    ISBN 0-8117-3033-6 : $16.95
    1. Hunting—West (U.S.) I. Title
SK45.R748   1990
799.2973—dc20   90-9884
                                                                            CIP

TO

JOHN BURROUGHS

DEAR OOM JOHN:—Every lover of outdoor life must feel a sense of affectionate obligation to you. Your writings appeal to all who care for the life of the woods and the fields, whether their tastes keep them in the homely, pleasant farm country or lead them into the wilderness. It is a good thing for our people that you should have lived; and surely no man can wish to have more said of him.

I wish to express my hearty appreciation of your warfare against the sham nature-writers—those whom you have called "the yellow journalists of the woods." From the days of Æsop to the days of Reinecke Fuchs, and from the days of Reinecke Fuchs to the present time, there has been a distinct and attractive place in literature for those who write avowed fiction in which the heroes are animals with human or semi-human attributes. This fiction serves a useful purpose in many ways, even in the way of encouraging people to take the right view of outdoor life and outdoor creatures; but it is unpardonable for any observer of nature to write fiction and then publish it as truth, and he who exposes and wars against such action is entitled to respect and support. You in your own person have illustrated what can be done by the lover of nature who has trained himself to keen observation, who describes accurately what is thus observed, and who, finally, possesses the additional gift of writing with charm and interest.

You were with me on one of the trips described in this volume, and I trust that to look over it will recall the pleasant days we spent together.

Your friend,

THEODORE ROOSEVELT.

THE WHITE HOUSE, October 2, 1905.

FOREWORD

As a sporting writer and naturalist—a man in two fields that have diverged all too far in modern America—Theodore Roosevelt was among the finest in American history. *Outdoor Pastimes of an American Hunter* is important proof of that reputation.

First produced in 1905, this book is said to have been the first ever published by a president while he was in the White House. However, Roosevelt already had established himself as one of the nation's leading writers on outdoor sports, and I think it quite likely that, had he done nothing else in his life but write his superb books on nature and hunting—never served in the military, never held public office, never written on other subjects—he would be only slightly less famous today among enthusiasts of sporting literature. His books are that good.

Roosevelt wrote three major works on hunting and outdoor life before this one: *Hunting Trips of a Ranchman* (1885), *Ranch Life and the Hunting Trail* (1888), and *The Wilderness Hunter* (1893). These three often are viewed by his biographers as his great "hunting trilogy," because the dates of their publication more or less span the period of his most active involvement in ranching and western adventure.

But seeing them as separate from his other outdoor writings does not do justice to the greater whole of his work. By the time *Outdoor Pastimes* appeared in 1905, he also had co-edited (with the great conservationist George Bird Grinnell) a series of classic hunting books for the Boone and Crockett Club and had contributed a number of chapters to other works. In fact, some of his contributions, those to the British *Cyclopedia of Sport,* were collected in a small book, *Some American Game* (1897). And of course *Outdoor Pastimes* was followed by other milestone volumes, including *African Game Trails* (1910), *Through the Brazilian Wilderness* (1914), and *A Book Lover's Holiday in the Open* (1916). After his death, Roosevelt's many writings on the outdoors and other subjects were gathered in a variety of forms, so don't be surprised to find a book by Roosevelt with a title not included here.

In a way, *Outdoor Pastimes* bridges the two eras of Roosevelt's outdoor career. Parts of it are the result of his experiences in the 1880s and 1890s, when he had the time and energy to roam the great western game lands, sometimes for several weeks at a stretch, absorbing the mood and spirit of the country as he gloried in the excitement and adventure of the hunt. Other parts of it were the result of more hurried trips, the kind a busy world leader could fit in here and there.

Like all of Roosevelt's American hunting books, *Outdoor Pastimes* is more a series of extended vignettes, each independent of the rest, than a single, long narrative. Even when Roosevelt was planning to eventually gather his work into a book, he wrote what essentially were long articles, as many of those that appear in this book had been. For that reason, feel no obligation to begin at the beginning. I own all of Roosevelt's hunting books, and I can't think of any of the American ones that I have read from front to back. Somehow it's just as satisfying to drop in here and there as the mood strikes.

However you choose to read *Outdoor Pastimes*, you're in for some surprises if you've never read Roosevelt before. For one thing, he was a true hunter–naturalist, and any story about hunting was a good opportunity for a digression on other things he saw on his outings. Indeed, some chapters are far more natural history than hunting. But even when he is not speaking directly of hunting, you will frequently hear the hunter's interests coming through in the natural history.

Some readers also may be surprised by the intensity and sophistication of Roosevelt's discussions of conservation. We now know much more about the animals he observed than was known in his day, and he has been proven wrong here and there, but all in all, you are about to read the work of an ardent, extraordinarily effective wildlife manager, one who felt and evoked the spiritual and aesthetic values of wild settings as strongly as he preached the protection of those settings. His account of a visit in 1903 to Yellowstone Park, my home, is one of my favorites of the hundreds of Yellowstone stories I've read over the years, though Roosevelt indulged in some shameful wildlife harassment—taking to his horse to chase park elk to exhaustion so he could have a closer look.

There are other surprises too, some a little less simple. Here and there we see him as a sportsman growing up or taking part in the evolution of the sporting tradition. His childhood Adirondack experiences jacklighting deer were common ones in the 1870s but, he notes, of questionable sporting quality. "Coursing" coyotes and pronghorn with dogs, an accepted activity in his time, has largely fallen out of favor, or become illegal. Indeed, Roosevelt lived in one of the most dynamic and eventful eras in American sport, and he witnessed—in fact, influenced—the growth and change of hunting ethics.

One of the nicest surprises is the wonderful essay on big-game books. Roosevelt had one of this country's finest libraries on big game and was a voracious reader. Chapter ten, "Books on Big Game," amounts to a literary tour through the history of hunting in all parts of the world. It was Roosevelt's exhaustive familiarity with the literature on big game that helped him gain the respect of the leading zoologists of his day for his knowledge of wildlife. And it is his frequent asides on international politics, the ethics of hunting, and other topics that make this essay so entertaining.

In some ways Roosevelt was ahead of his time. But for the most part, he was just an unusually vigorous personification of the optimism and enthusiasm of a fascinating era in American history. He knew what mattered, and he never hesitated to say so. Because he had so much to say on so many subjects, he generates strong opinions even today. Some people find him objectionable for his outdated views on race, politics, women, or some other subject; others love him for his adventurous nature and his heroic view of life. *Outdoor Pastimes* captures the strength of character that made him such a provocative figure, just as it shows the extent to which he was undisturbed by his detractors.

But you didn't buy this book to examine its complications. Don't concern yourself with all that, at least not the first time through. Just turn the page. You'll find yourself mounted next to T.R. (don't call him "Teddy"—he didn't like the nickname) in the Colorado mountains. It's well below zero, and the steel in your rifle barrel is too cold to touch. A thick steam is rising from the hunters, horses, and dogs as you all mill around waiting for the hunt to begin. Pull your coat's heavy, rough collar up so it almost touches the brim of your hat, lean back in your saddle, and let Roosevelt do the rest.

Paul Schullery

CONTENTS

xiii

CHAPTER VIII

CHAPTER IX

CHAPTER X

CHAPTER XI

*** Five of these Chapters have been recently written; the others have been revised and added to since they originally appeared in the publications of the Boone and Crockett Club and in Mr. Caspar Whitney's "Deer Family."

ILLUSTRATIONS

** The cuts for Chapter I are from photographs taken by Philip B. Stewart ; those in Chapter II, from photographs taken by Dr. Alexander Lambert and Philip B. Stewart ; those in Chapter III, from photographs taken by Dr. Lambert and Sloan Simpson ; those in Chapter IX were obtained through Major Pitcher ; most of the others are from photographs taken by me or by members of my family.

The photographs in Chapter XI are of the Roosevelt children by Roosevelt's second marriage: Theodore, Jr. (Ted), born 1887; Kermit, 1889; Ethel, 1891; Archibald (Archie), 1894; and Quentin, 1897.

OUTDOOR PASTIMES OF AN AMERICAN HUNTER

CHAPTER I

WITH THE COUGAR HOUNDS

IN January, 1901, I started on a five weeks' cougar hunt from Meeker in Northwest Colorado. My companions were Mr. Philip B. Stewart and Dr. Gerald Webb, of Colorado Springs; Stewart was the captain of the victorious Yale nine of '86. We reached Meeker on January 11th, after a forty mile drive from the railroad, through the bitter winter weather; it was eighteen degrees below zero when we started. At Meeker we met John B. Goff, the hunter, and left town the next morning on horseback for his ranch, our hunting beginning that same afternoon, when after a brisk run our dogs treed a bobcat. After a fortnight Stewart and Webb returned, Goff and I staying out three weeks longer. We did not have to camp out, thanks to the warm-hearted hospitality of the proprietor and manager of the Keystone Ranch, and of the Mathes Brothers and Judge Foreman, both of whose ranches I also visited. The five weeks were spent hunting north of the White River, most of the time in the neighborhood of Coyote Basin and Colorow Mountain. In midwinter, hunting on horseback in the Rockies is

apt to be cold work, but we were too warmly clad to
mind the weather. We wore heavy flannels, jackets lined
with sheepskin, caps which drew down entirely over our
ears, and on our feet heavy ordinary socks, german socks,
and overshoes. Galloping through the brush and among
the spikes of the dead cedars, meant that now and then
one got snagged; I found tough overalls better than
trousers; and most of the time I did not need the jacket,
wearing my old buckskin shirt, which is to my mind a
particularly useful and comfortable garment.

It is a high, dry country, where the winters are usually
very cold, but the snow not under ordinary circumstances
very deep. It is wild and broken in character, the hills
and low mountains rising in sheer slopes, broken by cliffs
and riven by deeply cut and gloomy gorges and ravines.
The sage-brush grows everywhere upon the flats and
hillsides. Large open groves of pinyon and cedar are
scattered over the peaks, ridges, and table-lands. Tall
spruces cluster in the cold ravines. Cottonwoods grow
along the stream courses, and there are occasional patches
of scrub-oak and quaking asp. The entire country is
taken up with cattle ranges wherever it is possible to get
a sufficient water-supply, natural or artificial. Some
thirty miles to the east and north the mountains rise
higher, the evergreen forest becomes continuous, the snow
lies deep all through the winter, and such Northern
animals as the wolverene, lucivee, and snow-shoe rabbit
are found. This high country is the summer home of the
Colorado elk, now woefully diminished in numbers, and
of the Colorado blacktail deer, which are still very plenti-

ful, but which, unless better protected, will follow the elk in the next few decades. I am happy to say that there are now signs to show that the State is waking up to the need of protecting both elk and deer; the few remaining mountain sheep in Colorado are so successfully protected that they are said to be increasing in numbers. In winter both elk and deer come down to the lower country, through a part of which I made my hunting trip. We did not come across any elk, but I have never, even in the old days, seen blacktail more abundant than they were in this region. The bucks had not lost their antlers, and were generally, but not always, found in small troops by themselves; the does, yearlings, and fawns—now almost yearlings themselves—went in bands. They seemed tame, and we often passed close to them before they took alarm. Of course at that season it was against the law to kill them; and even had this not been so none of our party would have dreamed of molesting them.

Flocks of Alaskan long-spurs and of rosy finches flitted around the ranch buildings; but at that season there was not very much small bird life.

The midwinter mountain landscape was very beautiful, whether under the brilliant blue sky of the day, or the starlight or glorious moonlight of the night, or when under the dying sun the snowy peaks, and the light clouds above, kindled into flame, and sank again to gold and amber and sombre purple. After the snow-storms the trees, almost hidden beneath the light, feathery masses, gave a new and strange look to the mountains, as if they were giant masses of frosted silver. Even the storms had a beauty of their own. The keen, cold air, the wonderful scenery, and the interest and excitement of the sport, made our veins thrill and beat with buoyant life.

In cougar hunting the success of the hunter depends absolutely upon his hounds. As hounds that are not perfectly trained are worse than useless, this means that success depends absolutely upon the man who trains and hunts the hounds. Goff was one of the best hunters with whom I have ever been out, and he had trained his pack to a point of perfection for its special work which I have never known another such pack to reach. With the exception of one new hound, which he had just purchased, and of a puppy, which was being trained, not one of the pack would look at a deer even when they were all as keen as mustard, were not on a trail, and when the deer got up but fifty yards or so from them. By the end of the hunt both the new hound and the puppy were entirely trustworthy; of course, Goff can only keep up his pack by continually including new or young dogs with the veterans. As cougar are only plentiful where deer are infinitely more plentiful, the first requisite for a good cougar hound is that it shall leave its natural prey, the deer, entirely alone. Goff's pack ran only bear, cougar, and bobcat. Under no circumstances were they ever permitted to follow elk, deer, antelope or, of course, rabbit. Nor were they allowed to follow a wolf unless it was wounded; for in such a rough country they would at once run out of sight and hearing, and moreover if they did overtake the wolf they would be so scattered as to come

GOFF AND THE PACK

From a photograph by Philip B. Stewart

up singly and probably be overcome one after another. Being bold dogs they were always especially eager after wolf and coyote, and when they came across the trail of either, though they would not follow it, they would usually challenge loudly. If the circumstances were such that they could overtake the wolf in a body, it could make no effective fight against them, no matter how large and powerful. On the one or two occasions when this had occurred, the pack had throttled " Isegrim " without getting a scratch.

As the dogs did all the work, we naturally became extremely interested in them, and rapidly grew to know the voice, peculiarities, and special abilities of each. There were eight hounds and four fighting dogs. The hounds were of the ordinary Eastern type, used from the Adirondacks to the Mississippi and the Gulf in the chase of deer and fox. Six of them were black and tan and two were mottled. They differed widely in size and voice. The biggest, and, on the whole, the most useful, was Jim, a very fast, powerful, and true dog with a great voice. When the animal was treed or bayed, Jim was especially useful because he never stopped barking; and we could only find the hounds, when at bay, by listening for the sound of their voices. Among the cliffs and precipices the pack usually ran out of sight and hearing if the chase lasted any length of time. Their business was to bring the quarry to bay, or put it up a tree, and then to stay with it and make a noise until the hunters came up. During this hunt there were two or three occasions when they had a cougar up a tree for at least three hours before we arrived, and on several occasions Goff had known them to keep a cougar up a tree overnight and to be still barking around the tree when the hunters at last found them the following morning. Jim always did his share of the killing, being a formidable fighter, though too wary to take hold until one of the professional fighting dogs had seized. He was a great bully with the other dogs, robbing them of their food, and yielding only to Turk. He possessed great endurance, and very stout feet.

On the whole the most useful dog next to Jim was old Boxer. Age had made Boxer slow, and in addition to this, the first cougar we tackled bit him through one hind leg, so that for the remainder of the trip he went on three legs, or, as Goff put it, " packed one leg "; but this seemed not to interfere with his appetite, his endurance, or his desire for the chase. Of all the dogs he was the best to puzzle out a cold trail on a bare hillside, or in any difficult place. He hardly paid any heed to the others, always insisting upon working out the trail for himself, and he never gave up. Of course, the dogs were much more apt to come upon the cold than upon the fresh trail of a cougar, and it was often necessary for them to spend several hours in working out a track which was at least two days old. Both Boxer and Jim had enormous appetites. Boxer was a small dog and Jim a very large one, and as the relations of the pack among themselves were those of brutal wild-beast selfishness, Boxer had to eat very quickly if he expected to get anything when Jim was around. He never ventured to fight Jim, but in deep-toned voice appealed to heaven against the unrighteousness with which he was treated; and time and again such appeal caused me to sally out and rescue his dinner from Jim's highway robbery. Once, when Boxer was given a biscuit, which he tried to bolt whole, Jim simply took his entire head in his jaws, and convinced him that he had his choice of surrendering the biscuit, or sharing its passage down Jim's capacious throat. Boxer promptly gave up the biscuit, then lay on his back and wailed a protest to fate—his voice being deep rather than loud, so that on the trail, when heard at a distance, it sounded a little as if he was croaking. After killing a cougar we usually cut up the carcass and fed it to the dogs, if we did not expect another chase that day. They devoured it eagerly, Boxer, after his meal, always looking as if he had swallowed a mattress.

Next in size to Jim was Tree'em. Tree'em was a good dog, but I never considered him remarkable until his feat on the last day of our hunt, to be afterward related. He was not a very noisy dog, and when " barking treed " he had a meditative way of giving single barks separated by intervals of several seconds, all the time gazing stolidly up at the big, sinister cat which he was baying. Early in the hunt, in the course of a fight with one of the cougars, he received some injury to his tail, which made it hang down like a piece of old rope. Apparently it hurt him a good deal and we let him rest for a fortnight. This put him in great spirits and made him fat and strong, but only enabled him to recover power over the root of the tail, while the tip hung down as before; it looked like a curved pump-handle when he tried to carry it erect.

Lil and Nel were two very stanch and fast bitches, the only two dogs that could keep up to Jim in a quick burst. They had shrill voices. Their only failing was a tendency to let the other members of the pack cow them so that they did not get their full share of the food. It was not a pack in which a slow or timid dog had much chance for existence. They would all unite in the chase and the fierce struggle which usually closed it; but the instant the quarry was killed each dog resumed his normal attitude of greedy anger or greedy fear toward the others.

Another bitch rejoiced in the not very appropriate name of Pete. She was a most ardent huntress. In the middle of our trip she gave birth to a litter of puppies, but before they were two weeks old she would slip away after us and join with the utmost ardor in the hunting and fighting. Her brother Jimmie, although of the same age (both were young), was not nearly as far advanced. He would run well on a fresh trail, but a cold trail or a long check always discouraged him and made him come back to Goff. He was rapidly learning; a single beating taught him to let deer alone. The remaining hound, Bruno, had just been added to the pack. He showed tendencies both to muteness and babbling, and at times, if he thought himself unobserved, could not resist making a sprint after a deer; but he occasionally rendered good service. If Jim or Boxer gave tongue every member of the pack ran to the sound; but not a dog paid any heed to Jimmie or Bruno. Yet both ultimately became first-class hounds.

The fighting dogs always trotted at the heels of the horses, which had become entirely accustomed to them, and made no objection when they literally rubbed against their heels. The fighters never left us until we came to where we could hear the hounds " barking treed," or with their quarry at bay. Then they tore in a straight line to the sound. They were the ones who were expected to do the seizing and take the punishment, though the minute they actually had hold of the cougar, the hounds all piled on too, and did their share of the killing; but the seizers fought the head while the hounds generally took hold behind. All of them, fighters and hounds alike, were exceedingly good-natured and affectionate with their human friends, though short-tempered to a degree with one another. The best of the fighters was old Turk, who was by blood half hound and half " Siberian blood-hound." Both his father and his mother were half-breeds of the same strains, and both were famous fighters. Once, when Goff had wounded an enormous gray wolf in the hind leg, the father had overtaken it and fought it to a standstill. The two dogs together were an over-match for any wolf. Turk had had a sister who was as good as he was; but she had been killed the year before by a cougar which bit her through the skull; accidents being, of course, frequent in the pack, for a big cougar is an even more formidable opponent to dogs than a wolf. Turk's head and body were seamed with scars.

He had lost his lower fangs, but he was still a most formidable dog. While we were at the Keystone Ranch
a big steer which had been driven in, got on the fight,
and the foreman, William Wilson, took Turk out to aid
him. At first Turk did not grasp what was expected of
him, because all the dogs were trained never to touch
anything domestic—at the different ranches where we
stopped the cats and kittens wandered about, perfectly
safe, in the midst of this hard-biting crew of bear and
cougar fighters. But when Turk at last realized that
he was expected to seize the steer, he did the business
with speed and thoroughness; he not only threw the steer,
but would have killed it then and there had he not been,
with much difficulty, taken away. Three dogs like Turk,
in their prime and with their teeth intact, could, I believe, kill an ordinary female cougar, and could hold
even a big male so as to allow it to be killed with the
knife.

Next to Turk were two half-breeds between bull and
shepherd, named Tony and Baldy. They were exceedingly game, knowing-looking little dogs, with a certain
alert swagger that reminded one of the walk of some
light-weight prize-fighters. In fights with cougars,
bears, and lynx, they too had been badly mauled and had
lost a good many of their teeth. Neither of the gallant
little fellows survived the trip. Their place was taken
by a white bulldog bitch, Queen, which we picked up
at the Keystone Ranch; a very affectionate and good-
humored dog, but, when her blood was aroused, a dauntless though rather stupid fighter. Unfortunately she did

not seize by the head, taking hold of any part that was nearest.

The pack had many interesting peculiarities, but none more so than the fact that four of them climbed trees. Only one of the hounds, little Jimmie, ever tried the feat; but of the fighters, not only Tony and Baldy but big Turk climbed every tree that gave them any chance. The pinyons and cedars were low, multi-forked, and usually sent off branches from near the ground. In consequence the dogs could, by industrious effort, work their way almost to the top. The photograph of Turk and the bobcat in the pinyon (facing p. 12) shows them at an altitude of about thirty feet above the ground. Now and then a dog would lose his footing and come down with a whack which sounded as if he must be disabled, but after a growl and a shake he would start up the tree again. They could not fight well while in a tree, and were often scratched or knocked to the ground by a cougar; and when the quarry was shot out of its perch and seized by the expectant throng below, the dogs in the tree, yelping with eager excitement, dived headlong down through the branches, regardless of consequences.

The horses were stout, hardy, surefooted beasts, not very fast, but able to climb like goats, and to endure an immense amount of work. Goff and I each used two for the trip.

The bear were all holed up for the winter, and so our game was limited to cougars and bobcats. In the books the bobcat is always called a lynx, which it of course is; but whenever a hunter or trapper speaks of a

lynx (which he usually calls " link," feeling dimly that
the other pronunciation is a plural), he means a lucivee.
Bobcat is a good distinctive name, and it is one which
I think the book people might with advantage adopt;
for wild-cat, which is the name given to the small lynx
in the East, is already pre-empted by the true wild-cat
of Europe. Like all people of European descent who
have gone into strange lands, we Americans have christened our wild beasts with a fine disregard for their
specific and generic relations. We called the bison
" buffalo " as long as it existed, and we still call the big
stag an " elk," instead of using for it the excellent term
wapiti; on the other hand, to the true elk and the reindeer we gave the new names moose and caribou—excellent names, too, by the way. The prong buck is always
called antelope, though it is not an antelope at all; and
the white goat is not a goat; while the distinctive name of
" bighorn " is rarely used for the mountain sheep. In
most cases, however, it is mere pedantry to try to upset
popular custom in such matters; and where, as with the
bobcat, a perfectly good name is taken, it would be better
for scientific men to adopt it. I may add that in this
particular of nomenclature we are no worse sinners than
other people. The English in Ceylon, the English and
Dutch in South Africa, and the Spanish in South America, have all shown the same genius for misnaming beasts
and birds.

Bobcats were very numerous where we were hunting.
They fed chiefly upon the rabbits, which fairly swarmed;
mostly cotton-tails, but a few jacks. Contrary to the

TURK AND A BOBCAT IN TOP OF A PINYON

From a photograph by Philip B. Stewart

popular belief, the winter is in many places a time of plenty for carnivorous wild beasts. In this place, for instance, the abundance of'deer and rabbits made good hunting for both cougar and bobcat, and all those we killed were as fat as possible, and in consequence weighed more than their inches promised. The bobcats are very fond of prairie dogs, and haunt the dog towns as soon as spring comes and the inhabitants emerge from their hibernation. They sometimes pounce on higher game. We came upon an eight months' fawn—very nearly a yearling—which had been killed by a big male bobcat; and Judge Foreman informed me that near his ranch, a few years previously, an exceptionally large bobcat had killed a yearling doe. Bobcats will also take lambs and young pigs, and if the chance occurs will readily seize their small kinsman, the house cat.

Bobcats are very fond of lurking round prairie-dog towns as soon as the prairie dogs come out in spring. In this part of Colorado, by the way, the prairie dogs were of an entirely different species from the common kind of the plains east of the Rockies.

We found that the bobcats sometimes made their lairs along the rocky ledges or in holes in the cut banks, and sometimes in thickets, prowling about during the night, and now and then even during the day. We never chased them unless the dogs happened to run across them by accident when questing for cougar, or when we were returning home after a day when we had failed to find cougar. Usually the cat gave a good run, occasionally throwing out the dogs by doubling or jack-knifing. Two or three times one of them gave us an hour's sharp trotting, cantering, and galloping through the open cedar and pinyon groves on the table-lands; and the runs sometimes lasted for a much longer period when the dogs had to go across ledges and through deep ravines.

On one of our runs a party of ravens fluttered along from tree to tree beside us, making queer gurgling noises and evidently aware that they might expect to reap a reward from our hunting. Ravens, multitudes of magpies, and golden and bald eagles were seen continually, and all four flocked to any carcass which was left in the open. The eagle and the raven are true birds of the wilderness, and in a way their presence both heightened and relieved the iron desolation of the wintry mountains.

Over half the cats we started escaped, getting into caves or deep holes in washouts. In the other instances they went up trees and were of course easily shot. Tony and Baldy would bring them out of any hole into which they themselves could get. After their loss, Lil, who was a small hound, once went into a hole in a washout after a cat. After awhile she stopped barking, though we could still hear the cat growling. What had happened to her we did not know. We spent a couple of hours calling to her and trying to get her to come out, but she neither came out nor answered, and, as sunset was approaching and the ranch was some miles off, we rode back there, intending to return with spades in the morning. However, by breakfast we found that Lil had come back. We supposed that she had got on the other side of the cat and had been afraid or unable to attack it; so that as Collins the cow-puncher, who was a Southerner, phrased it, " she just naturally stayed in the hole " until some time during the night the cat went out and she followed. When once hunters and hounds have come into the land, it is evident that the bobcats which take refuge in caves have a far better chance of surviving than those which make their lairs in the open and go up trees. But trees are sure havens against their wilderness foes. Goff informed me that he once came in the snow to a place where the tracks showed that some coyotes had put a bobcat up a tree, and had finally abandoned the effort to get at it. Any good fighting dog will kill a bobcat; but an untrained dog, even of large size, will probably fail, as the bobcat makes good use of both teeth and claws. The cats we caught frequently left marks on some of the pack. We found them very variable in size. My two largest—both of course males—weighed respectively thirty-one and thirty-nine pounds. The latter, Goff said, was of exceptional size, and as large as any he had ever killed. The full-grown females went down as low as eighteen pounds, or even lower.

When the bobcats were in the treetops we could get up very close. They looked like large malevolent pussies. I once heard one of them squall defiance when the dogs tried to get it out of a hole. Ordinarily they confined themselves to a low growling. Stewart and Goff went up the trees with their cameras whenever we got a bobcat in a favorable position, and endeavored to take its photograph. Sometimes they were very successful. Although they were frequently within six feet of a cat, and occasionally even poked it in order to make it change its position, I never saw one make a motion to jump on them. Two or three times on our approach the cat jumped from the tree almost into the midst of the pack, but it was so quick that it got off before they could seize it. They invariably put it up another tree before it had gone any distance.

Hunting the bobcat was only an incident. Our true quarry was the cougar. I had long been anxious to make a regular hunt after cougar in a country where the beasts were plentiful and where we could follow them with a good pack of hounds. Astonishingly little of a satisfactory nature has been left on record about the cougar by hunters, and in most places the chances for observation of the big cats steadily grow less. They have been thinned out almost to the point of extermination throughout the Eastern States. In the Rocky Mountain region they are still plentiful in places, but are growing less so; while on the contrary the wolf, which was exterminated even more quickly in the East, in the West has until recently been increasing in numbers. In northwestern Colorado a dozen years ago, cougars were far more plentiful than wolves; whereas at the present day the wolf is probably the more numerous. Nevertheless, there are large areas, here and there among the Rockies, in which cougars will be fairly plentiful for years to come.

No American beast has been the subject of so much loose writing or of such wild fables as the cougar. Even

BOBCAT IN PINYON

From a photograph by Philip B. Stewart

its name is unsettled. In the Eastern States it is usually called panther or painter; in the Western States, mountain lion, or, toward the South, Mexican lion. The Spanish-speaking people usually call it simply lion. It is, however, sometimes called cougar in the West and Southwest of our country, and in South America, puma. As it is desirable where possible not to use a name that is misleading and is already appropriated to some entirely different animal, it is best to call it cougar.

The cougar is a very singular beast, shy and elusive to an extraordinary degree, very cowardly and yet bloodthirsty and ferocious, varying wonderfully in size, and subject, like many other beasts, to queer freaks of character in occasional individuals. This fact of individual variation in size and temper is almost always ignored in treating of the animal; whereas it ought never to be left out of sight.

The average writer, and for the matter of that, the average hunter, where cougars are scarce, knows little or nothing of them, and in describing them merely draws upon the stock of well-worn myths which portray them as terrible foes of man, as dropping on their prey from trees where they have been lying in wait, etc., etc. Very occasionally there appears an absolutely trustworthy account like that by Dr. Hart Merriam in his "Adirondack Mammals." But many otherwise excellent writers are wholly at sea in reference to the cougar. Thus one of the best books on hunting in the far West in the old days is by Colonel Dodge. Yet when Colonel Dodge came to describe the cougar he actually treated of it as two species, one of which, the mountain lion, he painted as a most ferocious and dangerous opponent of man; while the other, the panther, was described as an abject coward, which would not even in the last resort defend itself against man—the two of course being the same animal.

However, the wildest of all fables about the cougar has been reserved not for hunter or popular writer, but for a professed naturalist. In his charmingly written book, "The Naturalist in La Plata," Mr. Hudson actually describes the cougar as being friendly to man, disinterestedly adverse to harming him, and at the same time an enemy of other large carnivores. Mr. Hudson bases his opinion chiefly upon the assertions of the Gauchos. The Gauchos, however, go one degree beyond Mr. Hudson, calling the puma the "friend of Christians"; whereas Mr. Hudson only ventures to attribute to the beast humanitarian, not theological, preferences. As a matter of fact, Mr. Hudson's belief in the cougar's peculiar friendship for man, and peculiar enmity to other large beasts of prey, has not one particle of foundation in fact as regards at any rate the North American form— and it is hardly to be supposed that the South American form would alone develop such extraordinary traits. For instance, Mr. Hudson says that the South American puma when hunted will attack the dogs in preference to the man. In North America he will fight the dog if the dog is nearest, and if the man comes to close quarters at the same time as the dog he will attack the man if anything more readily, evidently recognizing in him his chief opponent. He will often go up a tree for a single dog. On Mr. Hudson's theory he must do this because of his altruistic feeling toward the dog. In fact, Mr. Hudson could make out a better case of philo-humanity for the North American wolf than for the North American cougar. Equally absurd is it to talk, as Mr. Hudson does, of the cougar as the especial enemy of other ferocious beasts. Mr. Hudson speaks of it as attacking and conquering the jaguar. Of this I know nothing, but such an extraordinary statement should be well fortified with proofs; and if true it must mean that the jaguar is an infinitely less formidable creature than it has been painted. In support of his position Mr. Hudson alludes to the stories about the cougar attacking the grizzly bear. Here I am on ground that I do know. It is true that an occasional old hunter asserts that the cougar does this, but the old hunter who makes such an assertion also invariably insists that the cougar is a ferocious and habitual man-killer, and the two statements rest upon equally slender foundations of fact. I have never yet heard of a single authentic instance of a cougar interfering with a full-grown big bear. It will kill bear cubs if it gets a chance; but then so will the fox and the fisher, not to speak of the wolf. In 1894, a cougar killed a colt on a brushy river bottom a dozen miles below my ranch on the Little Missouri. I went down to visit the carcass and found that it had been taken possession of by a large grizzly. Both I and the hunter who was with me were very much interested in what had occurred, and after a careful examination of the tracks we concluded that the bear had arrived on the second night after the kill. He had feasted heartily on the remains, while the cougar, whose tracks were evident here and there at a little distance from the carcass, had seemingly circled around it, and had certainly not interfered with the bear, or even ventured to approach him. Now, if a cougar would ever have meddled with a large bear it would surely have been on such an occasion as this. If very much pressed by hunger, a large cougar will, if it gets the chance, kill a wolf; but this is only when other game has failed, and under all ordinary circumstances neither meddles with the other. When I was down in Texas, hunting peccaries on the Nueces, I was in a country where both cougar and jaguar were to be found; but no hunter had ever heard of either molesting the other, though they were all of the opinion that when the two met the cougar gave the path to his spotted brother. Of course, it is never safe to dogmatize about the unknown in zoology, or to generalize on insufficient evidence; but as regards the North American cougar there is not a particle of truth of any kind, sort, or description in the statement that he is the enemy of the larger carnivores, or the friend of man; and if the South American cougar, which so strongly resembles its Northern brother in its other habits, has developed on these two points the extraordinary peculiarities of which Mr. Hudson speaks, full and adequate proof should be forthcoming; and this proof is now wholly wanting.

Fables aside, the cougar is a very interesting creature. It is found from the cold, desolate plains of Patagonia to north of the Canadian line, and lives alike among the snow-clad peaks of the Andes and in the steaming forests of the Amazon. Doubtless careful investigation will disclose several varying forms in an animal found over such immense tracts of country and living under such utterly diverse conditions. But in its essential habits and traits, the big, slinking, nearly uni-colored cat seems to be much the same everywhere, whether living in mountain, open plain, or forest, under arctic cold or tropic heat. When the settlements become thick, it retires to dense forest, dark swamp or inaccessible mountain gorge, and moves about only at night. In wilder regions it not infrequently roams during the day and ventures freely into the open. Deer are its customary prey where they are plentiful, bucks, does, and fawns being killed indifferently. Usually the deer is killed almost instantaneously, but occasionally there is quite a scuffle, in which the cougar may get bruised, though, as far as I know, never seriously. It is also a dreaded enemy of sheep, pigs, calves, and especially colts, and when pressed by hunger a big male cougar will kill a full-grown horse or cow, moose or wapiti. It is the special enemy of mountain sheep. In 1886, while hunting white goats north of Clarke's fork of the Columbia, in a region where cougar were common, I found them preying as freely on the goats as on the deer. It rarely catches antelope, but is quick to seize rabbits, other small beasts, and even porcupines, as well as bobcats, coyotes and foxes.

No animal, not even the wolf, is so rarely seen or so difficult to get without dogs. On the other hand, no other wild beast of its size and power is so easy to kill by the aid of dogs. There are many contradictions in its character. Like the American wolf, it is certainly very much afraid of man; yet it habitually follows the trail of the hunter or solitary traveller, dogging his footsteps, itself always unseen. I have had this happen to me personally. When hungry it will seize and carry off any dog; yet it will sometimes go up a tree when pursued even by a single small dog wholly unable to do it the least harm. It is small wonder that the average frontier settler should grow to regard almost with superstition the great furtive cat which he never sees, but of whose presence he is ever aware, and of whose prowess sinister proof is sometimes afforded by the deaths not alone of his lesser stock, but even of his milch cow or saddle horse.

The cougar is as large, as powerful, and as formidably armed as the Indian panther, and quite as well able to attack man; yet the instances of its having done so are exceedingly rare. The vast majority of the tales to this effect are undoubtedly inventions. But it is foolish to deny that such attacks on human beings ever occur. There are a number of authentic instances, the latest that has come to my knowledge being related in the following letter, of May 15, 1893, written to Dr. Merriam by Professor W. H. Brewer, of Yale: " In 1880 I visited the base of Mount Shasta, and stopped a day to renew the memories of 1862, when I had climbed and measured this mountain. Panthers were numerous and were so destructive to sheep that poisoning by strychnine was common. A man living near who had (as a young hunter) gone up Mount Shasta with us in '62, now married (1880) and on a ranch, came to visit me, with a little son five or six years old. This boy when younger, but two or three years old, if I recollect rightly, had been attacked by a panther. He was playing in the yard by the house when a lean two-thirds grown panther came into the yard and seized the child by the throat. The child screamed, and alarmed the mother (who told me the story). She seized a broom and rushed out, while an old man at the house seized the gun. The panther let go the child and was shot. I saw the boy. He had the scars of the panther's teeth in the cheek, and below on the under side of the lower jaw, and just at the throat. This was the only case that came to my knowledge at first hand of a panther attacking a human being in that State, except one or two cases where panthers, exasperated by wounds, had fought with the hunters who had wounded them." This was a young cougar, bold, stupid, and very hungry. Goff told me of one similar case where a cougar stalked a young girl, but was shot just before it was close enough to make the final rush. As I have elsewhere related, I know of two undoubted cases, one in Mississippi, one in Florida, where a negro was attacked and killed by a cougar, while alone in a swamp at night. But these occurred many years ago. The instance related by Professor Brewer is the only one I have come across happening in recent years, in which the cougar actually seized a human being with the purpose of making prey of it; though doubtless others have occurred. I have never known the American wolf actually to attack a human being from hunger or to make prey of him; whereas the Old-World wolf, like the Old-World leopard, undoubtedly sometimes turns man-eater.

Even when hunted the cougar shows itself, as a rule, an abject coward, not to be compared in courage and prowess with the grizzly bear, and but little more dangerous to man than is the wolf under similar circumstances. Without dogs it is usually a mere chance that one is killed. Goff has killed some 300 cougars during the sixteen years he has been hunting in northwestern Colorado, yet all but two of them were encountered while he was with his pack; although this is in a region where they were plentiful. When hunted with good dogs their attention is so taken up with the pack that they have little time to devote to men. When hunted without dogs they never charge unless actually cornered, and, as a general rule, not even then, unless the man chooses to come right up to them. I knew of one Indian being killed in 1887, and near my ranch a cowboy was mauled; but in the first instance the cougar had been knocked down and the Indian was bending over it when it revived; and in the next instance, the cowboy literally came right on top of the animal. Now, under such circumstances either a bull elk or a blacktail buck will occasionally fight; twice I have known of wounded wapiti regularly charging, and one of my own cowboys, George Myer, was very roughly handled by a blacktail buck which he had wounded. In all his experience Goff says that save when he approached one too close when it was cornered by the dogs, he never but once had a cougar start to charge him, and on that occasion it was promptly killed by a bullet. Usually the cougar does not even charge at the dogs beyond a few feet, confining itself to seizing or striking any member of the pack which comes close up; although it will occasionally, when much irritated, make a rapid dash and seize some bold assailant. While I was on my hunt, one of Goff's brothers lost a hound in hunting a cougar; there were but two hounds, and the cougar would not tree for them, finally seizing and killing one that came too near. At the same time a ranchman not far off set his cattle dog on a cougar, which after a short run turned and killed the dog. But time and again cougars are brought to bay or treed by dogs powerless to do them the slightest damage; and they usually meet their death tamely when the hunter comes up. I have had no personal experience either with the South American jaguar or the Old-World leopard or panther; but these great spotted cats must be far more dangerous adversaries than the cougar.

It is true, as I have said, that a cougar will follow a man; but then a weasel will sometimes do the same thing. Whatever the cougar's motive, it is certain that in the immense majority of cases there is not the slightest danger of his attacking the man he follows. Dr. Hart Merriam informs me, however, that he is satisfied that he came across one genuine instance of a cougar killing a man whose tracks he had dogged. It cannot be too often repeated, that we must never lose sight of the individual variation in character and conduct among wild beasts. A thousand times a cougar might follow a man either not intending or not daring to attack him, while in the thousandth and first case it might be that the temper of the beast and the conditions were such that the attack would be made.

Other beasts show almost the same wide variation in temper. Wolves, for instance, are normally exceedingly wary of man. In this Colorado hunt I often came across their tracks, and often heard their mournful, but to my ears rather attractive, baying at night, but I never caught a glimpse of one of them; nor during the years when I spent much of my time on my ranch did I ever know of a wolf venturing to approach anywhere near a man in the day-time, though I have had them accompany me after nightfall, and have occasionally come across them by accident in daylight. But on the Keystone Ranch, where I spent three weeks on this particular trip, an incident which occurred before my arrival showed that wolves occasionally act with extraordinary boldness. The former owner of the ranch, Colonel Price, and one of the cowhands, Sabey (both of whom told me the story), were driving out in a buggy from Meeker to the ranch accompanied by a setter dog. They had no weapon with them. Two wolves joined them and made every effort to get at the dog. They accompanied the wagon for nearly a mile, venturing to within twenty yards of it. They paid no heed whatever to the shouts and gestures of the men, but did not quite dare to come to close quarters, and finally abandoned their effort. Now, this action on their part was, as far as my experience goes, quite as exceptional among American wolves as it is exceptional for a cougar to attack a man. Of course, these wolves were not after the men. They were simply after the dog; but I have never within my own experience come upon another instance of wolves venturing to attack a domestic animal in the immediate presence of and protected by a man. Exactly as these two wolves suddenly chose to behave with an absolutely unexpected daring, so a cougar will occasionally lose the fear of man which is inherent in its race.

Normally, then, the cougar is not in any way a formidable foe to man, and it is certainly by no means as dangerous to dogs as it could be if its courage and intelligence equalled its power to do mischief. It strikes with its forepaw like a cat, lacerating the foe with its sharp claws; or else it holds the animal with them, while the muscular forearm draws it in until the fatal bite may be inflicted. Whenever possible it strives to bite an assailant in the head. Occasionally, when fighting with a large dog, a cougar will throw itself on its back and try to rip open its antagonist with its hind feet. Male cougars often fight desperately among themselves.

Although a silent beast, yet at times, especially during the breeding season, the males utter a wild scream, and the females also wail or call. I once heard one cry repeatedly after nightfall, seemingly while prowling for game. On an evening in the summer of 1897 Dr. Merriam had a rather singular experience with a cougar. His party was camped in the forest by Tannum Lake, on the east slope of the Cascades, near the headwaters of a branch of the Yakima. The horses were feeding near by. Shortly after dark a cougar cried loudly in the gloom, and the frightened horses whinnied and stampeded. The cougar cried a number of times afterward, but the horses did not again answer. None of them was killed, however; and next morning, after some labor, all were again gathered together. In 1884 I had a somewhat similar experience with a bear, in the Big Horn Mountains.

Occasionally, but not often, the cougars I shot snarled or uttered a low, thunderous growl as we approached the tree, or as the dogs came upon them in the cave. In the death-grapple they were silent, excepting that one young cougar snarled and squalled as it battled with the dogs.

The cougar is sometimes tamed. A friend of mine had one which was as good-natured as possible until it was a year old, when it died. But one kept by another friend, while still quite young, became treacherous and dangerous. I doubt if they would ever become as trustworthy as a tame wolf, which, if taken when a very young puppy, will often grow up exactly like a dog. Two or three years ago there was such a tame wolf with the Colorado Springs greyhounds. It was safer and more friendly than many collies, and kept on excellent terms with the great greyhounds; though these were themselves solely used to hunt wolves and coyotes, and tackled them with headlong ferocity, having, unaided, killed a score or two of the large wolves and hundreds of coyotes.

Hunting in the snow we were able to tell very clearly what the cougars whose trails we were following had been doing. Goff's eye for a trail was unerring, and he read at a glance the lesson it taught. All the cougars which we came across were living exclusively upon deer, and their stomachs were filled with nothing else; much hair being mixed with the meat. In each case the deer was caught by stalking and not by lying in wait, and the cougar never went up a tree except to get rid of the dogs. In the day-time it retired to a ledge, or ravine, or dense thicket, starting to prowl as the dark came on. So far as I could see the deer in each case was killed by a bite in the throat or neck. The cougar simply rambled around in likely grounds until it saw or smelled its quarry, and then crept up stealthily until with one or two tremendous bounds it was able to seize its prey. If, as frequently happened, the deer took alarm in time to avoid the first few bounds, it always got away, for though the cougar is very fast for a short distance, it has no wind whatever. It cannot pursue a deer for any length of time, nor run before a dog for more than a few hundred yards, if the dog is close up at the start. I was informed by the ranchmen that when in May the deer leave the country, the cougars turn their attention to the stock, and are very destructive. They have a special fondness for horseflesh and kill almost every colt where they are plentiful, while the big males work havoc with the saddle bands on the ranches, as well as among the brood mares. Except in the case of a female with young they are roving, wandering beasts, and roam great distances. After leaving their day lairs, on a ledge, or in a gorge or thicket, they spend the night travelling across the flats, along the ridges, over the spurs. When they kill a deer they usually lie not very far away, and do not again wander until they are hungry. The males travel very long distances in the mating season. Their breeding-time is evidently irregular. We found kittens with their eyes not yet open in the middle of January. Two of the female cougars we killed were pregnant— in one case the young would have been born almost immediately, that is, in February; and in the other case in March. One, which had a partially grown young one of over fifty pounds with it, still had milk in its teats. At the end of January we found a male and female together, evidently mating. Goff has also found the young just dropped in May, and even in June. The females outnumber the males. Of the fourteen we killed, but three were males.

When a cougar kills a deer in the open it invariably drags it under some tree or shelter before beginning to eat. All the carcasses we came across had been thus dragged, the trail showing distinctly in the snow. Goff, however, asserted that in occasional instances he had known a cougar to carry a deer so that only its legs trailed on the ground.

The fourteen cougars we killed showed the widest variation not only in size but in color, as shown by the following table. Some were as slaty-gray as deer when in the so-called " blue "; others, rufous, almost as bright as deer in the " red." I use these two terms to describe the color phases; though in some instances the tint was very undecided. The color phase evidently has nothing to do with age, sex, season, or locality. In this table the first cougar is the one killed by Stewart, the sixth by

Webb. The length is measured in a straight line, " between uprights," from the nose to the extreme tip of the tail, when the beast was stretched out. The animals were weighed with the steelyard and also spring scales. Before measuring, we pulled the beast out as straight as we possibly could; and as the biggest male represents about, or very nearly, the maximum for the species, it is easy

Sex.	Color.	Length.		Weight.	Date.
		Feet.	Inches.	Pounds.	1901.
[1]Female.	Blue.	4	11	47	January 19
[1]Female.	Red.	4	11½	51	February 12
Female.	Blue.	6		80	January 14
Female.	Red.	6	4	102	January 28
Female.	Blue.	6	5	105	February 12
Female.	Blue.	6	5	107	January 18
Female.	Red.	6	9	108	·January 24
Female.	Blue.	6	7	118	January 15
Female.	Blue.	6	7	120	January 31
Female.	Red.	6	9	124	February 5
Female.	Blue.	7		133	February 8
Male.	Red.	7	6	160	February 13
Male.	Blue.	7	8	164	January 27
Male.	Red.	8		227	February 14

to see that there can be no basis for the talk one sometimes hears about ten and eleven foot cougars. No cougar, measured at all fairly, has ever come anywhere near reaching the length of nine feet. The fresh hide can easily be stretched a couple of feet extra. Except the first two, all were full grown; the biggest male was nearly three times the size of the smallest female.

I shot five bobcats: two old males weighing 39 and 31

[1] Young.

pounds respectively; and three females, weighing, respectively, 25, 21, and 18 pounds. Webb killed two, a male of 29 pounds and a female of 20; and Stewart two females, one of 22 pounds, and the other a young one of 11 pounds.

I sent the cougar and bobcat skulls to Dr. Merriam, at the Biological Survey, Department of Agriculture, Washington. He wrote me as follows: " The big [cougar] skull is certainly a giant. I have compared it with the largest in our collection from British Columbia and Wyoming, and find it larger than either. It'is in fact the largest skull of any member of the *Felis concolor* group I have seen. A hasty preliminary examination indicates that the animal is quite different from the northwest coast form, but that it is the same as my horse-killer from Wyoming—*Felis hippolestes*. In typical *Felis concolor* from Brazil the skull is lighter, the brain-case thinner and more smoothly rounded, devoid of the strongly developed sagittal crest; the under jaw straighter and lighter.

" Your series of skulls from Colorado is incomparably the largest, most complete and most valuable series ever brought together from any single locality, and will be of inestimable value in determining the amount of individual variation."

We rode in to the Keystone Ranch late on the evening of the second day after leaving Meeker. We had picked up a couple of bobcats on the way, and had found a cougar's kill (or bait, as Goff called it)—a doe, almost completely eaten. The dogs puzzled for several hours

STARTING FOR A HUNT

From a photograph by Philip B. Stewart

over the cold trail of the cougar; but it was old, and ran hither and thither over bare ground, so that they finally lost it. The ranch was delightfully situated at the foot of high wooded hills broken by cliffs, and it was pleasant to reach the warm, comfortable log buildings, with their clean rooms, and to revel in the abundant, smoking-hot dinner, after the long, cold hours in the saddle. As everywhere else in the cattle country nowadays, a successful effort had been made to store water on the Keystone, and there were great stretches of wire fencing—two improvements entirely unknown in former days. But the foreman, William Wilson, and the two punchers or cowhands, Sabey and Collins, were of the old familiar type—skilled, fearless, hardy, hard-working, with all the intelligence and self-respect that we like to claim as typical of the American character at its best. All three carried short saddle guns when they went abroad, and killed a good many coyotes, and now and then a gray wolf. The cattle were for the most part grade Herefords, very different from the wild, slab-sided, long-horned creatures which covered the cattle country a score of years ago.

The next day, January 14th, we got our first cougar. This kind of hunting was totally different from that to which I had been accustomed. In the first place, there was no need of always being on the alert for a shot, as it was the dogs who did the work. In the next place, instead of continually scanning the landscape, what we had to do was to look down so as to be sure not to pass over any tracks; for frequently a cold trail would be indicated so faintly that the dogs themselves might pass it

by, if unassisted by Goff's keen eyes and thorough knowledge of the habits of the quarry. Finally, there was no
object in making an early start, as what we expected to
find was not the cougar, but the cougar's trail; moreover,
the horses and dogs, tough though they were, could not
stand more than a certain amount, and to ride from sunrise to sunset, day in and day out, for five weeks, just
about tested the limits of their endurance.

We made our way slowly up the snow-covered, pin-
yon-clad side of the mountain back of the house, and
found a very old cougar trail which it was useless to try
to run, and a couple of fresh bobcat trails which it was
difficult to prevent the dogs from following. After criss-
crossing over the shoulders of this mountain for two or
three hours, and scrambling in and out of the ravines,
we finally struck another cougar trail, much more recent,
probably made thirty-six hours before. The hounds had
been hunting free to one side or the other of our path.
They were now summoned by a blast of the horn, and
with a wave of Goff's hand away they went on the trail.
Had it been fresh they would have run out of hearing
at once, for it was fearfully rough country. But they were
able to work but slowly along the loops and zigzags of
the trail, where it led across bare spaces, and we could
keep well in sight and hearing of them. Finally they
came to where it descended the sheer side of the mountain
and crossed the snow-covered valley beneath. They were
still all together, the pace having been so slow, and in
the snow of the valley the scent was fresh. It was a fine
sight to see them as they rushed across from one side to

the other, the cliffs echoing their chiming. Jim and the three bitches were in the lead, while Boxer fell behind, as he always did when the pace was fast.

Leading our horses, we slid and scrambled after the hounds; but when we reached the valley they had passed out of sight and sound, and we did not hear them again until we had toiled up the mountain opposite. They were then evidently scattered, having come upon many bare places; but while we were listening, and working our way over to the other side of the divide, the sudden increase in the baying told Goff that they had struck the fresh trail of the beast they were after; and in two or three minutes we heard Jim's deep voice " barking treed." The three fighters, who had been trotting at our heels, recognized the difference in the sound quite as quickly as we did, and plunged at full speed toward it down the steep hillside, throwing up the snow like so many snow-ploughs. In a minute or two the chorus told us that all the dogs were around the tree, and we picked our way down toward them.

While we were still some distance off we could see the cougar in a low pinyon moving about as the dogs tried to get up, and finally knocking one clean out of the top. It was the first time I had ever seen dogs with a cougar, and I was immensely interested; but Stewart's whole concern was with his camera. When we were within fifty yards of the tree, and I was preparing to take the rifle out of the scabbard, Stewart suddenly called " halt," with the first symptoms of excitement he had shown, and added, in an eager undertone: " Wait, there is a rabbit right here, and I want to take his picture." Accordingly we waited, the cougar not fifty yards off and the dogs yelling and trying to get up the tree after it, while Stewart crept up to the rabbit and got a kodak some six feet distant. Then we resumed our march toward the tree, and the cougar, not liking the sight of the reinforcements, jumped out. She came down just outside the pack and ran up hill. So quick was she that the dogs failed to seize her, and for the first fifty yards she went a great deal faster than they did. Both in the jump and in the run she held her tail straight out behind her; I found out afterward that sometimes one will throw its tail straight in the air, and when walking along, when first roused by the pack, before they are close, will, if angry, lash the tail from side to side, at the same time grinning and snarling.

In a minute the cougar went up another tree, but, as we approached, again jumped down, and on this occasion, after running a couple of hundred yards, the dogs seized it. The worry was terrific; the growling, snarling, and yelling rang among the rocks; and leaving our horses we plunged at full speed through the snow down the rugged ravine in which the fight was going on. It was a small though old female, only a few pounds heavier than either Turk or Jim, and the dogs had the upper hand when we arrived. They would certainly have killed it unassisted, but as it was doing some damage to the pack, and might at any moment kill a dog, I ended the struggle by a knife-thrust behind the shoulder. To shoot would have been quite as dangerous for the dogs

THE FIRST COUGAR KILLED

From a photograph by Philip B. Stewart

as for their quarry. Three of the dogs were badly scratched, and Turk had been bitten through one foreleg, and Boxer through one hind leg.

As will be seen by the measurements given before, this was much the smallest full-grown cougar we got. It was also one of the oldest, as its teeth showed, and it gave me a false idea of the size of cougars; although I knew they varied in size I was not prepared for the wide variation we actually found.

The fighting dogs were the ones that enabled me to use the knife. All three went straight for the head, and when they got hold they kept their jaws shut, worrying and pulling, and completely absorbing the attention of the cougar, so as to give an easy chance for the death-blow. The hounds meanwhile had seized the cougar behind, and Jim, with his alligator jaws, probably did as much damage as Turk. However, neither in this nor in any other instance, did any one of the dogs manage to get its teeth through the thick skin. When cougars fight among themselves their claws and fangs leave great scars, but their hides are too thick for the dogs to get their teeth through. On the other hand, a cougar's jaws have great power, and dogs are frequently killed by a single bite, the fangs being driven through the brain or spine; or they break a dog's leg or cut the big blood-vessels of the throat.

I had been anxious to get a set of measurements and weights of cougars to give to Dr. Hart Merriam. Accordingly I was carrying a tape, while Goff, instead of a rifle, had a steelyard in his gun scabbard. We weighed and measured the cougar, and then took lunch, making as impartial a distribution of it as was possible among ourselves and the different members of the pack; for, of course, we were already growing to have a hearty fellow-feeling for each individual dog.

The next day we were again in luck. After about two hours' ride we came upon an old trail. It led among low hills, covered with pinyon and cedar, and broken by gullies or washouts, in whose sharp sides of clay the water had made holes and caves. Soon the hounds left it to follow a bobcat, and we had a lively gallop through the timber, dodging the sharp snags of the dead branches as best we might. The cat got into a hole in a side washout; Baldy went in after it, and the rest of us, men and dogs, clustered about to look in. After a considerable time he put the cat out of the other end of the hole, nearly a hundred yards off, close to the main washout. The first we knew of it we saw it coming straight toward us, its tail held erect like that of a whitetail deer. Before either we or the dogs quite grasped the situation it bolted into another hole almost at our feet, and this time Baldy could not find it, or else could not get at it. Then we took up the cougar trail again. It criss-crossed in every direction. We finally found an old " bait," a buck. It was interesting to see the way in which the cougar had prowled from point to point, and the efforts it had made to approach the deer which it saw or smelled. Once we came to where it had sat down on the edge of a cliff, sitting on its haunches with its long tail straight behind it and looking out across the valley. After it had killed, according to the invariable custom of its kind, it had dragged the deer from the open, where it had over-taken it, to the shelter of a group of trees.

We finally struck the fresh trail; but it, also, led hither and thither, and we got into such a maze of tracks that the dogs were completely puzzled. After a couple of hours of vain travelling to and fro, we gave up the effort, called the dogs off, and started back beside a large washout which led along between two ridges. Goff, as usual, was leading, the dogs following and continually skirting to one side or the other. Suddenly they all began to show great excitement, and then one gave furious tongue at the mouth of a hole in some sunken and broken ground not thirty yards to our right. The whole pack rushed toward the challenge, the fighters leaped into the hole, and in another moment the row inside told us that they had found a cougar at home. We jumped off and ran down to see if we could be of assistance. To get into the hole was impossible, for two or three hounds had jumped down to join the fighters, and we could see noth-ing but their sterns. Then we saw Turk backing out with a dead kitten in his mouth. I had supposed that a cougar would defend her young to the last, but such was not the case in this instance. For some minutes she kept the dogs at bay, but then gradually gave ground, leaving her three kittens. Of course, the dogs killed them instantly, much to our regret, as we would have given a good deal to have kept them alive. As soon as she had abandoned them, away she went completely through the low cave or hole, leaped out of the other end, which was some thirty or forty yards off, scaled the bank, and galloped into the woods, the pack getting after her at once. She did not run more than a couple of hundred yards, and as we tore up on our horses we saw her standing in the lower branches of a pinyon only six or eight feet from the ground. She was not snarling or grinning, and looked at us as quietly as if nothing had happened. As we leaped out of the saddles she jumped down from the tree and ran off through the pack. They were after her at once, however, and a few yards farther on she started up another tree. Either Tony or Baldy grabbed her by the tip of the tail, she lost her footing for a moment, and the whole pack seized her. She was a powerful female of about the average size, being half as heavy again as the one we first got, and made a tremendous fight; and savage enough she looked, her ears tight back against her head, her yellow eyes flashing, and her great teeth showing as she grinned. For a moment the dogs had her down, but biting and striking she freed her head and fore quarters from the fighters, and faced us as we ran up, the hounds still having her from behind. This was another chance for the knife, and I cheered on the fighters. Again they seized her by the head, but though absolutely stanch dogs, their teeth, as I have said, had begun to suffer, and they were no longer always able to make their holds good. Just as I was about to strike her she knocked Turk loose with a blow, bit Baldy, and then, her head being free, turned upon me. Fortunately, Tony caught her free paw on that side, while I jammed the gun-butt into her jaws with my left hand and struck home with the right, the knife driving straight to the heart. The deep fang marks she left in the stock, biting the corner of the shoulder clean off, gave an idea of the power of her jaws. If it had been the very big male cougar which I afterward killed, the stock would doubtless have been bitten completely in two.

The dogs were pretty well damaged, and all retired and lay down under the trees, where they licked their wounds, and went to sleep; growling savagely at one another when they waked, but greeting us with demonstrative affection, and trotting eagerly out to share our lunch as soon as we began to eat it. Unaided, they would ultimately have killed the cougar, but the chance of one or two of them being killed or crippled was too great for us to allow this to be done; and in the mix-up of the struggle it was not possible to end it with the rifle. The writhing, yelling tangle offered too shifting a mark; one would have been as apt to hit a dog as the cougar. Goff told me that the pack had often killed cougars unassisted; but in the performance of such feats the best dogs were frequently killed, and this was not a risk to be taken lightly.

In some books the writers speak as if the male and female cougar live together and jointly seek food for the young. We never found a male cougar anywhere near either a female with young or a pregnant female. According to my observation the male only remains with the female for a short time, during the mating season, at which period he travels great distances in search of his temporary mates—for the females far outnumber the males. The cougar is normally a very solitary beast. The young—two to four in number, though more than one or two rarely grow up—follow the mother until over half grown. The mother lives entirely alone with the kittens while they are small. As the males fight so fiercely among themselves, it may be that the old he-cougars kill the young of their own sex; a ranchman whom I knew once found the body of a young male cougar which had evidently been killed by an old one; but I cannot say whether or not this was an exceptional case.

During the next ten days Stewart and Webb each shot a cougar. Webb's was got by as pretty an exhibition of trailing on the part of Goff and his hounds as one could wish to see. We ran across its old tracks while coming home on Wednesday, January 16th. The next day, Thursday, we took up the trail, but the animal had travelled a long distance; and, as cougars so often do, had spent much of its time walking along ledges, or at the foot of the cliffs, where the sun had melted the snow off the ground. In consequence, the dogs were often at fault. Moreover, bobcats were numerous, and twice the pack got after one, running a couple of hours before, in one instance, the cat went into a cave, and, in the other, took to a tree, where it was killed by Webb. At last, when darkness came on, we were forced to leave the cougar trail and ride home; a very attractive ride, too, loping rapidly over the snow-covered flats, while above us the great stars fairly blazed in the splendor of the winter night.

Early next morning we again took up the trail, and

after a little while found where it was less than thirty-six hours old. The dogs now ran it well, but were thrown out again on a large bare hillside, until Boxer succeeded in recovering the scent. They went up a high mountain and we toiled after them. Again they lost the trail, and while at fault jumped a big bobcat which they ran up a tree. After shooting him we took lunch, and started to circle for the trail. Most of the dogs kept with Goff, but Jim got off to one side on his own account; and suddenly his baying told us that he had jumped the cougar. The rest of the pack tore toward him and after a quarter of a mile run they had the quarry treed. The ground was too rough for riding, and we had to do some stiff climbing to get to it on foot.

Stewart's cougar was a young-of-the-year, and, according to his custom, he took several photographs of it. Then he tried to poke it so that it would get into a better position for the camera; whereupon it jumped out of the tree and ran headlong down hill, the yelling dogs but a few feet behind. Our horses had been left a hundred yards or so below, where they all stood, moping, with their heads drooped and their eyes half shut, in regular cow-pony style. The chase streamed by not a yard from their noses, but evidently failed to arouse even an emotion of interest in their minds, for they barely looked up, and made not a movement of any kind when the cougar treed again just below them.

We killed several bobcats; and we also got another cougar, this time in rather ignominious fashion. We had been running a bobcat, having an excellent gallop, during the course of which Stewart's horse turned a somersault. Without our knowledge the dogs changed to the fresh trail of a cougar, which they ran into its den in another cut bank. When we reached the place they had gone in after it, Baldy dropping into a hole at the top of the bank, while the others crawled into the main entrance, some twenty-five yards off at the bottom. It was evidently a very rough house inside, and above the baying, yelping, and snarling of the dogs we could hear the rumbling overtone of the cougar's growl. On this day we had taken along Queen, the white bull bitch, to " enter " her at cougar. It was certainly a lively experience for a first entry. We reached the place in time to keep Jim and the hound bitches out of the hole. It was evident that the dogs could do nothing with the cougar inside. They could only come at it in front, and under such circumstances its claws and teeth made the odds against them hopeless. Every now and then it would charge, driving them all back, and we would then reach in, seize a dog and haul him out. At intervals there would be an awful yelling and a hound would come out bleeding badly, quite satisfied, and without the slightest desire to go in again. Poor Baldy was evidently killed inside. Queen, Turk, and Tony were badly clawed and bitten, and we finally got them out too; Queen went in three times, and came out on each occasion with a fresh gash or bite; Turk was, at the last, the only one really anxious to go in again. Then we tried to smoke out the cougar, for as one of the dogs had gotten into the cave through an upper entrance, we supposed the cougar

AFTER THE FIGHT

From a photograph by Philip B. Stewart

could get out by the same route. However, it either could not or would not bolt; coming down close to the entrance where we had built the sage-brush fire, there it stayed until it was smothered. We returned to the ranch carrying its skin, but not over-pleased, and the pack much the worse for wear. Dr. Webb had to sew up the wounds of three of the dogs. One, Tony, was sent back to the home ranch, where he died. In such rough hunting as this, it is of course impossible to prevent occasional injuries to the dogs when they get the cougar in a cave, or overtake him on the ground. All that can be done is to try to end the contest as speedily as possible, which we always did.

Judging from the experience of certain friends of mine in the Argentine, I think it would be safe to crawl into a cave to shoot a cougar under normal circumstances; but in this instance the cave was a long, winding hole, so low that we could not get in on hands and knees, having to work our way on our elbows. It was pitch dark inside, so that the rifle sights could not be seen, and the cougar was evidently very angry and had on two or three occasions charged the dogs, driving them out of the entrance of the hole. In the dark, the chances were strongly against killing it with a single shot; while if only wounded, and if it had happened to charge, the man, in his cramped position, would have been utterly helpless.

The day after the death of the smoked-out cougar Stewart and Webb started home. Then it snowed for two days, keeping us in the ranch. While the snow was falling, there was no possibility of finding or following tracks; and as a rule wild creatures lie close during a storm. We were glad to have fresh snow, for the multitude of tracks in the old snow had become confusing; and not only the southern hillsides but the larger valleys had begun to grow bare, so that trailing was difficult.

The third day dawned in brilliant splendor, and when the sun arose all the land glittered dazzling white under his rays. The hounds were rested, we had fresh horses, and after an early breakfast we started to make a long circle. All the forenoon and early afternoon we plodded through the snowdrifts, up and down the valleys, and along the ridge crests, without striking a trail. The dogs trotted behind us or circled from one side to the other. It was no small test of their stanchness, eager and fresh as they were, for time after time we aroused bands of deer, to which they paid no heed whatever. At last, in mid-afternoon, we suddenly struck the tracks of two cougars, one a very large one, an old male. They had been playing and frolicking together, for they were evidently mating, and the snow in the tracks showed that they had started abroad before the storm was entirely over. For three hours the pack followed the cold trail, through an exceedingly rugged and difficult country, in which Goff helped them out again and again.

Just at sunset the cougars were jumped, and ran straight into and through a tangle of spurs and foothills, broken by precipices, and riven by long deep ravines. The two at first separated and then came together, with the result that Tree'em, Bruno, and Jimmie got on the back trail and so were left far behind; while old Boxer also fell to the rear, as he always did when the scent was hot, and Jim and the bitches were left to do the running by themselves.   In the gathering gloom we galloped along the main divide, my horse once falling on a slippery sidehill, as I followed headlong after Goff—whose riding was like the driving of the son of Nimshi.   The last vestige of sunlight disappeared, but the full moon was well up in the heavens when we came to a long spur, leading off to the right for two or three miles, beyond which we did not think the chase could have gone.   It had long run out of hearing.   Making our way down the rough and broken crest of this spur, we finally heard far off the clamorous baying which told us that the hounds had their quarry at bay.   We did not have the fighters with us, as they were still under the weather from the results of their encounter in the cave.

As it afterward appeared, the cougars had run three miles before the dogs overtook them, making their way up, down and along such difficult cliffs that the pack had to keep going round.   The female then went up a tree, while the pack followed the male.   He would not climb a tree and came to bay on the edge of a cliff.   A couple of hundred yards from the spot, we left the horses and scrambled along on foot, guided by the furious clamor of the pack.   When we reached them, the cougar had gone along the face of the cliff, most of the dogs could not see him, and it was some time before we could make him out ourselves.   Then I got up quite close.   Although the moonlight was bright I could not see the sights of my rifle, and fired a little too far back.   The bullet, however, inflicted a bad wound, and the cougar ran along a ledge, disappearing around the cliff shoulder. The conduct of the dogs showed that he had not left the cliff, but it was impossible to see him either from the sides or from below. The cliff was about a hundred feet high and the top overhung the bottom, while from above the ground sloped down to the brink at a rather steep angle, so that we had to be cautious about our footing. There was a large projecting rock on the brink; to this I clambered down, and, holding it with one hand, peeped over the edge. After a minute or two I made out first the tail and then the head of the cougar, who was lying on a narrow ledge only some ten feet below me, his body hidden by the overhang of the cliff. Thanks to the steepness of the incline, I could not let go of the rock with my left hand, because I should have rolled over; so I got Goff to come down, brace his feet against the projection, and grasp me by my legs. He then lowered me gently down until my head and shoulders were over the edge and my arms free; and I shot the cougar right between the ears, he being in a straight line underneath me. The dogs were evidently confident that he was going to be shot, for they had all gathered below the cliff to wait for him to fall; and sure enough, down he came with a crash, luckily not hitting any of them. We could hear them seize him, and they all, dead cougar and worrying dogs, rolled at least a hundred yards down the steep slope before they were stopped by a gully. It was an interesting experience, and one which I shall not soon forget. We clambered down to where the dogs were, admired our victim, and made up our minds not to try to skin him until the morning. Then we led down our horses, with some difficulty, into the snow-covered valley, mounted them, and cantered home to the ranch, under the cold and brilliant moon, through a white wonderland of shimmering light and beauty.

Next morning we came back as early as possible, intending first to skin the male and then to hunt up the female. A quarter of a mile before we reached the carcass we struck her fresh trail in the snow of the valley. Calling all the dogs together and hustling them forward, we got them across the trail without their paying any attention to it; for we wanted to finish the job of skinning before taking up the hunt. However, when we got off our horses and pulled the cougar down to a flat place to skin it, Nellie, who evidently remembered that there had been another cougar besides the one we had accounted for, started away on her own account while we were not looking. The first thing we knew we heard her giving tongue on the mountains above us, in such rough country that there was no use in trying to head her off. Accordingly we jumped on the horses again, rode down to where we had crossed the trail and put the whole pack on it. After crossing the valley the cougar had moved along the ledges of a great spur or chain of foothills, and as this prevented the dogs going too fast we were able to canter alongside them up the valley, watching them and listening to their chiming. We finally came to a large hillside bare of snow, much broken with rocks, among which grew patches of brush and scattered pinyons. Here the dogs were at fault for over an hour. It had evidently been a favorite haunt of the cougars; they had moved to and fro across it, and had lain sunning themselves in the dust under the ledges. Owing to the character of the ground we could give the hounds no assistance, but they finally puzzled out the trail for themselves. We were now given a good illustration of the impossibility of jumping a cougar without dogs, even when in a general way its haunt is known. We rode along the hillside, and quartered it to and fro, on the last occasion coming down a spur where we passed within two or three rods of the brush in which the cougar was actually lying; but she never moved and it was impossible to see her. When we finally reached the bottom, the dogs had disentangled the trail; and they passed behind us at a good rate, going up almost where we had come down. Even as we looked we saw the cougar rise from her lair, only fifty yards or so ahead of them, her red hide showing bright in the sun. It was a very pretty run to watch while it lasted. She left them behind at first, but after a quarter of a mile they put her up a pinyon. Approaching cautiously—for the climbing was hard work and I did not wish to frighten her out of the tree if it could be avoided, lest she might make such a run as that of the preceding evening—I was able to shoot her through the heart. She died in the branches, and I climbed the tree to throw her down. The only skill needed in such shooting is in killing the cougar outright so as to save the dogs. Six times on the hunt I shot the cougar through the heart. Twice the animal died in

COUGAR IN A TREE

From a photograph by Philip B. Stewart

the branches. In the other four cases it sprang out of the tree, head and tail erect, eyes blazing, and the mouth open in a grin of savage hate and anger; but it was practically dead when it touched the ground.

Although these cougars were mates, they were not of the same color, the female being reddish, while the male was slate-colored. In weighing this male we had to take off the hide and weigh it separately (with the head and paws attached), for our steelyard only went up to 150 pounds. When we came to weigh the biggest male we had to take off the quarters as well as the hide.

Thinking that we had probably exhausted the cougars around the Keystone Ranch, we spent the next fortnight off on a trip. We carried only what we could put in the small saddle-pockets—our baggage being as strictly limited as it ought to be with efficient cavalry who are on an active campaign. We worked hard, but, as so often happens, our luck was not in proportion to our labor.

The first day we rode to the Mathes brothers' ranch. On the high divides it was very cold, the thermometer standing at nearly twenty degrees below zero. But we were clad for just such weather, and were not uncomfortable. The three Mathes brothers lived together, with the wives and children of the two married ones. Their ranch was in a very beautiful and wild valley, the pinyon-crowned cliffs rising in walls on either hand. Deer were abundant and often in sight from the ranch doors. At night the gray wolves came down close to the buildings and howled for hours among the precipices, under the light of the full moon. The still cold was intense; but

I could not resist going out for half an hour at a time to listen to them. To me their baying, though a very eerie and lonesome sound, full of vaguely sinister associations, has, nevertheless, a certain wild music of its own which is far from being without charm.

We did not hear the cougars calling, for they are certainly nothing like as noisy as wolves; yet the Mathes brothers had heard them several times, and once one of them had crept up and seen the cougar, which remained in the same place for many minutes, repeating its cry continually. The Mathes had killed but two cougars, not having any dogs trained to hunt them. One of these was killed under circumstances which well illustrate the queer nature of the animal. The three men, with one of their two cattle dogs, were walking up the valley not half a mile above the ranch house, when they saw a cougar crossing in front of them, a couple of hundred yards off. As soon as she saw them she crouched flat down with her head toward them, remaining motionless. Two, with the dog, stayed where they were, while the other ran back to the ranch house for a rifle and for the other dog. No sooner had he gone than the cougar began deliberately to crawl toward the men who were left. She came on slowly but steadily, crouched almost flat to the ground. The two unarmed men were by no means pleased with her approach. They waved their hands and jumped about and shouted; but she kept approaching, although slowly, and was well within a hundred yards when the other brother arrived, out of breath, accompanied by the other dog. At sight of him she jumped up, ran off a couple of hundred yards, went up a tree, and was killed. I do not suppose she would have attacked the men; but as there was an unpleasant possibility that she might, they both felt distinctly more comfortable when their brother rejoined them with the rifle.

There was a good deal of snowy weather while we were at the Mathes ranch, but we had fair luck, killing two cougars. It was most comfortable, for the ranch was clean and warm, and the cooking delicious. It does not seem to me that I ever tasted better milk and butter, hot biscuits, rice, potatoes, pork and bulberry and wild-plum jam; and of course the long days on horseback in the cold weather gave an edge to our appetites. One stormy day we lost the hounds, and we spent most of the next day in finding such of them as did not come straggling in of their own accord. The country was very rough, and it was astounding to see some of the places up and down which we led the horses. Sometimes I found that my horse climbed rather better than I did, for he would come up some awkward-looking slope with such a rush that I literally had to scramble on all-fours to get out of his way.

There was no special incident connected with killing either of these two cougars. In one case Goff himself took the lead in working out the trail and preventing the hounds getting off after bobcats. In the other case the trail was fresher and the dogs ran it by themselves, getting into a country where we could not follow; it was very rough, and the cliffs and gorges rang with their baying. In both cases they had the cougar treed for about three hours before we were able to place them and walk up to them. It was hard work, toiling through the snow over the cliffs toward the baying; and on each occasion the cougar leaped from the tree at our approach, and ran a quarter of a mile or so before going up another, where it was shot. As I came up to shoot, most of the dogs paid no attention, but Boxer and Nellie always kept looking at me until I actually raised the rifle, when they began to spring about the spot where they thought the cougar would come down. The cougar itself always seemed to recognize the man as the dangerous opponent; and as I strode around to find a place from whence I could deliver an instantaneously fatal shot, it would follow me steadily with its evil yellow eyes. I came up very close, but the beasts never attempted to jump at me. Judging from what one reads in books about Indian and African game, a leopard under such circumstances would certainly sometimes charge.

Three days of our trip were spent on a ride to Colorow Mountain; we went down to Judge Foreman's ranch on White River to pass the night. We got another cougar on the way. She must really be credited to Jim. The other dogs were following in our footsteps through the snow, after having made various futile excursions of their own. When we found that Jim was missing, we tried in vain to recall him with the horn, and at last started to hunt him up. After an hour's ride we heard him off on the mountain, evidently following a trail, but equally evidently not yet having jumped the animal. The hounds heard him quite as quickly as we did, and started toward him. Soon we heard the music of the whole pack, which grew fainter and fainter, and was lost entirely as they disappeared around a spur, and then began to grow loud again, showing that they were coming toward us. Suddenly a change in the note convinced us that they had jumped the quarry. We stood motionless; nearer and nearer they came; and then a sudden burst of clamor proclaimed that they were barking treed. We had to ride only a couple of hundred yards; I shot the cougar from across a little ravine. She was the largest female we got.

The dogs were a source of unceasing amusement, not merely while hunting, but because of their relations to one another when off duty. Queen's temper was of the shortest toward the rest of the pack, although, like Turk, she was fond of literally crawling into my lap, when we sat down to rest after the worry which closed the chase. As soon as I began to eat my lunch, all the dogs clustered close around and I distributed small morsels to each in turn. Once Jimmie, Queen, and Boxer were sitting side by side, tightly wedged together. I treated them with entire impartiality; and soon Queen's feelings overcame her, and she unostentatiously but firmly bit Jimmie in the jaw. Jimmie howled tremendously and Boxer literally turned a back somersault, evidently fearing lest his turn should come next.

On February 11th we rode back to the Keystone Ranch, carrying the three cougar skins behind our saddles. It was again very cold, and the snow on the divides was so deep that our horses wallowed through it up to their saddle-girths. I supposed that my hunt was practically at an end, for I had but three days left; but as it turned out these were the three most lucky days of the whole trip.

The weather was beautiful, the snow lying deep enough to give the dogs easy trailing even on the southern slopes. Under the clear skies the landscape was dazzling, and I had to wear snow-glasses. On the first of the three days, February 12th, we had not ridden half an hour from the ranch before we came across the trail of a very big bobcat. It was so heavy that it had broken through the crust here and there, and we decided that it was worth following. The trail went up a steep mountain to the top, and we followed on foot after the dogs. Among the cliffs on the top they were completely at fault, hunting every which way. After awhile Goff suddenly spied the cat, which had jumped off the top of a cliff into a pinyon. I killed it before any of the dogs saw it, and at the shot they all ran in the wrong direction. When they did find us skinning it, they were evidently not at all satisfied that it was really their bobcat—the one which they had been trailing. Usually as soon as the animal was killed they all lay down and dozed off; but on this occasion they kept hurrying about and then in a body started on the back trail. It was some time before we could get them together again.

After we had brought them in we rode across one or two ridges, and up and down the spurs without finding anything, until about noon we struck up a long winding valley where we came across one or two old cougar trails. The pack were following in our footsteps behind the horses, except Jim, who took off to one side by himself. Suddenly he began to show signs that he had come across traces of game; and in another moment he gave tongue and all the hounds started toward him. They quartered around in the neighborhood of a little gulch for a short while, and then streamed off up the mountain-side; and before they had run more than a couple of minutes we heard them barking treed. By making a slight turn we rode almost up to the tree, and saw that their quarry was a young cougar. As we came up, it knocked Jimmie right out of the tree. On seeing us it jumped down and started to run, but it was not quite quick enough. Turk seized it and in a minute the dogs had it stretched out. It squawled, hissed, and made such a good fight that I put an end to the struggle with the knife, fearing lest it might maim one of the hounds.

While Goff was skinning it I wandered down to the kill near which it had been lying. This was a deer, almost completely devoured. It had been killed in the valley and dragged up perhaps a hundred yards to some cedars. I soon saw from the tracks around the carcass that there was an older cougar with the younger one—doubtless its mother—and walked back to Goff with the information. Before I got there, however, some of the pack had made the discovery for themselves. Jim, evidently feeling that he had done his duty, had curled up and gone to sleep, with most of the others; but old Boxer and the three bitches (Pete had left her pups and joined us about the time we roused the big bobcat), hunted about until they struck the fresh trail of the old female. They went off at a great rate, and the sleeping dogs heard them and scampered away to the sound. The trail led them across a spur, into a valley, and out of it up the precipitous side of another mountain. When we got to the edge of the valley we could hear them barking treed nearly at the summit of the mountain opposite. It was over an hour's stiff climbing before we made our way around to them, although we managed to get the horses up to within a quarter of a mile of the spot. On approaching we found the cougar in a leaning pinyon on a ledge at the foot of a cliff. Jimmie was in the lower branches of the pinyon, and Turk up above him, within a few feet of the cougar. Evidently he had been trying to tackle her and had been knocked out of the tree at least once, for he was bleeding a good deal and there was much blood on the snow beneath. Yet he had come back into the tree, and was barking violently not more than three feet beyond her stroke. She kept up a low savage growling, and as soon as I appeared, fixed her yellow eyes on me, glaring and snarling as I worked around into a place from which I could kill her outright. Meanwhile Goff took up his position on the other side, hoping to get a photograph when I shot. My bullet went right through her heart. She bit her paw, stretched up her head and bit a branch, and then died where she was, while Turk leaped forward at the crack of the rifle and seized her in the branches. I had some difficulty in bundling him and Jimmie out of the tree as I climbed up to throw down the cougar.

Next morning we started early, intending to go to Juniper Mountain, where we had heard that cougars were plentiful; but we had only ridden about half an hour from the ranch when we came across a trail which by the size we knew must belong to an old male. It was about thirty-six hours old and led into a tangle of bad lands where there was great difficulty in working it out. Finally, however, we found where it left these bad lands and went straight up a mountain-side, too steep for the horses to follow. From the plains below we watched the hounds working to and fro until they entered a patch of pinyons in which we were certain the cougar had killed a deer, as ravens and magpies were sitting around in the trees. In these pinyons the hounds were again at fault for a little while, but at last evidently found the right trail, and followed it up over the hill-crest and out of sight. We then galloped hard along the plain to the left, going around the end of the ridge and turning to our right on the other side. Here we entered a deep narrow valley or gorge which led up to a high plateau at the farther end. On our right, as we rode up the valley, lay the high and steep ridge over which the hounds had followed the trail. On the left it was still steeper, the slope being broken by ledges and precipices. Near the mouth of the gorge we encountered the hounds, who had worked the trail down and across the gorge, and were now hunting up the steep cliff-shoulder on our left. Evidently the cougar had wandered to and fro over this shoulder, and the dogs were much puzzled and worked in zigzags and circles around it, gradually getting clear to the top. Then old Boxer suddenly gave tongue with renewed zest and started off at a run almost on top of the ridge, the other dogs following. Immediately afterward they jumped the cougar.

We had been waiting below to see which direction the chase would take and now put spurs to our horses and galloped up the ravine, climbing the hillside on our right so as to get a better view of what was happening. A few hundred yards of this galloping and climbing brought us again in sight of the hounds. They were now barking treed and were clustered around a pinyon below the ridge crest on the side hill opposite us. The two fighters, Turk and Queen, who had been following at our horses' heels, appreciated what had happened as soon as we did, and, leaving us, ran down into the valley and began to work their way through the deep snow up the hillside opposite, toward where the hounds were. Ours was an ideal position for seeing the whole chase. In a minute the cougar jumped out of the tree down among the hounds, who made no attempt to seize him, but followed him as soon as he had cleared their circle. He came down hill at a great rate and jumped over a low cliff, bringing after him such an avalanche of snow that it was a moment before I caught sight of him again, this time crouched on a narrow ledge some fifteen or twenty feet below the brink from which he had jumped, and about as far above the foot of the cliff, where the steep hill-slope again began. The hounds soon found him and came along the ledge barking loudly, but not venturing near where he lay facing them, with his back arched like a great cat. Turk and Queen were meanwhile working their way up hill. Turk got directly under the ledge and could not find a way up. Queen went to the left and in a minute we saw her white form as she made her way through the dark-colored hounds straight for the cougar. "That's the end of Queen," said Goff; "he'll kill her now, sure." In another moment she had made her rush and the cougar, bounding forward, had seized her, and as we afterward discovered had driven his great fangs right through the side of her head, fortunately missing the brain. In the struggle he lost his footing and rolled off the ledge, and when they struck the ground below he let go of the bitch. Turk, who was near where they struck, was not able to spring for the hold he desired, and in another moment the cougar was coming down hill like a quarter horse. We stayed perfectly still, as he was travelling in our direction. Queen was on her feet almost as quick as the cougar, and she and Turk tore after him, the hounds following in a few seconds, being delayed in getting off the ledge. It was astonishing to see the speed of the cougar. He ran considerably more than a quarter of a mile down hill, and at the end of it had left the dogs more than a hundred yards behind. But his bolt was shot, and after going perhaps a hundred yards or so up the hill on our side and below us, he climbed a tree, under which the dogs began to bay frantically, while we scrambled toward them. When I got down I found him standing half upright on a big branch, his forepaws hung over another higher branch, his sides puffing like bellows, and evidently completely winded. In scrambling up the pinyon he must have struck a patch of resin, for it had torn a handful of hair off from behind his right forearm. I shot him through the heart. At the shot he sprang clean into the top of the tree, head and tail up, and his face fairly demoniac with rage; but before he touched the ground he was dead. Turk jumped up, seized him as he fell, and the two rolled over a low ledge, falling about eight feet into the snow, Turk never losing his hold.

No one could have wished to see a prettier chase under better circumstances. It was exceedingly interesting. The only dog hurt was Queen, and very miserable indeed she looked. She stood in the trail, refusing to lie down or to join the other dogs, as, with prodigious snarls at one another, they ate the pieces of the carcass we cut out for them. Dogs hunting every day, as these were doing, and going through such terrific exertion, need enormous quantities of meat, and as old horses and crippled steers were not always easy to get, we usually fed them the cougar carcasses. On this occasion, when they had eaten until they could eat no longer, I gave most of my lunch to Queen—Boxer, who after his feast could hardly move, nevertheless waddling up with his ears forward to beg a share. Queen evidently felt that the lunch was a delicacy, for she ate it, and then trotted home behind us with the rest of the dogs. Rather to my astonishment, next day she was all right, and as eager to go with us as ever. Though one side of her head was much swollen, in her work she showed no signs of her injuries.

Early the following morning, February 14th, the last day of my actual hunting, we again started for Juniper Mountain, following the same course on which we had

"BARKING TREED"

started the previous day. Before we had gone a mile, that is, only about half-way to where we had come across the cougar track the preceding day, we crossed another, and as we deemed a fresher, trail, which Goff pronounced to belong to a cougar even larger than the one we had just killed. The hounds were getting both weary and footsore, but the scent put heart into them and away they streamed. They followed it across a sage-brush flat, and then worked along under the base of a line of cliffs—cougar being particularly apt thus to travel at the foot of cliffs. The pack kept well together, and it was pleasant, as we cantered over the snowy plain beside them, to listen to their baying, echoed back from the cliffs above. Then they worked over the hill and we spurred ahead and turned to the left, up the same gorge or valley in which we had killed the cougar the day before. The hounds followed the trail straight to the cliff-shoulder where the day before the pack had been puzzled until Boxer struck the fresh scent. Here they seemed to be completely at fault, circling everywhere, and at one time following their track of yesterday over to the pinyon-tree up which the cougar had first gone.

We made our way up the ravine to the head of the plateau, and then, turning, came back along the ridge until we reached the top of the shoulder where the dogs had been; but when we got there they had disappeared. It did not seem likely that the cougar had crossed the ravine behind us—although as a matter of fact this was exactly what had happened—and we did not know what to make of the affair.

We could barely hear the hounds; they had followed their back trail of the preceding day, toward the place where we had first come across the tracks of the cougar we had already killed. We were utterly puzzled, even Goff being completely at fault, and we finally became afraid that the track which the pack had been running was one which, instead of having been made during the night, had been there the previous morning, and had been made by the dead cougar. This meant, of course, that we had passed it without noticing it, both going and coming, on the previous day, and knowing Goff's eye for a track I could not believe this. He, however, thought we might have confused it with some of the big wolf tracks, of which a number had crossed our path. After some hesitation, he said that at any rate we could find out the truth by getting back into the flat and galloping around to where we had begun our hunt the day before; because if the dogs really had a fresh cougar before them he must have so short a start that they were certain to tree him by the time they got across the ridge-crest. Accordingly we scrambled down the precipitous mountain-side, galloped along the flat around the end of the ridge and drew rein at about the place where we had first come across the cougar trail on the previous day. Not a dog was to be heard anywhere, and Goff's belief that the pack was simply running a back track became a certainty both in his mind and mine, when Jim suddenly joined us, evidently having given up the chase. We came to the conclusion that Jim, being wiser than the other dogs, had discovered his mistake while they had not; " he just naturally quit," said Goff.

After some little work we found where the pack had crossed the broad flat valley into a mass of very rough broken country, the same in which I had shot my first big male by moonlight. Cantering and scrambling through this stretch of cliffs and valleys, we began to hear the dogs, and at first were puzzled because once or twice it seemed as though they were barking treed or had something at bay; always, however, as we came nearer we could again hear them running a trail, and when we finally got up tolerably close we found that they were all scattered out. Boxer was far behind, and Nellie, whose feet had become sore, was soberly accompanying him, no longer giving tongue. The others were separated one from the other, and we finally made out Tree'em all by himself, and not very far away. In vain Goff called and blew his horn; Tree'em disappeared up a high hillside, and with muttered comments on his stupidity we galloped our horses along the valley around the foot of the hill, hoping to intercept him. No sooner had we come to the other side, however, than we heard Tree'em evidently barking treed. We looked at one another, wondering whether he had come across a bobcat, or whether it had really been a fresh cougar trail after all.

Leaving our horses we scrambled up the canyon until we got in sight of a large pinyon on the hillside, underneath which Tree'em was standing, with his preposterous tail arched like a pump-handle, as he gazed solemnly up in the tree, now and then uttering a bark at a huge cougar, which by this time we could distinctly make out standing in the branches. Turk and Queen had already left us and were running hard to join Tree'em, and in another minute or two all of the hounds, except the belated Boxer and Nellie, had also come up. The cougar having now recovered his wind, jumped down and cantered off. He had been running for three hours before the dogs and evidently had been overtaken again and again, but had either refused to tree, or if he did tree had soon come down and continued his flight, the hounds not venturing to meddle with him, and he paying little heed to them. It was a different matter, however, with Turk and Queen along. He went up the hill and came to bay on the top of the cliffs, where we could see him against the skyline. The hounds surrounded him, but neither they nor Turk came to close quarters. Queen, however, as soon as she arrived rushed straight in, and the cougar knocked her a dozen feet off. Turk tried to seize him as soon as Queen had made her rush; the cougar broke bay, and they all disappeared over the hill-top, while we hurried after them. A quarter of a mile beyond, on the steep hillside, they again had him up a pinyon-tree. I approached as cautiously as possible so as not to alarm him. He stood in such an awkward position that I could not get a fair shot at the heart, but the bullet broke his back, and the dogs seized him as he struck the ground. There was still any amount of fight in him, and I ran in as fast as possible, jumping and slipping over the rocks and the bushes as the cougar and dogs rolled and slid down the steep mountain-side—for, of course, every minute's delay meant the chance of a dog being killed or crippled. It was a day of misfortunes for Jim, who was knocked completely out of the fight by a single blow. The cougar was too big for the dogs to master, even crippled as he was; but when I came up close Turk ran in and got the great beast by one ear, stretching out the cougar's head, while he kept his own forelegs tucked way back so that the cougar could not get hold of them. This gave me my chance and I drove the knife home, leaping back before the creature could get round at me. Boxer did not come up for half an hour, working out every inch of the trail for himself, and croaking away at short intervals, while Nellie trotted calmly beside him. Even when he saw us skinning the cougar he would not hurry nor take a short cut, but followed the scent to where the cougar had gone up the tree, and from the tree down to where we were; then he meditatively bit the carcass, strolled off, and lay down, satisfied.

It was a very large cougar, fat and heavy, and the men at the ranch believed it was the same one which had at intervals haunted the place for two or three years, killing on one occasion a milch cow, on another a steer, and on yet another a big work horse. Goff stated that he had on two or three occasions killed cougars that were quite as long, and he believed even an inch or two longer, but that he had never seen one as large or as heavy. Its weight was 227 pounds, and as it lay stretched out it looked like a small African lioness. It would be impossible to wish a better ending to a hunt.

The next day Goff and I cantered thirty miles into Meeker, and my holiday was over.

CHAPTER II

A COLORADO BEAR HUNT

IN mid-April, nineteen hundred and five, our party, consisting of Philip B. Stewart, of Colorado Springs, and Dr. Alexander Lambert, of New York, in addition to myself, left Newcastle, Col., for a bear hunt. As guides and hunters we had John Goff and Jake Borah, than whom there are no better men at their work of hunting bear in the mountains with hounds. Each brought his own dogs; all told, there were twenty-six hounds, and four half-blood terriers to help worry the bear when at bay. We travelled in comfort, with a big pack train, spare horses for each of us, and a cook, packers, and horse wranglers. I carried one of the new model Springfield military rifles, a 30–40, with a soft-nosed bullet—a very accurate and hard-hitting gun.

This first day we rode about twenty miles to where camp was pitched on the upper waters of East Divide Creek. It was a picturesque spot. At this altitude it was still late winter and the snow lay in drifts, even in the creek bottom, while the stream itself was not yet clear from ice. The tents were pitched in a grove of leafless aspens and great spruces, beside the rushing, ice-rimmed brook. The cook tent, with its stove, was an attractive place on the cool mornings and in stormy weather. Fry,

STARTING FOR CAMP

From a stereograph, copyright, 1905, by Underwood and Underwood

the cook, a most competent man, had rigged up a table, and we had folding camp-chairs—luxuries utterly unknown to my former camping trips. Each day we breakfasted early and dined ten or twelve hours later, on returning from the day's hunt; and as we carried no lunch, the two meals were enjoyed with ravenous pleasure by the entire company. The horses were stout, tough, shaggy beasts, of wonderful staying power, and able to climb like cats. The country was very steep and rugged; the mountain-sides were greasy and slippery from the melting snow, while the snow bucking through the deep drifts on their tops and on the north sides was exhausting. Only sure-footed animals could avoid serious tumbles, and only animals of great endurance could have lasted through the work. Both Johnny Goff and his partner, Brick Wells, who often accompanied us on the hunts, were frequently mounted on animals of uncertain temper, with a tendency to buck on insufficient provocation; but they rode them with entire indifference up and down any incline. One of the riders, " Al," a very good tempered man, a tireless worker, had as one of his horses a queer, big-headed dun beast, with a black stripe down its back and traces of zebra-like bands on the backs of his front legs. He was an atavistic animal, looking much as the horses must have looked which an age or two ago lived in this very locality and were preyed on by sabre-toothed tigers, hyenadons, and other strange and terrible beasts of a long-vanished era. Lambert remarked to him: " Al, you ought to call that horse of yours ' Fossil '; he is a hundred thousand years old." To which Al, with immovable face, replied: "Gee! and that man sold him to me for a seven-year-old! I'll have the law on him!"

The hounds were most interesting, and showed all the variations of character and temper to be expected in such a pack; a pack in which performance counted for everything and pedigree for nothing. One of the best hounds was half fox terrier. Three of Johnny's had been with us four years before, when he and I hunted cougars together; these three being Jim, now an old dog, who dropped behind in a hard run, but still excellent on a cold trail; Tree'em, who, like Jim, had grown aged, but was very sure; and Bruno, who had become one of the best of all the pack on a hot trail, but who was apt to overrun it if it became at all difficult and cold. The biggest dog of the pack, a very powerful animal, was Badge, who was half foxhound and half what Johnny called Siberian bloodhound—I suppose a Great Dane or Ulm dog. His full brother Bill came next to him. There was a Rowdy in Jake's pack and another Rowdy in Johnny's, and each got badly hurt before the hunt was through. Jake's Rowdy, as soon as an animal was killed, became very cross and wished to attack any dog that came near. One of Jake's best hounds was old Bruise, a very sure, although not a particularly fast dog. All the members of the pack held the usual wild-beast attitude toward one another. They joined together for the chase and the fight, but once the quarry was killed, their relations among themselves became those of active hostility or selfish indifference. At feeding time each took whatever his strength permitted, and each paid abject deference to whichever animal was his known superior in prowess. Some of the younger dogs would now and then run deer or coyote. But the older dogs paid heed only to bear and bobcat; and the pack, as a body, discriminated sharply between the hounds they could trust and those which would go off on a wrong trail. The four terriers included a heavy, liver-colored half-breed bull-dog, a preposterous animal who looked as if his ancestry had included a toadfish. He was a terrible fighter, but his unvarying attitude toward mankind was one of effusive and rather foolish affection. In a fight he could whip any of the hounds save Badge, and he was far more willing than Badge to accept punishment. There was also a funny little black and tan, named Skip, a most friendly little fellow, especially fond of riding in front or behind the saddle of any one of us who would take him up, although perfectly able to travel forty miles a day on his own sturdy legs if he had to, and then to join in the worry of the quarry when once it had been shot. Porcupines abounded in the woods, and one or two of the terriers and half a dozen of the hounds positively refused to learn any wisdom, invariably attacking each porcupine they found; the result being that we had to spend many minutes in removing the quills from their mouths, eyes, etc. A white bull-terrier would come in from such a combat with his nose literally looking like a glorified pincushion, and many of the spines we had to take out with nippers. The terriers never ran with the hounds, but stayed behind with the horses until they heard the hounds barking " bayed " or " treed," when they forthwith tore toward them. Skip adopted me as his special master, rode with me whenever I would let him, and slept on the foot of my bed at night, growling defiance at anything that came near. I grew attached to the friendly, bright little fellow, and at the end of the hunt took him home with me as a playmate for the children.

It was a great, wild country. In the creek bottoms there were a good many ranches; but we only occasionally passed by these, on our way to our hunting grounds in the wilderness along the edge of the snow-line. The mountains crowded close together in chain, peak, and table-land; all the higher ones were wrapped in an unrent shroud of snow. We saw a good many deer, and fresh sign of elk, but no elk themselves, although we were informed that bands were to be found in the high spruce timber where the snows were so deep that it would have been impossible to go on horseback, while going on foot would have been inconceivably fatiguing. The country was open. The high peaks were bare of trees. Cotton-woods, and occasionally dwarfed birch or maple and willows, fringed the streams; aspens grew in groves higher up. There were pinyons and cedars on the slopes of the foothills; spruce clustered here and there in the cooler ravines and valleys and high up the mountains. The dense oak brush and thick growing cedars were hard on our clothes, and sometimes on our bodies.

Bear and cougars had once been very plentiful throughout this region, but during the last three or four years the cougars have greatly diminished in numbers throughout northern Colorado, and the bears have diminished also, although not to the same extent. The great grizzlies which were once fairly plentiful here are now very rare, as they are in most places in the United States. There remain plenty of the black and brown bears, which are simply individual color phases of the same species.

Bears are interesting creatures and their habits are always worth watching. When I used to hunt grizzlies my experience tended to make me lay special emphasis on their variation in temper. There are savage and cowardly bears, just as there are big and little ones; and sometimes these variations are very marked among bears of the same district, and at other times all the bears of one district will seem to have a common code of behavior which differs utterly from that of the bears of another district. Readers of Lewis and Clark do not need to be reminded of the great difference they found in ferocity between the bears of the upper Missouri and the bears of the Columbia River country; and those who have lived in the upper Missouri country nowadays know how widely the bears that still remain have altered in character from what they were as recently as the middle of the last century.

This variability has been shown in the bears which I have stumbled upon at close quarters. On but one occasion was I ever regularly charged by a grizzly. To this animal I had given a mortal wound, and without any effort at retaliation he bolted into a thicket of what, in my hurry, I thought was laurel (it being composed in reality, I suppose, of thick-growing berry bushes). On my following him and giving him a second wound, he charged very determinedly, taking two more bullets without flinching. I just escaped the charge by jumping to one side, and he died almost immediately after striking at me as he rushed by. This bear charged with his mouth open, but made very little noise after the growl or roar with which he greeted my second bullet. I mention the fact of his having kept his mouth open, because one or two of my friends who have been charged have informed me that in their cases they particularly noticed that the bear charged with his mouth shut. Perhaps the fact that my bear was shot through the lungs may account for the difference, or it may simply be another example of individual variation.

On another occasion, in a windfall, I got up within eight or ten feet of a grizzly, which simply bolted off, paying no heed to a hurried shot which I delivered as I poised unsteadily on the swaying top of an overthrown dead pine. On yet another occasion, when I roused a big bear from his sleep, he at the first moment seemed to pay little or no heed to me, and then turned toward me in a leisurely way, the only sign of hostility he betrayed being to ruffle up the hair on his shoulders and the back of his neck. I hit him square between the eyes, and he dropped like a pole-axed steer.

On another occasion I got up quite close to and mortally wounded a bear, which ran off without uttering a sound until it fell dead; but another of these grizzlies, which I shot from ambush, kept squalling and yelling every time I hit him, making a great rumpus. On one occasion one of my cow hands and myself were able to

AT DINNER

From a photograph by Philip B. Stewart

run down on foot a she grizzly bear and her cub, which had obtained a long start of us, simply because of the foolish conduct of the mother. The cub—or more properly the yearling, for it was a cub of the second year— ran on far ahead, and would have escaped if the old she had not continually stopped and sat up on her hind legs to look back at us. I think she did this partly from curiosity, but partly also from bad temper, for once or twice she grinned and roared at us. The upshot of it was that I got within range and put a bullet in the old she, who afterward charged my companion and was killed; and we also got the yearling.

One young grizzly which I killed many years ago dropped to the first bullet, which entered its stomach. It then let myself and my companion approach closely, looking up at us with alert curiosity, but making no effort to escape. It was really not crippled at all, but we thought from its actions that its back was broken, and my companion advanced to kill it with his pistol. The pistol, however, did not inflict a mortal wound, and the only effect was to make the young bear jump to its feet as if unhurt, and race off at full speed through the timber; for though not full grown it was beyond cubhood, being probably about eighteen months old. By desperate running I succeeded in getting another shot, and more by luck than by anything else knocked it over, this time permanently.

Black bear are not, under normal conditions, formidable brutes. If they do charge and get home they may maul a man severely, and there are a number of instances on record in which they have killed men. Ordinarily, however, a black bear will not charge home, though he may bluster a good deal. I once shot one very close up which made a most lamentable outcry, and seemed to lose its head, its efforts to escape resulting in its bouncing about among the trees with such heedless hurry that I was easily able to kill it. Another black bear, which I also shot at close quarters, came straight for my companions and myself, and almost ran over the white hunter who was with me. This bear made no sound whatever when I first hit it, and I do not think it was charging. I believe it was simply dazed, and by accident ran the wrong way, and so almost came into collision with us. However, when it found itself face to face with the white hunter, and only four or five feet away, it prepared for hostilities, and I think would have mauled him if I had not brained it with another bullet; for I was myself standing but six feet or so to one side of it. None of the bears shot on this Colorado trip made a sound when hit; they all died silently, like so many wolves.

Ordinarily, my experience has been that bears were not flurried when I suddenly came upon them. They impressed me as if they were always keeping in mind the place toward which they wished to retreat in the event of danger, and for this place, which was invariably a piece of rough ground or dense timber, they made off with all possible speed, not seeming to lose their heads.

Frequently I have been able to watch bears for some time while myself unobserved. With other game I have very often done this even when within close range, not

THE PACK STRIKES THE FRESH BEAR TRAIL
From a photograph by Philip B. Stewart

wishing to kill creatures needlessly, or without a good object; but with bears, my experience has been that chances to secure them come so seldom as to make it very distinctly worth while improving any that do come, and I have not spent much time watching any bear unless he was in a place where I could not get at him, or else was so close at hand that I was not afraid of his getting away. On one occasion the bear was hard at work digging up squirrel or gopher *caches* on the side of a pine-clad hill; while at this work he looked rather like a big badger. On two other occasions the bear was fussing around a carcass preparatory to burying it. On these occasions I was very close, and it was extremely interesting to note the grotesque, half-human movements, and giant, awkward strength of the great beast. He would twist the carcass around with the utmost ease, sometimes taking it in his teeth and dragging it, at other times grasping it in his forepaws and half lifting, half shoving it. Once the bear lost his grip and rolled over during the course of some movement, and this made him angry, and he struck the carcass a savage whack, just as a pettish child will strike a table against which it has knocked itself. At another time I watched a black bear some distance off getting his breakfast under stumps and stones. He was very active, turning the stone or log over, and then thrusting his muzzle into the empty space to gobble up the small creatures below before they recovered from their surprise and the sudden inflow of light. From under one log he put a chipmunk, and danced hither and thither with even more agility than awkwardness, slapping at the chipmunk with his paw while it zigzagged about, until finally he scooped it into his mouth.

All this was in the old days when I was still-hunting, with only the rifle. This Colorado trip was the first on which I hunted bears with hounds. If we had run across a grizzly there would doubtless have been a chance to show some prowess, at least in the way of hard riding. But the black and brown bears cannot, save under exceptional circumstances, escape from such a pack as we had with us; and the real merit of the chase was confined to the hounds and to Jake and Johnny for their skill in handling them. Perhaps I should add the horses, for their extraordinary endurance and surefootedness. As for the rest of us, we needed to do little more than to sit ten or twelve hours in the saddle and occasionally lead the horses up or down the most precipitous and cliff-like of the mountain sides. But it was great fun, nevertheless, and usually a chase lasted long enough to be interesting.

The first day after reaching camp we rode for eleven hours over a very difficult country, but without getting above the snow-line. Finally the dogs got on the fresh trail of a bobcat, and away they went. A bobcat will often give a good run, much better, on the average, than a cougar; and this one puzzled the dogs not a little at first. It scrambled out of one deep valley, crossing and recrossing the rock ledges where its scent was hard to follow; then plunged into another valley. Meanwhile we had ridden up on the high mountain spur between the two valleys, and after scrambling and galloping to and fro as the cry veered from point to point when the dogs changed directions, we saw them cross into the second valley. Here again they took a good deal of time to puzzle out the trail, and became somewhat scattered. We had dismounted and were standing by the horses' heads, listening to the baying and trying to decide which way we should go, when Stewart suddenly pointed us out a bear. It was on the other side of the valley from us, and perhaps half a mile away, galloping down hill, with two of the hounds after it, and in the sunlight its fur looked glossy black. In a minute or two it passed out of sight in the thick-growing timber at the bottom of the valley; and as we afterward found, the two hounds, getting momentarily thrown out, and hearing the others still baying on the cat trail, joined the latter. Jake started off to go around the head of the valley, while the rest of us plunged down into it. We found from the track that the bear had gone up the valley, and Jake found where he had come out on the high divide, and then turned and retraced his steps. But the hounds were evidently all after the cat. There was nothing for us to do but follow them. Sometimes riding, sometimes leading the horses, we went up the steep hillside, and as soon as we reached the crest heard the hounds barking treed. Shorty and Skip, who always trotted after the horses while the hounds were in full cry on a trail, recognized the change of note immediately, and tore off in the direction of the bay, while we followed as best we could, hoping to get there in time for Stewart and Lambert to take photographs of the lynx in a tree. But we were too late. Both Shorty and Skip could climb trees, and although Skip was too light to tackle a bobcat by himself, Shorty, a heavy, formidable dog, of unflinching courage and great physical strength, was altogether too much for any bobcat. When we reached the place we found the bobcat in the top of a pinyon, and Shorty steadily working his way up through the branches and very near the quarry. Evidently the bobcat felt that the situation needed the taking of desperate chances, and just before Shorty reached it out it jumped, Shorty yelling with excitement as he plunged down through the branches after it. But the cat did not jump far enough. One of the hounds seized it by the hind leg and in another second everything was over.

Shorty was always the first of the pack to attack dangerous game, and in attacking bear or cougar even Badge was much less reckless and more wary. In consequence, Shorty was seamed over with scars; most of them from bobcats, but one or two from cougars. He could speedily kill a bobcat single-handed; for these small lynxes are not really formidable fighters, although they will lacerate a dog quite severely. Shorty found a badger a much more difficult antagonist than a bobcat. A bobcat in a hole makes a hard fight, however. On this hunt we once got a bobcat under a big rock, and Jake's Rowdy in trying to reach it got so badly mauled that he had to join the invalid class for several days.

The bobcat we killed this first day was a male, weighing twenty-five pounds. It was too late to try after the bear, especially as we had only ten or a dozen dogs out, while the bear's tracks showed it to be a big one; and we rode back to camp.

Next morning we rode off early, taking with us all twenty-six hounds and the four terriers. We wished first to find whether the bear had gone out of the country in which we had seen him, and so rode up a valley and then scrambled laboriously up the mountain-side to the top of the snow-covered divide. Here the snow was three feet deep in places, and the horses plunged and floundered as we worked our way in single file through the drifts. But it had frozen hard the previous night, so that a bear could walk on the crust and leave very little sign. In consequence we came near passing over the place where the animal we were after had actually crossed out of the canyon-like ravine in which we had seen him and gone over the divide into another set of valleys. The trail was so faint that it puzzled us, as we could not be certain how fresh it was, and until this point could be cleared up we tried to keep the hounds from following it. Old Jim, however, slipped off to one side and speedily satisfied himself that the trail was fresh. Along it he went, giving tongue, and the other dogs were maddened by the sound, while Jim, under such circumstances, paid no heed whatever to any effort to make him come back. Accordingly, the other hounds were slipped after him, and down they ran into the valley, while we slid, floundered, and scrambled along the ridge crest parallel to them, until a couple of miles farther on we worked our way down to some great slopes covered with dwarf scrub-oak. At the edge of these slopes, where they fell off in abrupt descent to the stream at the bottom of the valley, we halted. Opposite us was a high and very rugged mountain-side cov-

ered with a growth of pinyon—never a close-grow-
ing tree—its precipitous flanks broken by ledges and
scored by gullies and ravines. It was hard to follow the
scent across such a mountain-side, and the dogs speedily
became much scattered. We could hear them plainly,
and now and then could see them, looking like ants as
they ran up and down hill and along the ledges. Finally
we heard some of them barking bayed. The volume of
sound increased steadily as the straggling dogs joined
those which had first reached the hunted animal. At
about this time, to our astonishment, Badge, usually a
stanch fighter, rejoined us, followed by one or two other
hounds, who seemed to have had enough of the matter.
Immediately afterward we saw the bear, half-way up the
opposite mountain-side. The hounds were all around
him, and occasionally bit at his hind quarters; but he had
evidently no intention of climbing a tree. When we first
saw him he was sitting up on a point of rock surrounded
by the pack, his black fur showing to fine advantage.
Then he moved off, threatening the dogs, and making
what in Mississippi is called a walking bay. He was a
sullen, powerful beast, and his leisurely gait showed how
little he feared the pack, and how confident he was in his
own burly strength. By this time the dogs had been after
him for a couple of hours, and as there was no water on
the mountain-side we feared they might be getting exhausted, and rode toward them as rapidly as we could.
It was a hard climb up to where they were, and we had
to lead the horses. Just as we came in sight of him, across
a deep gully which ran down the sheer mountain-side,

DEATH OF THE BIG BEAR

From a photograph by Philip B. Stewart

he broke bay and started off, threatening the foremost of the pack as they dared to approach him. They were all around him, and for a minute I could not fire; then as he passed under a pinyon I got a clear view of his great round stern and pulled trigger. The bullet broke both his hips, and he rolled down hill, the hounds yelling with excitement as they closed in on him. He could still play havoc with the pack, and there was need to kill him at once. I leaped and slid down my side of the gully as he rolled down his; at the bottom he stopped and raised himself on his fore quarters; and with another bullet I broke his back between the shoulders.

Immediately all the dogs began to worry the carcass, while their savage baying echoed so loudly in the narrow, steep gully that we could with difficulty hear one another speak. It was a wild scene to look upon, as we scrambled down to where the dead bear lay on his back between the rocks. He did not die wholly unavenged, for he had killed one of the terriers and six other dogs were more or less injured. The chase of the bear is grim work for the pack. Jim, usually a very wary fighter, had a couple of deep holes in his thigh; but the most mishandled of the wounded dogs was Shorty. With his usual dauntless courage he had gone straight at the bear's head. Being such a heavy, powerful animal, I think if he had been backed up he could have held the bear's head down, and prevented the beast from doing much injury. As it was, the bear bit through the side of Shorty's head, and bit him in the shoulder, and again in the hip, inflicting very bad wounds. Once the fight was over Shorty lay down on the hillside, unable to move. When we started home we put him beside a little brook, and left a piece of bear meat by him, as it was obvious we could not get him to camp that day. Next day one of the boys went back with a pack-horse to take him in; but half-way out met him struggling toward camp, and returned. Late in the afternoon Shorty turned up while we were at dinner, and staggered toward us, wagging his tail with enthusiastic delight at seeing his friends. We fed him until he could not hold another mouthful; then he curled up in a dry corner of the cook-tent and slept for forty-eight hours; and two or three days afterward was able once more to go hunting.

The bear was a big male, weighing three hundred and thirty pounds. On examination at close quarters, his fur, which was in fine condition, was not as black as it had seemed when seen afar off, the roots of the hairs being brown. There was nothing whatever in his stomach. Evidently he had not yet begun to eat, and had been but a short while out of his hole. Bear feed very little when they first come out of their dens, sometimes beginning on grass, sometimes on buds. Occasionally they will feed at carcasses and try to kill animals within a week or two after they have left winter quarters, but this is rare, and as a usual thing for the first few weeks after they have come out they feed much as a deer would. Although not hog fat, as would probably have been the case in the fall, this bear was in good condition. In the fall, however, he would doubtless have weighed over four hundred pounds. The three old females we got on this trip weighed one hundred and eighty, one hundred and seventy-five, and one hundred and thirty-five pounds apiece. The year-lings weighed from thirty-one to forty pounds. The only other black bears I ever weighed all belonged to the sub-species *Luteolus,* and were killed on the Little Sun-flower River, in Mississippi, in the late fall of nineteen hundred and two. A big old male, in poor condition, weighed two hundred and eighty-five pounds, and two very fat females weighed two hundred and twenty and two hundred and thirty-five pounds respectively.

The next few days we spent in hunting perseveringly, but unsuccessfully. Each day we were from six to twelve hours in the saddle, climbing with weary toil up the mountains and slipping and scrambling down them. On the tops and on the north slopes there was much snow, so that we had to pick our trails carefully, and even thus the horses often floundered belly-deep as we worked along in single file; the men on the horses which were best at snow bucking took turns in breaking the trail. In the worst places we had to dismount and lead the horses, often over such bad ground that nothing less sure-footed than the tough mountain ponies could even have kept their legs. The weather was cold, with occasional sharp flurries of snow, and once a regular snow-storm. We found the tracks of one or two bears, but in each case several days old, and it was evident either that the bears had gone back to their dens, finding the season so late, or else that they were lying quiet in sheltered places, and travelling as little as possible. One day, after a long run of certainly five or six miles through very difficult coun-try, the dogs treed a bobcat in a big cedar. It had run so far that it was badly out of breath. Stewart climbed the tree and took several photographs of it, pushing the camera up to within about four feet of where the cat sat. Lambert obtained photographs of both Stewart and the cat. Shorty was at this time still an invalid from his encounter with the bear, but Skip worked his way thirty feet up the tree in his effort to get at the bobcat. Lambert shot the latter with his revolver, the bobcat dying stuck in the branches; and he then had to climb the tree to get both the bobcat and Skip, as the latter was at such a height that we thought he would hurt himself if he fell. Another bobcat when treed sealed his own fate by stepping on a dead branch and falling right into the jaws of the pack.

At this camp, as everywhere, the tiny four-striped chipmunks were plentiful and tame; they are cheerful, attractive little animals. We also saw white-footed mice and a big meadow mouse around camp; and we found a young brushy-tailed pack-rat. The snowshoe rabbits were still white on the mountains, but in the lower valleys they had changed to the summer pelage. On the mountains we occasionally saw woodchucks and rock squirrels of two kinds, a large and a small—*Spermophilus grammurus* and *armatus*. The noisy, cheerful pine squirrels were common where the woods were thick. There were eagles and ravens in the mountains, and once we saw sandhill cranes soaring far above the highest peaks. The long-crested jays came familiarly around camp, but on this occasion we only saw the whiskey-jacks, Clark's nut-crackers and magpies, while off in the mountains.

STEWART AND THE BOBCAT

From a photograph, copyright, 1905, by Alexander Lambert, M.D.

Among the pinyons, we several times came across straggling flocks of the queer pinyon jays or blue crows, with
their unmistakable calls and almost blackbird-like habits.
There were hawks of several species, and blue grouse,
while the smaller birds included flickers, robins, and the
beautiful mountain bluebirds. Juncos and mountain
chickadees were plentiful, and the ruby-crowned kinglets
were singing with astonishing power for such tiny birds.
We came on two nests of the red-tailed hawk; the birds
were brooding, and seemed tame and unwary.

After a week of this we came to the conclusion that
the snow was too deep and the weather too cold for us to
expect to get any more bear in the immediate neighborhood, and accordingly shifted camp to where Clear Creek
joins West Divide Creek.

The first day's hunt from the new camp was successful. We were absent about eleven hours and rode some
forty miles. The day included four hours' steady snow
bucking, for the bear, as soon as they got the chance, went
through the thick timber where the snow lay deepest.
Some two hours after leaving camp we found the old
tracks of a she and a yearling, but it took us a much longer
time before we finally struck the fresh trail made late the
previous night or early in the morning. It was Jake who
first found this fresh track, while Johnny with the pack
was a couple of miles away, slowly but surely puzzling
out the cold trail and keeping the dogs up to their work.
As soon as Johnny came up we put all the hounds on the
tracks, and away they went, through and over the snow,
yelling their eager delight. Meanwhile we had fixed our

saddles and were ready for what lay ahead. It was wholly impossible to ride at the tail of the pack, but we did our best to keep within sound of the baying. Finally, after much hard work and much point riding through snow, slush, and deep mud, on the level, and along, up, and down sheer slopes, we heard the dogs barking treed in the middle of a great grove of aspens high up the mountain-side. The snow was too deep for the horses, and leaving them, we trudged heavily up on foot. The yearling was in the top of a tall aspen. Lambert shot it with his rifle and we then put the dogs on the trail of the old she. Some of the young ones did not know what to make of this, evidently feeling that the tracks must be those of the bear that they had already killed; but the veterans were in full cry at once. We scrambled after them up the steep mountain, and then downward along ridges and spurs, getting all the clear ground we could. Finally we had to take to the snow, and floundered and slid through the drifts until we were in the valley. Most of the time the dogs were within hearing, giving tongue as they followed the trail. Finally a total change in the note showed that they were barking treed; and as rapidly as possible we made our way toward the sound. Again we found ourselves unable to bring the horses up to where the bear had treed, and scrambled thither on foot through the deep snow.

The bear was some thirty or forty feet up a tall spruce; it was a big she, with a glossy black-brown coat. I was afraid that at our approach she might come down; but she had been running hard for some four hours, had

THE PACK BAYING THE BEAR

From a photograph, copyright, 1905, by Alexander Lambert, M.D.

been pressed close, and evidently had not the slightest idea of putting herself of her own free will within the reach of the pack, which was now frantically baying at the foot of the tree. I shot her through the heart. As the bullet struck she climbed up through the branches with great agility for six or eight feet; then her muscles relaxed, and down she came with a thud, nearly burying herself in the snow. Little Skip was one of the first dogs to seize her as she came down; and in another moment he literally disappeared under the hounds as they piled on the bear. As soon as possible we got off the skin and pushed campward at a good gait, for we were a long way off. Just at nightfall we came out on a bluff from which we could overlook the rushing, swirling brown torrent, on the farther bank of which the tents were pitched.

The stomach of this bear contained nothing but buds. Like the other shes killed on this trip, she was accompanied by her yearling young, but had no newly born cub; sometimes bear breed only every other year, but I have found the mother accompanied not only by her cub but by her young of the year before. The yearling also had nothing but buds in its stomach. When its skin was taken off, Stewart looked at it, shook his head, and turning to Lambert said solemnly, " Alex., that skin isn't big enough to use for anything but a doily." From that time until the end of the hunt the yearlings were only known as " doily bears."

Next morning we again went out, and this time for twelve hours steadily, in the saddle, and now and then on foot. Most of the time we were in snow, and it was extraordinary that the horses could get through it at all, especially in working up the steep mountain-sides. But until it got so deep that they actually floundered—that is, so long as they could get their legs down to the bottom— I found that they could travel much faster than I could. On this day some twenty good-natured, hard-riding young fellows from the ranches within a radius of a dozen miles had joined our party to " see the President kill a bear." They were a cheerful and eagerly friendly crowd, as hardy as so many young moose, and utterly fear- less horsemen; one of them rode his wild, nervous horse bareback, because it had bucked so when he tried to put the saddle on it that morning that he feared he would get left behind, and so abandoned the saddle outright. Whenever they had a chance they all rode at headlong speed, paying no heed to the slope of the mountain-side or the character of the ground. In the deep snow they did me a real service, for of course they had to ride their horses single file through the drifts, and by the time my turn came we had a good trail.

After a good deal of beating to and fro, we found where an old she-bear with two yearlings had crossed a hill during the night and put the hounds on their tracks. Johnny and Jake, with one or two of the cowboys, fol- lowed the hounds over the exceedingly difficult hillside where the trail led; or rather, they tried to follow them, for the hounds speedily got clear away, as there were many places where they could run on the crust of the snow, in which the horses wallowed almost helpless. The

A DOILY BEAR

From a photograph, copyright, 1905, by Alexander Lambert, M.D.

rest of us went down to the valley, where the snow was light and the going easier. The bear had travelled hither and thither through the woods on the sidehill, and the dogs became scattered. Moreover, they jumped several deer, and four or five of the young dogs took after one of the latter. Finally, however, the rest of the pack put up the three bears. We had an interesting glimpse of the chase as the bears quartered up across an open spot of the hillside. The hounds were but a short distance behind them, strung out in a long string, the more powerful, those which could do best in the snow-bucking, taking the lead. We pushed up the mountain-side after them, horse after horse getting down in the snow, and speedily heard the redoubled clamor which told us that something had been treed. It was half an hour before we could make our way to the tree, a spruce, in which the two yearlings had taken refuge, while around the bottom the entire pack was gathered, crazy with excitement. We could not take the yearlings alive, both because we lacked the means of carrying them, and because we were anxious to get after the old bear. We could not leave them where they were, because it would have been well-nigh impossible to get the dogs away, and because, even if we had succeeded in getting them away, they would not have run any other trail as long as they knew the yearlings were in the tree. It was therefore out of the question to leave them unharmed, as we should have been glad to do, and Lambert killed them both with his revolver; the one that was first hit immediately biting its brother. The ranchmen took them home to eat.

The hounds were immediately put on the trail of the old one and disappeared over the snow. In a few minutes we followed. It was heavy work getting up the mountain-side through the drifts, but once on top we made our way down a nearly bare spur, and then turned to the right, scrambled a couple of miles along a slippery side-hill, and halted. Below us lay a great valley, on the farther side of which a spruce forest stretched up toward the treeless peaks. Snow covered even the bottom of the valley, and lay deep and solid in the spruce forest on the mountain-side. The hounds were in full cry, evidently on a hot trail, and we caught glimpses of them far on the opposite side of the valley, crossing little open glades in the spruce timber. If the crust was hard they scattered out. Where it was at all soft they ran in single file. We worked our way down toward them, and on reaching the bottom of the valley, went up it as fast as the snow would allow. Finally we heard the pack again barking treed and started toward them. They had treed the bear far up the mountain-side in the thick spruce timber, and a short experiment showed us that the horses could not possibly get through the snow. Accordingly, off we jumped and went toward the sound on foot, all the young ranchmen and cowboys rushing ahead, and thereby again making me an easy trail. On the way to the tree the rider of the bareback horse pounced on a snowshoe rabbit which was crouched under a bush and caught it with his hands. It was half an hour before we reached the tree, a big spruce, up which the bear had gone to a height of some forty feet. I broke her neck with a single bullet.

She was smaller than the one I had shot the day before, but full grown. In her stomach, as in those of the two yearlings, there were buds of rose-bushes and quaking aspens. One yearling had also swallowed a mouse. It was a long ride to camp, and darkness had fallen by the time we caught the gleam from the lighted tents, across the dark stream.

With neither of these last two bear had there been any call for prowess; my part was merely to kill the bear dead at the first shot, for the sake of the pack. But the days were very enjoyable, nevertheless. It was good fun to be twelve hours in the saddle in such wild and beautiful country, to look at and listen to the hounds as they worked, and finally to see the bear treed and looking down at the maddened pack baying beneath.

For the next two or three days I was kept in camp by a touch of Cuban fever. On one of these days Lambert enjoyed the longest hunt we had on the trip, after an old she-bear and three yearlings. The yearlings treed one by one, each of course necessitating a stoppage, and it was seven in the evening before the old bear at last went up a cottonwood and was shot; she was only wounded, however, and in the fight she crippled Johnny's Rowdy before she was killed. When the hunters reached camp it was thirteen hours since they had left it. The old bear was a very light brown; the first yearling was reddish-brown, the second light yellowish-brown, the third dark black-brown, though all were evidently of the same litter.

Following this came a spell of bad weather, snow-storm and blizzard steadily succeeding one another.

This lasted until my holiday was over. Some days we had to stay in camp. On other days we hunted; but there was three feet of new snow on the summits and foothills, making it difficult to get about. We saw no more bear, and, indeed, no more bear-tracks that were less than two or three weeks old.

We killed a couple of bobcats. The chase of one was marked by several incidents. We had been riding through a blizzard on the top of a plateau, and were glad to plunge down into a steep sheer-sided valley. By the time we reached the bottom there was a lull in the storm and we worked our way with considerable difficulty through the snow, down timber, and lava rock, toward Divide Creek. After a while the valley widened a little, spruce and aspens fringing the stream at the bottom while the sides were bare. Here we struck a fresh bobcat trail leading off up one of the mountain-sides. The hounds followed it nearly to the top, then turned and came down again, worked through the timber in the bottom, and struck out on the hillside opposite. Suddenly we saw the bobcat running ahead of them and doubling and circling. A few minutes afterward the hounds followed the trail to the creek bottom and then began to bark treed. But on reaching the point we found there was no cat in the tree, although the dogs seemed certain that there was; and Johnny and Jake speedily had them again running on the trail. After making its way for some distance through the bottom, the cat had again taken to the side-hill, and the hounds went after it hard. Again they went nearly to the top, again they streamed down to the bottom

THE BIG BEAR

From a photograph by Philip B. Stewart

and crossed the creek. Soon afterward we saw the cat ahead of them. For the moment it threw them off the track by making a circle and galloping around close to the rearmost hounds. It then made for the creek bottom, where it climbed to the top of a tall aspen. The hounds soon picked up the trail again, and followed it full cry; but unfortunately just before they reached where it had treed they ran on to a porcupine. When we reached the foot of the aspen, in the top of which the bobcat crouched, with most of the pack baying beneath, we found the porcupine dead and half a dozen dogs with their muzzles and throats filled full of quills. Before doing anything with the cat it was necessary to take these quills out. One of the terriers, which always found porcupines an irresistible attraction, was a really extraordinary sight, so thickly were the quills studded over his face and chest. But a big hound was in even worse condition; the quills were stuck in abundance into his nose, lips, cheeks, and tongue, and in the roof of his mouth they were almost as thick as bristles in a brush. Only by use of pincers was it possible to rid these two dogs of the quills, and it was a long and bloody job. The others had suffered less.

The dogs seemed to have no sympathy with one another, and apparently all that the rest of the pack felt was that they were kept a long time waiting for the cat. They never stopped baying for a minute, and Shorty, as was his habit, deliberately bit great patches of bark from the aspens, to show his impatience; for the tree in which the cat stood was not one which he could climb. After attending to the porcupine dogs one of the men climbed the tree and with a stick pushed out the cat. It dropped down through the branches forty or fifty feet, but was so quick in starting and dodging that it actually rushed through the pack, crossed the stream, and, doubling and twisting, was off up the creek through the timber. It ran cunning, and in a minute or two lay down under a bush and watched the hounds as they went by, overrunning its trail. Then it took off up the hillside; but the hounds speedily picked up its track, and running in single file, were almost on it. Then the cat turned down hill, but too late, for it was overtaken within fifty yards. This ended our hunting.

One Sunday we rode down some six miles from camp to a little blue school-house and attended service. The preacher was in the habit of riding over every alternate Sunday from Rifle, a little town twenty or twenty-five miles away; and the ranchmen with their wives and children, some on horseback, some in wagons, had gathered from thirty miles round to attend the service. The crowd was so large that the exercises had to take place in the open air, and it was pleasant to look at the strong frames and rugged, weather-beaten faces of the men; while as for the women, one respected them even more than the men.

In spite of the snow-storms spring was coming; some of the trees were beginning to bud and show green, more and more flowers were in bloom, and bird life was steadily increasing. In the bushes by the streams the handsome white-crowned sparrows and green-tailed towhees were in full song, making attractive music; although the song of neither can rightly be compared in point of plaintive beauty with that of the white-throated sparrow, which, except some of the thrushes, and perhaps the winter wren, is the sweetest singer of the Northeastern forests. The spurred towhees were very plentiful; and one morning a willow-thrush sang among the willows like a veery. Both the crested jays and the Woodhouse jays came around camp. Lower down the Western meadow larks were singing beautifully, and vesper finches were abundant. Say's flycatcher, a very attractive bird, with pretty, soft-colored plumage, continually uttering a plaintive single note, and sometimes a warbling twitter, flitted about in the neighborhood of the little log ranch houses. Gangs of blackbirds visited the corrals. I saw but one song sparrow, and curiously enough, though I think it was merely an individual peculiarity, this particular bird had a song entirely different from any I have heard from the familiar Eastern bird—always a favorite of mine.

While up in the mountains hunting, we twice came upon owls, which were rearing their families in the deserted nests of the red-tailed hawk. One was a long-eared owl, and the other a great horned owl, of the pale Western variety. Both were astonishingly tame, and we found it difficult to make them leave their nests, which were in the tops of cottonwood trees.

On the last day we rode down to where Glenwood Springs lies, hemmed in by lofty mountain chains, which are riven in sunder by sheer-sided, cliff-walled canyons. As we left ever farther behind us the wintry desolation of our high hunting grounds we rode into full spring.

The green of the valley was a delight to the eye; bird songs sounded on every side, from the fields and from the trees and bushes beside the brooks and irrigation ditches; the air was sweet with the spring-time breath of many budding things. The sarvice bushes were white with bloom, like shadblow on the Hudson; the blossoms of the Oregon grape made yellow mats on the ground. We saw the chunky Say's ground squirrel, looking like a big chipmunk, with on each side a conspicuous white stripe edged with black. In one place we saw quite a large squirrel, grayish, with red on the lower back. I suppose it was only a pine squirrel, but it looked like one of the gray squirrels of southern Colorado. Mountain mockers and the handsome, bold Arkansaw king birds were numerous. The black-tail sage sparrow was conspicuous in the sagebrush, and high among the cliffs the white-throated swifts were soaring. There were numerous warblers, among which I could only make out the black-throated gray, Audubon's, and McGillivray's. In Glenwood Springs itself the purple finches, house finches, and Bullock's orioles were in full song. Flocks of siskins passed with dipping flight. In one rapid little stream we saw a water ousel. Humming-birds—I suppose the broad-tailed— were common, and as they flew they made, intermittently and almost rhythmically, a curious metallic sound; seemingly it was done with their wings.

But the thing that interested me most in the way of bird life was something I saw in Denver. To my delight I found that the huge hotel at which we took dinner was monopolized by the pretty, musical house finches, to the exclusion of the ordinary city sparrows. The latter are all too plentiful in Denver, as in every other city, and, as always, are noisy, quarrelsome—in short, thoroughly unattractive and disreputable. The house finch, on the contrary, is attractive in looks, in song, and in ways. It was delightful to hear the males singing, often on the wing. They went right up to the top stories of the high hotel, and nested under the eaves and in the cornices. The cities of the Southwestern States are to be congratulated on having this spirited, attractive little songster as a familiar dweller around their houses and in their gardens.

CHAPTER III

WOLF-COURSING

ON April eighth, nineteen hundred and five, we left the town of Frederick, Oklahoma, for a few days' coyote coursing in the Comanche Reserve. Lieut.-Gen. S. B. M. Young, U. S. A., retired, Lieutenant Fortescue, U. S. A., formerly of my regiment, Dr. Alexander Lambert, of New York, Colonel Cecil Lyon, of Texas, and Sloan Simpson, also of Texas, and formerly of my regiment, were with me. We were the guests of two old-style Texas cattlemen, Messrs. Burnett and Wagner, who had leased great stretches of wire-fenced pasture from the Comanches and Kiowas; and I cannot sufficiently express my appreciation of the kindness of these my two hosts. Burnett's brand, the Four Sixes, has been owned by him for forty years. Both of them had come to this country thirty years before, in the days of the buffalo, when all game was very plentiful and the Indians were still on the war-path. Several other ranchmen were along, including John Abernethy, of Tesca, Oklahoma, a professional wolf hunter. There were also a number of cowhands of both Burnett and Wagner; among them were two former riders for the Four Sixes, Fi Taylor and Uncle Ed Gillis, who seemed to make it their special mission to see that everything went right with me.

STARTING TOWARDS THE WOLF GROUNDS

From a photograph, copyright, 1905, by Alexander Lambert, M.D.

Furthermore there was Captain McDonald of the Texas Rangers, a game and true man, whose name was one of terror to outlaws and violent criminals of all kinds; and finally there was Quanah Parker, the Comanche chief, in his youth a bitter foe of the whites, now painfully teaching his people to travel the white man's stony road.

We drove out some twenty miles to where camp was pitched in a bend of Deep Red Creek, which empties into the Red River of the South. Cottonwood, elm, and pecans formed a belt of timber along the creek; we had good water, the tents were pitched on short, thick grass, and everything was in perfect order. The fare was delicious. Altogether it was an ideal camp, and the days we passed there were also ideal. Cardinals and mocking-birds—the most individual and delightful of all birds in voice and manner—sang in the woods; and the beautiful, many-tinted fork-tailed fly-catchers were to be seen now and then, perched in trees or soaring in curious zigzags, chattering loudly.

In chasing the coyote only greyhounds are used, and half a dozen different sets of these had been brought to camp. Those of Wagner, the " Big D " dogs, as his cow-punchers called them, were handled by Bony Moore, who, with Tom Burnett, the son of our host Burke Burnett, took the lead in feats of daring horsemanship, even in that field of daring horsemen. Bevins had brought both greyhounds and rough-haired staghounds from his Texas ranch. So had Cecil Lyon, and though his dogs had chiefly been used in coursing the black-tailed Texas jack-rabbit, they took naturally to the coyote chases.

Finally there were Abernethy's dogs, which, together with their master, performed the feats I shall hereafter relate. Abernethy has a homestead of his own not far from Frederick, and later I was introduced to his father, an old Confederate soldier, and to his sweet and pretty wife, and their five little children. He had run away with his wife when they were nineteen and sixteen respectively; but the match had turned out a happy one. Both were particularly fond of music, including the piano, horn, and violin, and they played duets together. General Young, whom the Comanches called "War Bonnet," went in a buggy with Burke Burnett, and as Burnett invariably followed the hounds at full speed in his buggy, and usually succeeded in seeing most of the chase, I felt that the buggy men really encountered greater hazards than anyone else. It was a thoroughly congenial company all through. The weather was good; we were in the saddle from morning until night; and our camp was in all respects all that a camp should be; so how could we help enjoying ourselves?

The coursing was done on the flats and great rolling prairies which stretched north from our camp toward the Wichita Mountains and south toward the Red River. There was a certain element of risk in the gallops, because the whole country was one huge prairie-dog town, the prairie-dogs being so numerous that the new towns and the abandoned towns were continuous with one another in every direction. Practically every run we had was through these prairie-dog towns, varied occasionally by creeks and washouts. But as we always ran scattered out, the wonderfully quick cow-ponies, brought up in this country and spending all their time among the prairie-dog towns, were able, even while running at headlong speed, to avoid the holes with a cleverness that was simply marvellous. During our hunt but one horse stepped in a hole; he turned a complete somerset, though neither he nor his rider was hurt. Stunted mesquite bushes grew here and there in the grass, and there was cactus. As always in prairie-dog towns, there were burrowing owls and rattlesnakes. We had to be on our guard that the dogs did not attack the latter. Once we thought a greyhound was certainly bitten. It was a very fast blue bitch, which seized the rattler and literally shook it to pieces. The rattler struck twice at the bitch, but so quick were the bitch's movements that she was not hit either time, and in a second the snake was not merely dead, but in pieces. We usually killed the rattlers with either our quirts or ropes. One which I thus killed was over five feet long.

By rights there ought to have been carts in which the greyhounds could be drawn until the coyotes were sighted, but there were none, and the greyhounds simply trotted along beside the horses. All of them were fine animals, and almost all of them of recorded pedigree. Coyotes have sharp teeth and bite hard, while greyhounds have thin skins, and many of them were cut in the worries. This was due to the fact that only two or three of them seized by the throat, the others taking hold behind, which of course exposed them to retaliation. Few of them would have been of much use in stopping a big wolf.

Abernethy's hounds, however, though they could not kill a big wolf, would stop it, permitting their owner to seize it exactly as he seized coyotes, as hereafter described. He had killed but a few of the big gray wolves; one weighed ninety-seven pounds. He said that there were gradations from this down to the coyotes. A few days before our arrival, after a very long chase, he had captured a black wolf, weighing between fifty and sixty pounds.

These Southern coyotes or prairie-wolves are only about one-third the size of the big gray timber wolves of the Northern Rockies. They are too small to meddle with full-grown horses and cattle, but pick up young calves and kill sheep, as well as any small domesticated animal that they can get at. The big wolves flee from the neighborhood of anything like close settlements, but coyotes hang around the neighborhood of man much more persistently. They show a fox-like cunning in catching rabbits, prairie-dogs, gophers, and the like. After nightfall they are noisy, and their melancholy wailing and yelling are familiar sounds to all who pass over the plains. The young are brought forth in holes in cut banks or similar localities. Within my own experience I have known of the finding of but two families. In one there was but a single family of five cubs and one old animal, undoubtedly the mother; in the other case there were ten or eleven cubs and two old females which had apparently shared the burrow or cave, though living in separate pockets. In neither case was any full-grown male coyote found in the neighborhood; as regards these particular

GREYHOUNDS RESTING AFTER A RUN

From a photograph by W. Sloan Simpson

litters, the father seemingly had nothing to do with taking care of or supporting the family. I am not able to say whether this was accidental or whether it is a rule, that only the mother lives with and takes care of the litter; I have heard contrary statements about the matter from hunters who should know. Unfortunately I have learned from long experience that it is only exceptional hunters who can be trusted to give accurate descriptions of the habits of any beast, save such as are connected with its chase.

Coyotes are sharp, wary, knowing creatures, and on most occasions take care to keep out of harm's way. But individuals among them have queer freaks. On one occasion while Sloan Simpson was on the round-up he waked at night to find something on the foot of his bed, its dark form indistinctly visible against the white tarpaulin. He aroused a friend to ask if it could be a dog. While they were cautiously endeavoring to find out what it was, it jumped up and ran off; they then saw that it was a coyote. In a short time it returned again, coming out of the darkness toward one of the cowboys who was awake, and the latter shot it, fearing it might have hydrophobia. But I doubt this, as in such case it would not have curled up and gone to sleep on Simpson's bedding. Coyotes are subject to hydrophobia, and when under the spell of the dreadful disease will fearlessly attack men. In one case of which I know, a mad coyote coming into camp sprang on a sleeping man who was rolled in his bedding and bit and worried the bedding in the effort to get at him. Two other men hastened to his rescue, and the coyote first attacked them and then suddenly sprang aside and again worried the bedding, by which time one of them was able to get in a shot and killed it. All coyotes, like big wolves, die silently and fight to the last. I had never weighed any coyotes until on this trip. I weighed the twelve which I myself saw caught, and they ran as follows: male, thirty pounds; female, twenty-eight pounds; female, thirty-six pounds; male, thirty-two pounds; male, thirty-four pounds; female, thirty pounds; female, twenty-seven pounds; male, thirty-two pounds; male, twenty-nine pounds; young male, twenty-two pounds; male, twenty-nine pounds; female, twenty-seven pounds. Disregarding the young male, this makes an average of just over thirty pounds.[1] Except the heaviest female, they were all gaunt and in splendid running trim; but then I do not remember ever seeing a really fat coyote.

The morning of the first day of our hunt dawned bright and beautiful, the air just cool enough to be pleasant. Immediately after breakfast we jogged off on horseback, Tom Burnett and Bony Moore in front, with six or eight greyhounds slouching alongside, while Burke Burnett and "War Bonnet" drove behind us in the buggy. I was mounted on one of Tom Burnett's favorites, a beautiful Kiowa pony. The chuck wagon, together with the

---

[1] I sent the skins and skulls to Dr. Hart Merriam, the head of the Biological Survey. He wrote me about them : "All but one are the plains coyote, *Canis nebracensis*. They are not perfectly typical, but are near enough for all practical purposes. The exception is a yearling pup of a much larger species. Whether this is *frustor* I dare not say in the present state of knowledge of the group."

relay of greyhounds to be used in the afternoon, was to join us about midday at an appointed place where there was a pool of water.

We shuffled along, strung out in an irregular line, across a long flat, in places covered with bright-green wild onions; and then up a gentle slope where the stunted mesquite grew, while the prairie-dogs barked spasmodically as we passed their burrows. The low crest, if such it could be called, of the slope was reached only some twenty minutes after we left camp, and hardly had we started down the other side than two coyotes were spied three or four hundred yards in front. Immediately horses and dogs were after them at a headlong, breakneck run, the coyotes edging to the left where the creek bottom, with its deep banks and narrow fringes of timber, was about a mile distant. The little wolves knew their danger and ran their very fastest, while the long dogs stretched out after them, gaining steadily. It was evident the chase would be a short one, and there was no need to husband the horses, so every man let his pony go for all there was in him. At such a speed, and especially going down hill, there was not the slightest use in trying to steer clear of the prairie-dog holes; it was best to let the veteran cow-ponies see to that for themselves. They were as eager as their riders, and on we dashed at full speed, curving to the left toward the foot of the slope; we jumped into and out of a couple of broad, shallow washouts, as we tore after the hounds, now nearing their quarry. The rearmost coyote was overtaken just at the edge of the creek; the foremost, which was a few yards

in advance, made good its escape, as all the dogs promptly
tackled the rearmost, tumbling it over into a rather deep
pool. The scuffling and splashing told us what was going
on, and we reined our horses short up at the brink of
the cut bank. The water had hampered the dogs in killing their quarry, only three or four of them being in the
pool with him; and of those he had seized one by the
nose and was hanging on hard. In a moment one of the
cowboys got hold of him, dropped a noose over his head,
and dragged him out on the bank, just as the buggy came
rattling up at full gallop. Burnett and the general, taking advantage of the curve in our course, had driven
across the chord of the arc, and keeping their horses at a
run, had seen every detail of the chase and were in at the
death.

In a few minutes the coyote was skinned, the dogs
rested, and we were jogging on once more. Hour after
hour passed by. We had a couple more runs, but in each
case the coyote had altogether too long a start and got
away; the dogs no longer being as fresh as they had been.
As a rule, although there are exceptions, if the greyhounds cannot catch the coyote within two or three miles
the chances favor the escape of the little wolf. We found
that if the wolf had more than half a mile start he got
away. As greyhounds hunt by sight, cut banks enable the
coyote easily to throw off his pursuers unless they are
fairly close up. The greyhounds see the wolf when he is
far off, for they have good eyes; but in the chase, if the
going is irregular, they tend to lose him, and they do not
depend much on one another in recovering sight of him;

AT THE TAIL OF THE CHUCK WAGON
From a photogragh by W. Sloan Simpson

on the contrary, the dog is apt to quit when he no longer has the quarry in view.

At noon we joined the chuck wagon where it stood drawn up on a slope of the treeless, bushless prairie; and the active round-up cook soon had the meal ready. It was the Four Sixes wagon, the brand burned into the wood of the chuck box. Where does a man take more frank enjoyment in his dinner than at the tail end of a chuck wagon?

Soon after eating we started again, having changed horses and dogs. I was mounted on a Big D cow pony, while Lambert had a dun-colored horse, hard to hold, but very tough and swift. An hour or so after leaving camp we had a four-mile run after a coyote, which finally got away, for it had so long a start that the dogs were done out by the time they came within fair distance. They stopped at a little prairie pool, some of them lying or standing in it, panting violently; and thus we found them as we came stringing up at a gallop. After they had been well rested we started toward camp; but we were down in the creek bottom before we saw another coyote. This one again was a long distance ahead, and I did not suppose there was much chance of our catching him; but away all the dogs and all the riders went at the usual run, and catch him we did, because, as it turned out, the "morning" dogs, which were with the wagon, had spied him first and run him hard, until he was in sight of the "afternoon" dogs, which were with us. I got tangled in a washout, scrambled out, and was galloping along, watching the country in front, when Lambert passed me as hard as he could go; I saw him disappear into another washout, and then come out on the other side, while the dogs were driving the coyote at an angle down toward the creek. Pulling short to the right, I got through the creek, hoping the coyote would cross, and the result was that I galloped up to the worry almost as soon as the foremost riders from the other side—a piece of good fortune for which I had only luck to thank. The hounds caught the coyote as he was about crossing the creek. From this point it was but a short distance into camp.

Again next morning we were off before the sun had risen high enough to take away the cool freshness from the air. This day we travelled several miles before we saw our first coyote. It was on a huge, gently sloping stretch of prairie, which ran down to the creek on our right. We were travelling across it strung out in line when the coyote sprang up a good distance ahead of the dogs. They ran straight away from us at first. Then I saw the coyote swinging to the right toward the creek and I half-wheeled, riding diagonally to the line of the chase. This gave me an excellent view of dogs and wolf, and also enabled me to keep nearly abreast of them. On this particular morning the dogs were Bevin's greyhounds and staghounds. From where the dogs started they ran about three miles, catching their quarry in the flat where the creek circled around in a bend, and when it was not fifty yards from the timber. By this time the puncher, Bony Moore, had passed me, most of the other riders having been so far to the left when the run began that they were unable to catch up. The little wolf ran well, and the greyhounds had about reached their limit when they caught up with it. But they lasted just long enough to do the work. A fawn-colored greyhound and a black staghound were the first dogs up. The staghound tried to seize the coyote, which dodged a little to one side; the fawn-colored greyhound struck and threw it; and in another moment the other dogs were up and the worry began. I was able to see the run so well, because Tom Burnett had mounted me on his fine roan cutting horse. We sat around in a semicircle on the grass until the dogs had been breathed, and then started off again. After some time we struck another coyote, but rather far off, and this time the dogs were not fresh. After running two or three miles he pulled away and we lost him, the dogs refreshing themselves by standing and lying in a shallow prairie pool.

In the afternoon we again rode off, and this time Abernethy, on his white horse, took the lead, his greyhounds trotting beside him. There was a good deal of rivalry among the various owners of the hounds as to which could do best, and a slight inclination among the cowboys to be jealous of Abernethy. No better riders could be imagined than these same cowboys, and their greyhounds were stanch and fast; but Abernethy, on his tough white horse, not only rode with great judgment, but showed a perfect knowledge of the coyote, and by his own exertions greatly assisted his hounds. He had found out in his long experience that while the greyhounds could outpace a coyote in a two or three mile run, they would then fall behind; but that after going eight or ten miles, a coyote in turn became exhausted, and if he had been able to keep his hounds going until that time, they could, with his assistance, then stop the quarry.

We had been shogging along for an hour or more when we put up a coyote and started after it. I was riding the Big D pony I had ridden the afternoon before. It was a good and stout horse, but one which my weight was certain to distress if I tried to go too fast for too long a time. Moreover, the coyote had a long start, and I made up my mind that he would either get away or give us a hard run. Accordingly, as the cowboys started off at their usual headlong pace, I rode behind at a gallop, husbanding my horse. For a mile or so the going was very rough, up over and down stony hills and among washouts. Then we went over gently rolling country for another mile or two, and then came to a long broken incline which swept up to a divide some four miles ahead of us. Lambert had been riding alongside of Abernethy, at the front, but his horse began to play out, and needed to be nursed along, so that he dropped back level with me. By the time I had reached the foot of this incline the punchers, riding at full speed, had shot their bolts, and one by one I passed them, as well as most of the greyhounds. But Abernethy was far ahead, his white horse loping along without showing any signs of distress. Up the long slope I did not dare press my animal, and Abernethy must have been a mile ahead of me when he struck the divide, while where the others were I had no idea, except that they were behind me. When I reached

THE BIG D. COW PONY

From a photograph by W. Sloan Simpson

the divide I was afraid I might have missed Abernethy, but to my delight he was still in sight, far ahead. As we began to go down hill I let the horse fairly race; for by Abernethy's motions I could tell that he was close to the wolf and that it was no longer running in a straight line, so that there was a chance of my overtaking them. In a couple of miles I was close enough to see what was going on. But one greyhound was left with Abernethy. The coyote was obviously tired, and Abernethy, with the aid of his perfectly trained horse, was helping the greyhound catch it. Twice he headed it, and this enabled me to gain rapidly. They had reached a small unwooded creek by the time I was within fifty yards; the little wolf tried to break back to the left; Abernethy headed it and rode almost over it, and it gave a wicked snap at his foot, cutting the boot. Then he wheeled and came toward it; again it galloped back, and just as it crossed the creek the greyhound made a rush, pinned it by the hind leg and threw it. There was a scuffle, then a yell from the greyhound as the wolf bit it. At the bite the hound let go and jumped back a few feet, and at the same moment Abernethy, who had ridden his horse right on them as they struggled, leaped off and sprang on top of the wolf. He held the reins of the horse with one hand and thrust the other, with a rapidity and precision even greater than the rapidity of the wolf's snap, into the wolf's mouth, jamming his hand down crosswise between the jaws, seizing the lower jaw and bending it down so that the wolf could not bite him. He had a stout glove on his hand, but this would have been of no avail whatever had he not seized the animal just as he did; that is, behind the canines, while his hand pressed the lips against the teeth; with his knees he kept the wolf from using its forepaws to break the hold, until it gave up struggling. When he thus leaped on and captured this coyote it was entirely free, the dog having let go of it; and he was obliged to keep hold of the reins of his horse with one hand. I was not twenty yards distant at the time, and as I leaped off the horse he was sitting placidly on the live wolf, his hand between its jaws, the greyhound standing beside him, and his horse standing by as placid as he was. In a couple of minutes Fortescue and Lambert came up. It was as remarkable a feat of the kind as I have ever seen.

Through some oversight we had no straps with us, and Abernethy had lost the wire which he usually carried in order to tie up the wolves' muzzles—for he habitually captured his wolves in this fashion. However, Abernethy regarded the lack of straps as nothing more than a slight bother. Asking one of us to hold his horse, he threw the wolf across in front of the saddle, still keeping his grip on the lower jaw, then mounted and rode off with us on the back track. The wolf was not tied in any way. It was unhurt, and the only hold he had was on its lower jaw. I was surprised that it did not strive to fight with its legs, but after becoming satisfied that it could not bite, it seemed to resign itself to its fate, was fairly quiet, and looked about with its ears pricked forward. The wolves which I subsequently saw him capture, and, having tied up their muzzles, hold before him on the saddle, acted in precisely the same manner.

The run had been about ten miles in an almost straight line. At the finish no other riders were in sight, but soon after we crossed the divide on our return, and began to come down the long slope toward the creek, we were joined by Tom Burnett and Bony Moore; while some three or four miles ahead on a rise of the prairie we could see the wagon in which Burke Burnett was driving General Young. Other punchers and straggling greyhounds joined us, and as the wolf, after travelling some five miles, began to recover his wind and show a tendency to fight for his freedom, Abernethy tied up his jaws with his handkerchief and handed him over to Bony Moore, who packed him on the saddle with entire indifference, the wolf himself showing a curious philosophy. Our horses had recovered their wind and we struck into a gallop down the slope; then as we neared the wagon we broke into a run, Bony Moore brandishing aloft with one hand the live wolf, its jaws tied up with a handkerchief, but otherwise unbound. We stopped for a few minutes with Burnett and the general to tell particulars of the hunt. Then we loped off again toward camp, which was some half dozen miles off. I shall always remember this run and the really remarkable feat Abernethy performed. Colonel Lyon had seen him catch a big wolf in the same way that he caught this coyote. It was his usual method of catching both coyotes and wolves. Almost equally noteworthy were the way in which he handled and helped his greyhounds, and the judgment, resolution, and fine horsemanship he displayed. His horse showed extraordinary endurance.

The third day we started out as usual, the chuck wagon driving straight to a pool far out on the prairie, where we were to meet it for lunch. Chief Quanah's three wives had joined him, together with a small boy and a baby, and they drove in a wagon of their own. Meanwhile the riders and hounds went south nearly to Red River. In the morning we caught four coyotes and had a three miles run after one which started too far ahead of the dogs, and finally got clean away. All the four that we got were started fairly close up, and the run was a breakneck scurry, horses and hounds going as hard as they could put feet to the ground. Twice the cowboys distanced me; and twice the accidents of the chase, the sudden twists and turns of the coyote in his efforts to take advantage of the ground, favored me and enabled me to be close up at the end, when Abernethy jumped off his horse and ran in to where the dogs had the coyote. He was even quicker with his hands than the wolf's snap, and in a moment he always had the coyote by the lower jaw.

Between the runs we shogged forward across the great reaches of rolling prairie in the bright sunlight. The air was wonderfully clear, and any object on the sky-line, no matter how small, stood out with startling distinctness. There were few flowers on these dry plains; in sharp contrast to the flower prairies of southern Texas, which we had left the week before, where many acres for a stretch would be covered by masses of red or white or blue or yellow blossoms—the most striking of all, perhaps, being the fields of the handsome buffalo clover. As we plodded

ABERNETHY AND COYOTE

From a photograph, copyright, 1905, by Alexander Lambert, M.D.

over the prairie the sharp eyes of the punchers were scanning the ground far and near, and sooner or later one of them would spy the motionless form of a coyote, or all would have their attention attracted as it ran like a fleeting gray or brown shadow among the grays and browns of the desolate landscape. Immediately dogs and horses would stretch at full speed after it, and everything would be forgotten but the wild exhilaration of the run.

It was nearly noon when we struck the chuck wagon. Immediately the handy round-up cook began to prepare a delicious dinner, and we ate as men have a right to eat, who have ridden all the morning and are going to ride fresh horses all the afternoon. Soon afterward the horse-wranglers drove up the saddle band, while some of the cow-punchers made a rope corral from the side of the wagon. Into this the horses were driven, one or two breaking back and being brought into the bunch again only after a gallop more exciting than most coyote chases. Fresh ponies were roped out and the saddle band again turned loose. The dogs that had been used during the morning then started campward with the chuck wagon. One of the punchers was riding a young and partially broken horse; he had no bridle, simply a rope around the horse's neck. This man started to accompany the wagon to the camp.

The rest of us went off at the usual cow-pony trot or running walk. It was an hour or two before we saw anything; then a coyote appeared a long way ahead and the dogs raced after him. The first mile was up a gentle slope; then we turned, and after riding a couple of miles on the level the dogs had shot their bolt and the coyote drew away. When he got too far in front the dogs and foremost riders stopped and waited for the rest of us to overtake them, and shortly afterward Burke Burnett and the general appeared in their buggy. One of the greyhounds was completely done out and we took some time attending to it. Suddenly one of the men, either Tom Burnett or Bony Moore, called out that he saw the coyote coming back pursued by a horseman. Sure enough, the unfortunate little wolf had run in sight of the wagons, and the puncher on the young unbridled horse immediately took after him, and, in spite of a fall, succeeded in heading him back and bringing him along in our direction, although some three-quarters of a mile away. Immediately everyone jumped into his saddle and away we all streamed down a long slope diagonally to the course the coyote was taking. He had a long start, but the dogs were rested, while he had been running steadily, and this fact proved fatal to him. Down the slope to the creek bottom at its end we rode at a run. Then there came a long slope upward, and the heavier among us fell gradually to the rear. When we topped the divide, however, we could see ahead of us the foremost men streaming after the hounds, and the latter running in a way which showed that they were well up on their game. Even a tired horse can go pretty well down hill, and by dint of hard running we who were behind got up in time to see the worry when the greyhounds caught the coyote, by some low ponds in a treeless creek-bed. We had gone about seven miles, the unlucky coyote at least ten. Our journey to camp was enlivened by catching another coyote after a short run.

Next day was the last of our hunt. We started off in the morning as usual, but the buggy men on this occasion took with them some trail hounds, which were managed by a sergeant of the regular army, a game sportsman. They caught two coons in the timber of a creek two or three miles to the south of the camp. Meanwhile the rest of us, riding over the prairie, saw the greyhounds catch two coyotes, one after a rather long run and one after a short one. Then we turned our faces toward camp. I saw Abernethy, with three or four of his own hounds, riding off to one side, but unfortunately I did not pay any heed to him, as I supposed the hunting was at an end. But when we reached camp Abernethy was not there, nor did he turn up until we were finishing lunch. Then he suddenly appeared, his tired greyhounds trotting behind him, while he carried before him on the saddle a live coyote, with its muzzle tied up, and a dead coyote strapped behind his saddle. Soon after leaving us he had found a coyote, and after a good run the dogs had stopped it and he had jumped off and captured it in his usual fashion. Then while riding along, holding the coyote before him on the saddle, he put up another one. His dogs were tired, and he himself was of course greatly hampered in such a full-speed run by having the live wolf on the saddle in front of him. One by one the dogs gave out, but his encouragement and assistance kept two of them to their work, and after a run of some seven miles the coyote was overtaken. It was completely done out and would probably have died by itself, even if the hounds had not taken part in the killing. Hampered as he was, Abernethy could not take it alive in his usual fashion. So when it was dead he packed it behind his horse and rode back in triumph. The live wolf, as in every other case where one was brought into camp, made curiously little effort to fight with its paws, seeming to acquiesce in its captivity, and looking around, with its ears thrust forward, as if more influenced by curiosity than by any other feeling.

After lunch we rode toward town, stopping at nightfall to take supper by the bank of a creek. We entered the town after dark, some twenty of us on horseback. Wagner was riding with us, and he had set his heart upon coming into and through the town in true cowboy style; and it was he who set the pace. We broke into a lope a mile outside the limits, and by the time we struck the main street the horses were on a run and we tore down like a whirlwind until we reached the train. Thus ended as pleasant a hunting trip as any one could imagine. The party got seventeen coyotes all told, for there were some runs which I did not see at all, as now and then both men and dogs would get split into groups.

On this hunt we did not see any of the big wolves, the so-called buffalo or timber wolves, which I hunted in the old days on the Northern cattle plains. Big wolves are found in both Texas and Oklahoma, but they are rare compared to the coyotes; and they are great wanderers. Alone or in parties of three or four or half a dozen they travel to and fro across the country, often leaving a district at once if they are molested. Coyotes are more or less plentiful everywhere throughout the West in thinly settled districts, and they often hang about in the immediate neighborhood of towns. They do enough damage to make farmers and ranchers kill them whenever the chance offers. But this damage is not appreciable when compared with the ravages of their grim big brother, the gray wolf, which, wherever it exists in numbers, is a veritable scourge to the stockmen.

Colonel Lyon's hounds were, as I have said, used chiefly after jack-rabbits. He had frequently killed coyotes with them, however, and on two or three occasions one of the big gray wolves. At the time when he did most of his wolf-hunting he had with the greyhounds a huge fighting dog, a Great Dane, weighing one hundred and forty-five pounds. In spite of its weight this dog could keep up well in a short chase, and its ferocious temper and enormous weight and strength made it invaluable at the bay. Whether the quarry were a gray wolf or coyote mattered not in the least to it, and it made its assaults with such headlong fury that it generally escaped damage. On the two or three occasions when the animal bayed was a big wolf the greyhounds did not dare tackle it, jumping about in an irregular circle and threatening the wolf until the fighting dog came up. The latter at once rushed in, seizing its antagonist by the throat or neck and throwing it. Doubtless it would have killed the wolf unassisted, but the greyhounds always joined in the killing; and once thrown, the wolf could never get on his legs. In these encounters the dog was never seriously hurt. Rather curiously, the only bad wound it ever received was from a coyote; the little wolf, not one-third of its weight, managing to inflict a terrific gash down its huge antagonist's chest, nearly tearing it open. But of course a coyote against such a foe could not last much longer than a rat pitted against a terrier.

Big wolves and coyotes are found side by side throughout the Western United States, both varying so in size that if a sufficient number of specimens, from different localities, are examined it will be found that there is a complete intergradation in both stature and weight. To the northward the coyotes disappear, and the big wolves grow larger and larger until in the arctic regions they become veritable giants. At Point Barrow Mr. E. A. McIlhenny had six of the eight " huskies " of his dog team killed and eaten by a huge white dog wolf. At last he shot it, and found that it weighed one hundred and sixty-one pounds.

Good trail hounds can run down a wolf. A year ago Jake Borah's pack in northwestern Colorado ran a big wolf weighing one hundred and fifteen pounds to bay in but little over an hour. He then stood with his back to a rock, and though the dogs formed a semicircle around him, they dared not tackle him. Jake got up and shot him. Unless well trained and with the natural fighting edge neither trail hounds (fox-hounds) nor greyhounds can or will kill a big wolf, and under ordinary circumstances, no matter how numerous, they make but a poor showing against one. But big ninety-pound or one hundred-pound greyhounds, specially bred and trained for the purpose, stand on an entirely different footing. Three or four of these dogs, rushing in together and seizing the wolf by the throat, will kill him, or worry him until he is helpless. On several occasions the Colorado Springs greyhounds have performed this feat. Johnny Goff owned a large, fierce dog, a cross between what he called a Siberian bloodhound (I suppose some animal like a Great Dane) and an ordinary hound, which, on one occasion when he had shot at and broken the hind leg of a big wolf, ran it down and killed it. On the other hand, wolves will often attack dogs. In March of the present year— nineteen hundred and five—Goff's dogs were scattered over a hillside hunting a bobcat, when he heard one of them yell, and looking up saw that two wolves were chasing it. The other dogs were so busy puzzling out the cat's trail that they never noticed what was happening. Goff called aloud, whereupon the wolves stopped. He shot one and the other escaped. He thinks that they would have overtaken and killed the hound in a minute or two if he had not interfered.

The big wolves shrink back before the growth of the thickly settled districts, and in the Eastern States they often tend to disappear even from districts that are uninhabited save by a few wilderness hunters. They have thus disappeared almost entirely from Maine, the Adirondacks, and the Alleghanies, although here and there they are said to be returning to their old haunts. Their disappearance is rather mysterious in some instances, for they are certainly not all killed off. The black bear is much easier killed, yet the black bear holds its own in many parts of the land from which the wolf has vanished. No animal is quite so difficult to kill as is the wolf, whether by poison or rifle or hound. Yet, after a comparatively few have been slain, the entire species will perhaps vanish from certain localities. In some localities even the cougar, the easiest of all game to kill with hounds, holds its own better. This, however, is not generally true.

But with all wild animals, it is a noticeable fact that a course of contact with man continuing over many generations of animal life causes a species so to adapt itself to its new surroundings that it can hold its own far better than formerly. When white men take up a new country, the game, and especially the big game, being entirely unused to contend with the new foe, succumb easily, and are almost completely killed out. If any individuals survive at all, however, the succeeding generations are far more difficult to exterminate than were their ancestors, and they cling much more tenaciously to their old homes. The game to be found in old and long-settled countries is of course much more wary and able to take care of itself than the game of an untrodden wilderness; it is the wilderness life, far more than the actual killing of the wilderness game, which tests the ability of the wilderness hunter.

After a time, game may even, for the time being, increase in certain districts where settlements are thin. This was true of the wolves throughout the northern cattle country, in Montana, Wyoming, Colorado, and the western ends of the Dakotas. In the old days wolves were

ABERNETHY RETURNS FROM THE HUNT

From a photograph, copyright, 1905, by Alexander Lambert, M.D.

very plentiful throughout this region, closely following the huge herds of buffaloes. The white men who followed these herds as professional buffalo-hunters were often accompanied by other men, known as wolfers, who poisoned these wolves for the sake of their fur. With the disappearance of the buffalo the wolves diminished in numbers so that they also seemed to disappear. Then in the late eighties or early nineties the wolves began again to increase in numbers until they became once more as numerous as ever and infinitely more wary and difficult to kill; though as they were nocturnal in their habits they were not often seen. Along the Little Missouri and in many parts of Montana and Wyoming this increase was very noticeable during the last decade of the nineteenth century. They were at that time the only big animals of the region which had increased in numbers. Such an increase following a previous decrease in the same region was both curious and interesting. I never knew the wolves to be so numerous or so daring in their assaults upon stock in the Little Missouri country as in the years 1894 to 1896 inclusive. I am unable wholly to account for these changes. The first great diminution in the numbers of the wolves is only partially to be explained by the poisoning; yet they seemed to disappear almost everywhere and for a number of years continued scarce. Then they again became plentiful, reappearing in districts from whence they had entirely vanished, and appearing in new districts where they had been hitherto unknown. Then they once more began to diminish in number. In northwestern Colorado, in the White River country, cougars fairly swarmed in the early nineties, while up to that time the big gray wolves were almost or entirely unknown. Then they began to come in, and increased steadily in numbers, while the cougars diminished, so that by the winter of 1902–3 they much outnumbered the big cats, and committed great ravages among the stock. The settlers were at their wits' ends how to deal with the pests. At last a trapper came in, a shiftless fellow, but extraordinarily proficient in his work. He had some kind of scent, the secret of which he would not reveal, which seemed to drive the wolves nearly crazy with desire. In one winter in the neighborhood of the Keystone Ranch he trapped forty-two big gray wolves; they still outnumber the cougars, which in that neighborhood have been nearly killed out, but they are no longer abundant.

At present wolves are decreasing in numbers all over Colorado, as they are in Montana, Wyoming, and the Dakotas. In some localities traps have been found most effective; in others, poison; and in yet others, hounds. I am inclined to think that where they have been pursued in one manner for a long time any new method will at first prove more efficacious. After a very few wolves have been poisoned or trapped, the survivors become so wary that only a master in the art can do anything with them, while there are always a few wolves which cannot be persuaded to touch a bait save under wholly exceptional circumstances. From association with the old she wolves the cubs learn as soon as they are able to walk to avoid man's traces in every way, and to look out for traps and poison. They are so shy and show such extraordinary cunning in hiding and slinking out of the way of the hunter that they are rarely killed with the rifle. Personally I never shot but one. A bold and good rider on a first-rate horse can, however, run down even a big gray wolf in fair chase, and either rope or shoot it. I have known a number of cow-punchers thus to rope wolves when they happened to run across them after they had gorged themselves on their quarry. A former Colorado ranchman, Mr. Henry N. Pancoast, who had done a good deal of wolf-hunting, and had killed one which, judging by its skin, was a veritable monster, wrote me as follows about his experiences:

"I captured nearly all my wolves by running them down and then either roped or shot them. I had one mount that had great endurance, and when riding him never failed to give chase to a wolf if I had the time to spare; and never failed to get my quarry but two or three times. I roped four full-grown and two cubs and shot five full-grown and three cubs—the large wolf in question being killed that way. And he was by far the hardest proposition I ever tried, and I candidly think I run him twenty miles before overhauling and shooting him (he showed too much fight to use a rope). As it was almost dark, concluded to put him on horse and skin at ranch, but had my hands full to get him on the saddle, was so very heavy. My plan in running wolves down was to get about three hundred yards from them, and then to keep that distance until the wolf showed signs of fatigue, when a little spurt would generally succeed in landing him. In the case of the large one, however, I reckoned without my host, as the wolf had as much go left as the horse, so I tried slowing down to a walk and let the wolf go; he . . . came down to a little trot and soon placed a half mile between us, and finally went out of sight over a high hill. I took my time and on reaching top of hill saw wolf about four hundred yards off, and as I now had a down grade managed to get my tired horse on a lope and was soon up to the wolf, which seemed all stiffened up, and one shot from my Winchester finished him. We always had poison out, as wolves and coyotes killed a great many calves. Never poisoned but two wolves, and those were caught with fresh antelope liver and entrails (coyotes were easily poisoned)."

In the early nineties the ravages of the wolves along the Little Missouri became so serious as thoroughly to arouse the stockmen. Not only colts and calves, and young trail stock, but in midwinter full-grown horses and steers were continually slain. The county authorities put a bounty of three dollars each on wolf scalps, to which the ranchmen of the neighborhood added a further bounty of five dollars. This made eight dollars for every wolf, and as the skin was also worth something, the business of killing wolves became profitable. Quite a number of men tried poisoning or trapping, but the most successful wolf hunter on the Little Missouri at that time was a man who did not rely on poison at all, but on dogs. He was named Massingale, and he always had a pack of at least twenty hounds. The number varied, for a wolf at bay is a terrible fighter, with jaws like those of a steel

BONY MOORE AND THE COYOTE

From a photograph, copyright, 1905, by Alexander Lambert, M.D.

trap, and teeth that cut like knives, so that the dogs were continually disabled and sometimes killed, and the hunter had always to be on the watch to add animals to his pack. It was not a good-looking pack, but it was thoroughly fit for its own work. Most of the dogs were greyhounds, whether rough or smooth haired, but many of them were big mongrels, part greyhound and part some other breed, such as bulldog, mastiff, Newfoundland, bloodhound, or collie. The only two requisites were that the dogs should run fast and fight gamely; and in consequence they formed as wicked, hard-biting a crew as ever ran down and throttled a wolf. They were usually taken out ten at a time, and by their aid Massingale killed over two hundred wolves, including cubs. Of course there was no pretence of giving the game fair play. The wolves were killed as vermin, not for sport. The greatest havoc was in the spring-time, when the she-wolves were followed to their dens. Some of the hounds were very fast, and they could usually overtake a young or weak wolf; but an old dog-wolf, with a good start, unless run into at once, would ordinarily get away if he were in running trim. Frequently, however, he was caught when not in running trim, for the hunter was apt to find him when he had killed a calf or taken part in dragging down a horse or steer, and was gorged with meat. Under these circumstances he could not run long before the pack. If possible, as with all such packs, the hunter himself got up in time to end the worry by a stab of his hunting-knife; but unless he was quick he had nothing to do, for the pack was thoroughly competent to do its own killing. Grim

fighter though a great dog-wolf is, he stands no show before the onslaught of ten such hounds, agile and powerful, who rush on their antagonist in a body. Massingale's
dogs possessed great power in their jaws, and unless he
was up within two or three minutes after the wolf was
overtaken, they tore him to death, though one or more
of their number might be killed or crippled in the fight.
The wolf might be throttled without having the hide
on its neck torn; but when it was stretched out the dogs
ripped open its belly. Dogs do not get their teeth
through the skin of an old cougar; but they will tear up
either a bobcat or coyote.

In 1894 and 1896 I saw a number of wolves on the
Little Missouri, although I was not looking for them. I
frequently came upon the remains of sheep and young
stock which they had killed; and once, upon the top of
a small plateau, I found the body of a large steer, while
the torn and trodden ground showed that he had fought
hard for his life before succumbing. There had been
two wolves engaged in the work, and the cunning beasts
had evidently acted in concert. Apparently, while one
attracted the steer's attention in front, the other, according to the invariable wolf habit, attacked him from behind, hamstringing him and tearing out his flanks. His
body was still warm when I came up, but the marauders
had slunk off, either seeing or smelling me. There was
no mistaking the criminals, however, for, unlike bears,
which usually attack an animal at the withers, or cougars,
which attack the throat or head, wolves almost invariably
attack their victim at the hind quarters and begin first

on the hams or flanks, if the animal is of any size. Owing to their often acting in couples or in packs, the big wolves do more damage to horned stock than cougars, but they are not as dangerous to colts, and they are not nearly as expert as the big cats in catching deer and mountain sheep. When food is plentiful, good observers say that they will not try to molest foxes; but, if hungry, they certainly snap them up as quickly as they would fawns. Ordinarily they show complete tolerance of the coyotes; yet one bitter winter I knew of a coyote being killed and eaten by a wolf.

Not only do the habits of wild beasts change under changing conditions as time goes on, but there seems to be some change even in their appearance. Thus the early observers of the game of the Little Missouri, those who wrote in the first half of the nineteenth century, spoke much of the white wolves which were then so common in the region. These white wolves represented in all probability only a color variety of the ordinary gray wolf; and it is difficult to say exactly why they disappeared. Yet when about the year 1890 wolves again grew common these white wolves were very, very rare; indeed I never personally heard of but one being seen. This was on the Upper Cannonball in 1892. A nearly black wolf was killed not far from this spot in the year 1893. At the present day black wolves are more common than white wolves, which are rare indeed. But all these big wolves are now decreasing in numbers, and in most places are decreasing rapidly.

It will be noticed that on some points my observations

about wolves are in seeming conflict with those of other observers as competent as I am; but I think the conflict is more seeming than real, and I have concluded to let my words stand. The great book of nature contains many pages which are hard to read, and at times conscientious students may well draw different interpretations of the obscure and least-known texts. It may not be that either observer is at fault, but what is true of an animal in one locality may not be true of the same animal in another, and even in the same locality two individuals of the same species may differ widely in their traits and habits.

CHAPTER IV

THE prongbuck is the most characteristic and distinctive of American game animals. Zoologically speaking, its position is unique. It is the only hollow-horned ruminant which sheds its horns, or rather the horn sheaths. We speak of it as an antelope, and it does of course represent on our prairies the antelopes of the Old World; but it stands apart from all other horned animals. Its place in the natural world is almost as lonely as that of the giraffe. In all its ways and habits it differs as much from deer and elk as from goat and sheep. Now that the buffalo has gone, it is the only game really at home on the wide plains. It is a striking-looking little creature, with its prominent eyes, single-pronged horns, and the sharply contrasted white, brown and reddish of its coat. The brittle hair is stiff, coarse and springy; on the rump it is brilliantly white, and is erected when the animal is alarmed or excited, so as to be very conspicuous. In marked contrast to deer, antelope never seek to elude observation; all they care for is to be able themselves to see. As they have good noses and wonderful eyes, and as they live by preference where there is little or no cover, shots at them are usually obtained at far longer range than is the case with other game; and yet, as they are easily seen, and often stand looking at the hunter just barely within very long rifle-range, they are always tempting their pursuer to the expenditure of cartridges. More shots are wasted at antelope than at any other game. They would be even harder to secure were it not that they are subject to fits of panic folly, or excessive curiosity, which occasionally put them fairly at the mercy of the rifle-bearing hunter.

In the old days the prongbuck was found as soon as the westward-moving traveller left the green bottom-lands of the Mississippi, and from thence across to the dry, open valleys of California, and northward to Canada and southward into Mexico. It has everywhere been gradually thinned out, and has vanished altogether from what were formerly the extreme easterly and westerly limits of its range. The rates of extermination of the different kinds of big game have been very unequal in different localities. Each kind of big game has had its own peculiar habitat in which it throve best, and each has also been found more or less plentifully in other regions where the circumstances were less favorable; and in these comparatively unfavorable regions it early tends to disappear before the advance of man. In consequence, where the ranges of the different game animals overlap and are intertwined, one will disappear first in one locality, and another will disappear first where the conditions are different. Thus the whitetail deer had thrust forward along the very narrow river bottoms into the domain of the mule-deer and the prongbuck among the foothills of the Rocky Mountains, and in these places it was exterminated from the narrow strips which it inhabited long before the mule-deer vanished from the high hills, or the prongbuck from the great open plains. But along great portions of the Missouri there are plenty of white-tails yet left in the river bottoms, while the mule-deer that once dwelt in the broken hills behind them, and the prongbuck which lived on the prairie just back of these bluffs, have both disappeared. In the same way the mule-deer and the prongbuck are often found almost inter-mingled through large regions in which plains, hills, and mountains alternate. If such a region is mainly moun-tainous, but contains a few valleys and table-lands, the prongbuck is sure to vanish from the latter before the mule-deer vanishes from the broken country. But if the region is one primarily of plains, with here and there rows of rocky hills in which the mule-deer is found, the latter is killed off long before the prongbuck can be hunted out of the great open stretches. The same is true of the pronghorn and the wapiti. The size and value of the wapiti make it an object of eager persecution on the part of hunters. But as it can live in the forest-clad fast-nesses of the Rockies, into which settlement does not go, it outlasts over great regions the pronghorn, whose abode is easily penetrated by sheep and cattle men. Under any-thing like even conditions, however, the prongbuck, of course, outlasts the wapiti. This was the case on the Lit-tle Missouri. On that stream the bighorn also outlasted the wapiti. In 1881 wapiti were still much more plenti-ful than bighorns. Within the next decade they had almost totally disappeared, while the bighorn was still to be found; I shot one and saw others in 1893, at which time I had not authentic information of a single wapiti remaining anywhere on the river in my neighborhood, although it is possible that one or two still lurked in some out-of-the-way recess. In Colorado at one time the bighorn was nearly exterminated, while the wapiti still withstood the havoc made among its huge herds; then followed a period in which the rapidity of destruction of the wapiti increased far beyond that of the bighorn.

I mention these facts partly because they are of interest in themselves, but chiefly because they tend to explain the widely different opinions expressed by competent observers about what superficially seem to be similar facts. It cannot be too often repeated that allowance must be made for the individual variability in the traits and characters of animals of the same species, and especially of the same species under different circumstances and in different localities; and allowance must also be made for the variability of the individual factor in the observers themselves. Many seemingly contradictory observations of the habits of deer, wapiti, and prongbuck will be found in books by the best hunters. Take such questions as the keenness of sight of the deer as compared with the prongbuck, and of the pugnacity of the wapiti, both actual and relative, and a wide difference of opinion will be found in three such standard works as Dodge's " The Hunting-grounds of the Great West," Caton's " Deer and Antelope of America," and the contributions of Mr. Grinnell to the " Century Book of Sports." Sometimes the difference will be in mere matters of opinion, as, for instance, in the belief as to the relative worth of the sport furnished by the chase of the different creatures; but sometimes there is a direct conflict of fact. Colonel Dodge, for instance, has put it upon record that the wapiti is an exceedingly gentle animal, less dangerous than a whitetail or blacktail buck in a close encounter, and that the bulls hardly ever fight among themselves. My own experience leads me to traverse in the most emphatic manner every one of these conclusions, and all hunters whom I have met feel exactly as I do; yet no one would question for a moment Colonel Dodge's general competency as an observer. In the same way Mr. Grinnell has a high opinion of the deer's keenness of sight. Judge Caton absolutely disagrees with him, and my own experience tends to agree with that of the Judge—at least to the extent of placing the deer's vision far below that of the prongbuck and even that of the bighorn, and only on a par with that of the wapiti. Yet Mr. Grinnell is an unusually competent observer, whose opinion on any such subject is entitled to unqualified respect.

Difference in habits may be due simply to difference of locality, or to the need of adaptation to new conditions. The prongbuck's habits about migration offer examples of the former kind of difference. Over portions of its range the prongbuck is not migratory at all. In other parts the migrations are purely local. In yet other regions the migrations are continued for great distances, immense multitudes of the animals going to and fro in the spring and fall along well-beaten tracks. I know of one place in New Mexico where the pronghorn herds are tenants of certain great plains throughout the entire year. I know another region in northwestern Colorado where the very few prongbucks still left, though they shift from valley to valley, yet spend the whole year in the same stretch of rolling, barren country. On the Little Missouri, however, during the eighties and early nineties, there was a very distinct though usually local migration. Before the Black Hills had been settled they were famous wintering places for the antelope, which swarmed from great distances to them when cold weather approached; those which had summered east of the Big Missouri actually swam the river in great herds, on their journey to the Hills. The old hunters around my ranch insisted that formerly the prongbuck had for the most part travelled from the Little Missouri Bad Lands into the Black Hills for the winter.

When I was ranching on that river, however, this custom no longer obtained, for the Black Hills were too well settled, and the herds of prongbuck that wintered there were steadily diminishing in numbers. At that time, from 1883 to 1896, the seasonal change in habits, and shift of position, of the prongbucks were well marked. As soon as the new grass sprang they appeared in great numbers upon the plains. They were especially fond of the green, tender blades that came up where the country had been burned over. If the region had been devastated by prairie fires in the fall, the next spring it was certain to contain hundreds and thousands of prongbucks. All through the summer they remained out on these great open plains, coming to drink at the little pools

ON THE LITTLE MISSOURI

in the creek beds, and living where there was no shelter of any kind. As winter approached they began to gather in bands. Some of these bands apparently had regular wintering places to the south of us, in Pretty Buttes and beyond; and close to my ranch, at the crossing of the creek called Beaver, there were certain trails which these antelope regularly travelled, northward in the spring and southward in the fall. But other bands would seek out places in the Bad Lands near by, gathering together on some succession of plateaus which were protected by neighboring hills from the deep drifts of snow. Here they passed the winter, on short commons, it is true (they graze, not browsing like deer), but without danger of perishing in the snow-drifts. On the other hand, if the skin hunters discovered such a wintering place, they were able to butcher practically the entire band, if they so desired, as the prongbucks were always most reluctant to leave such a chosen ground.

Normally the prongbuck avoids both broken ground and timber. It is a queer animal, with keen senses, but with streaks of utter folly in its character. Time and again I have known bands rush right by me, when I happened to surprise them feeding near timber or hills, and got between them and the open plains. The animals could have escaped without the least difficulty if they had been willing to go into the broken country, or through even a few rods of trees and brush; and yet they preferred to rush madly by me at close range, in order to get out to their favorite haunts. But nowadays there are certain localities where the prongbucks spend a large part of their time in the timber or in rough, hilly country, feeding and bringing up their young in such localities.

Typically, however, the prongbuck is preeminently a beast of the great open plains, eating their harsh, dry pasturage, and trusting to its own keen senses and speed for its safety. All the deer are fond of skulking; the whitetail preeminently so. The prongbuck, on the contrary, never endeavors to elude observation. Its sole aim is to be able to see its enemies, and it cares nothing whatever about its enemies seeing it. Its coloring is very conspicuous, and is rendered still more so by its habit of erecting the white hair on its rump. It has a very erect carriage, and when it thinks itself in danger it always endeavors to get on some crest or low hill from which it can look all about. The big bulging eyes, situated at the base of the horns, scan the horizon far and near like twin telescopes. They pick out an object at such a distance that it would entirely escape the notice of a deer. When suspicious, they have a habit of barking, uttering a sound something like " kau," and repeating it again and again, as they walk up and down, endeavoring to find out if danger lurks in the unusual object. They are extremely curious, and in the old days it was often possible to lure them toward the hunter by waving a red handkerchief to and fro on a stick, or even by lying on one's back and kicking the legs. Nowadays, however, there are very few localities indeed in which they are sufficiently unsophisticated to make it worth while trying these time-honored tricks of the long-vanished trappers and hunters.

Along the Little Missouri the fawns, sometimes one and sometimes two in number, were dropped in May or early in June. At that time the antelope were usually found in herds which the mother did not leave until she was about to give birth to the fawn. During the first few days the fawn's safety is to be found only in its not attracting attention. During this time it normally lies perfectly flat on the ground, with its head outstretched, and makes no effort to escape. While out on the spring round-up I have come across many of these fawns. Once, in company with several cowboys, I was riding behind a bunch of cattle which, as we hurried them, spread out in open order ahead of us. Happening to cast down my eyes I saw an antelope fawn directly ahead of me. The bunch of cattle had passed all around it, but it made not the slightest sign, not even when I halted, got off my pony, and took it up in my arms. It was useless to take it to camp and try to rear it, and so I speedily put it down again. Scanning the neighborhood, I saw the doe hanging about some half a mile off, and when I looked back from the next divide I could see her gradually drawing near to the fawn.

If taken when very young, antelope make cunning and amusing pets, and I have often seen them around the ranches. There was one in the ranch of a Mrs. Blank who had a station on the Deadwood stage line some eighteen years ago. She was a great worker in buckskin, and I got her to make me the buckskin shirt I still use. There was an antelope fawn that lived at the house, wandering wherever it wished; but it would not permit me to touch it. As I sat inside the house it would come in and hop up on a chair, looking at me sharply all the while. No matter how cautiously I approached, I could never put my hand upon it, as at the last moment it would spring off literally as quick as a bird would fly. One of my neighbors on the Little Missouri, Mr. Howard Eaton, had at one time upon his ranch three little antelope whose foster-mother was a sheep, and who were really absurdly tame. I was fond of patting them and of giving them crusts, and the result was that they followed me about so closely that I had to be always on the lookout to see that I did not injure them. They were on excellent terms with the dogs, and were very playful. It was a comic sight to see them skipping and hopping about the old ewe when anything happened to alarm her and she started off at a clumsy waddle. Nothing could surpass the tameness of the antelope that are now under Mr. Hornaday's care at the Bronx Zoological Garden in New York. The last time that I visited the garden some repairs were being made inside the antelope enclosure, and a dozen workmen had gone in to make them. The antelope regarded the workmen with a friendliness and curiosity untempered by the slightest touch of apprehension. When the men took off their coats the little creatures would nose them over to see if they contained anything edible, and they would come close up and watch the men plying the pick with the utmost interest. Mr. Hornaday took us inside, and they all came up in the most friendly manner. One or two of the bucks would put their heads against our legs and try to push us around, but not roughly. Mr.

Hornaday told me that he was having great difficulty, exactly as with the mule-deer, in acclimatizing the antelope, especially as the food was so different from what they were accustomed to in their native haunts.

The wild fawns are able to run well a few days after they are born. They then accompany the mother everywhere. Sometimes she joins a band of others; more often she stays alone with her fawn, and perhaps one of the young of the previous year, until the rut begins. Of all game the prongbuck seems to me the most excitable during the rut. The males run the does much as do the bucks of the mule and whitetail deer. If there are no does present, I have sometimes watched a buck run to and fro by himself. The first time I saw this I was greatly interested, and could form no idea of what the buck was doing. He was by a creek bed in a slight depression or shallow valley, and was grazing uneasily. After a little while he suddenly started and ran just as hard as he could, off in a straight direction, nearly away from me. I thought that somehow or other he had discovered my presence; but he suddenly wheeled and came back to the original place, still running at his utmost speed. Then he halted, moved about with the white hairs on his rump outspread, and again dashed off at full speed, halted, wheeled, and came back. Two or three times he did this, and let me get very close to him before he discovered me. I was too much interested in what he was doing to desire to shoot him.

In September, sometimes not earlier than October, the big bucks begin to gather the does into harems. Each buck is then constantly on the watch to protect his harem from outsiders, and steal another doe if he can get a chance. I have seen a comparatively young buck who had appropriated a doe, hustle her hastily out of the country as soon as he saw another antelope in the neighborhood; while, on the other hand, a big buck, already with a good herd of does, will do his best to appropriate any other that comes in sight. The bucks fight fearlessly but harmlessly among themselves, locking their horns and then pushing as hard as they can.

Although their horns are not very formidable weapons, they are bold little creatures, and if given a chance will stand at bay before either hound or coyote. A doe will fight most gallantly for her fawn, and is an overmatch for a single coyote, but of course she can do but little against a large wolf. The wolves are occasionally very destructive to the herds. The cougar, however, which is a much worse foe than the wolf to deer and mountain sheep, can but rarely molest the prongbuck, owing to the nature of the latter's haunts. Eagles, on occasion, take the fawns, as they do those of deer.

I have always been fond of the chase of the prongbuck. While I lived on my ranch on the Little Missouri it was, next to the mule-deer, the game which I most often followed, and on the long wagon strips which I occasionally took from my ranch to the Black Hills, to the Big Horn Mountains, or into eastern Montana, prongbuck venison was our usual fresh meat, save when we could kill prairie-chickens and ducks with our rifles, which was not always feasible. In my mind the prong-

buck is always associated with the open prairies during
the spring, summer, or early fall. It has happened that
I have generally pursued the bighorn in bitter weather;
and when we laid in our stock of winter meat, mule-
deer was our usual game. Though I have shot prongbuck
in winter, I never liked to do so, as I felt the animals
were then having a sufficiently hard·struggle for existence
anyhow. But in the spring the meat of the prongbuck
was better than that of any other game, and, moreover,
there was not the least danger of mistaking the sexes,
and killing a doe accidentally, and accordingly I rarely
killed anything but pronghorns at that season. In those
days we never got any fresh meat, whether on the ranch or
while on the round-up or on a wagon trip, unless we shot
it, and salt pork became a most monotonous diet after a
time.

Occasionally I killed the prongbuck in a day's hunt
from my ranch. If I started with the intention of prongbuck hunting, I always went on horseback; but twice I
killed them on foot when I happened to run across them
by accident while looking for mule-deer. I shall always
remember one of these occasions. I was alone in the Elkhorn ranch-house at the time, my foreman and the only
cowpuncher who was not on the round-up having driven
to Medora, some forty miles away, in order to bring down
the foreman's wife and sister, who were going to spend
the summer with him. It was the fourth day of his absence. I expected him in the evening and wanted to have
fresh meat, and so after dinner I shouldered my rifle and
strolled off through the hills. It was too early in the

day to expect to see anything, and my intention was simply to walk out until I was five or six miles from the ranch, and then work carefully home through a likely country toward sunset, as by this arrangement I would be in a good game region at the very time that the animals were likely to stir abroad. It was a glaring, late-spring day, and in the hot sun of mid-afternoon I had no idea that anything would be moving, and was not keeping a very sharp lookout. After an hour or two's steady tramping I came into a long, narrow valley, bare of trees and brushwood, and strolled along it, following a cattle trail that led up the middle. The hills rose steeply into a ridge crest on each side, sheer clay shoulders breaking the mat of buffalo-grass which elsewhere covered the sides of the valley as well as the bottom. It was very hot and still, and I was paying but little attention to my surroundings, when my eye caught a sudden movement on the ridge crest to my right, and, dropping on one knee as I wheeled around, I saw the head and neck of a prong-buck rising above the crest. The animal was not above a hundred yards off, and stood motionless as it stared at me. At the crack of the rifle the head disappeared; but as I sprang clear of the smoke I saw a cloud of dust rise on the other side of the ridge crest, and felt convinced that the quarry had fallen. I was right. On climbing the ridge crest I found that on the other side it sank abruptly in a low cliff of clay, and at the foot of this, thirty feet under me, the prongbuck lay with its neck broken. After dressing it I shouldered the body entire, thinking that I should like to impress the new-comers by the sight of so tangible a proof of my hunting prowess as whole prongbuck hanging up in the cottonwoods by the house. As it was a well-grown buck the walk home under the hot sun was one of genuine toil.

The spot where I ran across this prongbuck was miles away from the nearest plains, and it was very unusual to see one in such rough country. In fact, the occurrence was wholly exceptional; just as I once saw three bighorn rams, which usually keep to the roughest country, deliberately crossing the river bottom below my ranch, and going for half a mile through the thick cottonwood timber. Occasionally, however, parties of prongbuck came down the creek bottoms to the river. Once I struck a couple of young bucks in the bottom of a creek which led to the Chimney Butte ranch-house, and stalked them without difficulty; for as prongbuck make no effort to hide, if there is good cover even their sharp eyes do not avail them. On another occasion several does and fawns, which we did not molest, spent some time on what we called "the corral bottom," which was two or three miles above the ranch-house. In the middle of this bottom we had built a corral for better convenience in branding the calves when the round-up came near our ranch—as the bottom on which the ranch-house stood was so thickly wooded as to make it difficult to work cattle thereon. The does and fawns hung around the corral bottom for some little time, and showed themselves very curious and by no means shy.

When I went from the ranch for a day's prongbuck hunting of set purpose, I always rode a stout horse and started by dawn. The prongbucks are almost the only game that can be hunted as well during the heat of the day as at any other time. They occasionally lie down for two or three hours about noon in some hollow where they cannot be seen, but usually there is no place where they are sure they can escape observation even when resting; and when this is the case they choose a somewhat conspicuous station and trust to their own powers of observation, exactly as they do when feeding. There is therefore no necessity, as with deer, of trying to strike them at dawn or dusk. The reason why I left the ranch before sunrise and often came back long after dark was because I had to ride at least a dozen miles to get out to the ground and a dozen to get back, and if after industrious walking I failed at first to find my game, I would often take the horse again and ride for an hour or two to get into new country. Prongbuck water once a day, often travelling great distances to or from some little pool or spring. Of course, if possible, I liked to leave the horse by such a pool or spring. On the great plains to which I used to make these excursions there was plenty of water in early spring, and it would often run, here and there, in the upper courses of some of the creeks—which, however, usually contained running water only when there had been a cloudburst or freshet. As the season wore on the country became drier and drier. Water would remain only in an occasional deep hole, and few springs were left in which there was so much as a trickle. In a strange country I could not tell where these water-holes were, but in the neighborhood of the ranch I of course knew where

I was likely to find them. Often, however, I was disappointed; and more than once after travelling many miles to where I hoped to find water, there would be nothing but sun-cracked mud, and the horse and I would have eighteen hours of thirst in consequence. A ranch horse, however, is accustomed to such incidents, and of course when a man spends half the time riding, it is merely a matter of slight inconvenience to go so long without a drink.

Nevertheless, if I did reach a spring, it turned the expedition into pleasure instead of toil. Even in the hot weather the ride toward the plains over the hills was very lovely. It was beautiful to see the red dawn quicken from the first glimmering gray in the east, and then to watch the crimson bars glint on the tops of the fantastically shaped barren hills when the sun flamed, burning and splendid, above the horizon. In the early morning the level beams threw into sharp relief the strangely carved and channelled cliff walls of the buttes. There was rarely a cloud to dim the serene blue of the sky. By the time the heat had grown heavy I had usually reached the spring or pool, where I unsaddled the horse, watered him, and picketed him out to graze. Then, under the hot sun, I would stride off for the hunting proper. On such occasions I never went to where the prairie was absolutely flat. There were always gently rolling stretches broken by shallow watercourses, slight divides, and even low mounds, sometimes topped with strangely shaped masses of red scoria or with petrified trees. My object, of course, was, either with my unaided eyes or with the help of my glasses, to catch sight of the prongbucks before they saw me. I speedily found, by the way, that if they were too plentiful this was almost impossible. The more abundant deer are in a given locality the more apt one is to run across them, and of course if the country is sufficiently broken, the same is true of prongbucks; but where it is very flat and there are many different bands in sight at the same time, it is practically impossible to keep out of sight of all of them, and as they are also all in sight of one another, if one flees the others are certain to take the alarm. Under such circumstances I have usually found that the only pronghorns I got were obtained by accident, so to speak; that is, by some of them unexpectedly running my way, or by my happening to come across them in some nook where I could not see them, or they me.

Prongbucks are very fast runners indeed, even faster than deer. They vary greatly in speed, however, precisely as is the case with deer; in fact, I think that the average hunter makes altogether too little account of this individual variation among different animals of the same kind. Under the same conditions different deer and antelope vary in speed and wariness, exactly as bears and cougars vary in cunning and ferocity. When in perfect condition a full-grown buck antelope, from its strength and size, is faster and more enduring than an old doe; but a fat buck, before the rut has begun, will often be pulled down by a couple of good greyhounds much more speedily than a flying yearling or two-year-old doe. Under favorable circumstances, when the antelope was jumped near by, I have seen one overhauled and seized by a first-class greyhound; and, on the other hand, I have more than once seen a pronghorn run away from a whole pack of just as good dogs. With a fair start, and on good ground, a thoroughbred horse, even though handicapped by the weight of a rider, will run down an antelope; but this is a feat which should rarely be attempted, because such a race, even when carried to a successful issue, is productive of the utmost distress to the steed.

Ordinary horses will sometimes run down an antelope which is slower than the average. I once had on my ranch an under-sized old Indian pony named White Eye, which, when it was fairly roused, showed a remarkable turn of speed, and had great endurance. One morning on the round-up, when for some reason we did not work the cattle, I actually ran down an antelope in fair chase on this old pony. It was a nursing doe, and I came over the crest of the hill, between forty and fifty yards away from it. As it wheeled to start back, the old cayuse pricked up his ears with great interest, and the moment I gave him a sign was after it like a shot. Whether, being a cow-pony, he started to run it just as if it were a calf or a yearling trying to break out of the herd, or whether he was overcome by dim reminiscences of buffalo-hunting in his Indian youth, I know not. At any rate, after the doe he went, and in a minute or two I found I was drawing up to her. I had a revolver, but of course did not wish to kill her, and so got my rope ready to try to take her alive. She ran frantically, but the old pony, bending level to the ground, kept up his racing lope and closed right in beside her. As I came up she fairly bleated. An expert with the rope would have captured her with the utmost ease; but I missed, sending the coil across her shoulders. She again gave an agonized bleat, or bark, and wheeled around like a shot. The cow-pony stopped almost, but not quite, as fast, and she got a slight start, and it was some little time before I overhauled her again. When I did I repeated the performance, and this time when she wheeled she succeeded in getting on some ground where I could not follow, and I was thrown out.

Normally, a horseman without greyhounds can hope for nothing more than to get within fair shooting range; and this only by taking advantage of the prongbucks' peculiarity of running straight ahead in the direction in which they are pointed, when once they have settled into their pace. Usually, as soon as they see a hunter they run straight away from him; but sometimes they make their flight at an angle, and as they do not like to change their course when once started, it is thus possible, with a good horse, to cut them off from the point toward which they are headed, and get a reasonably close shot.

I have done a good deal of coursing with greyhounds at one time or another, but always with scratch packs. There are a few ranchmen who keep leashes of grey-hounds of pure blood, bred and trained to antelope coursing, and who do their coursing scientifically, carrying the dogs out to the hunting-grounds in wagons and exercising every care in the sport; but these men are rare. The average man who dwells where antelope are sufficiently abundant to make coursing a success, simply follows the pursuit at odd moments, with whatever long-legged dogs he and his neighbors happen to have; and his methods of coursing are apt to be as rough as his outfit. My own coursing was precisely of this character. At different times I had on my ranch one or two high-classed greyhounds and Scotch deerhounds, with which we coursed deer and antelope, as well as jack-rabbits, foxes, and coyotes; and we usually had with them one or two ordinary hounds, and various half-bred dogs. I must add, however, that some of the latter were very good. I can recall in particular one fawn-colored beast, a cross between a greyhound and a foxhound, which ran nearly as fast as the former, though it occasionally yelped in shrill tones. It could also trail well, and was thoroughly game; on one occasion it ran down and killed a coyote single-handed.

On going out with these dogs, I rarely chose a day when I was actually in need of fresh meat. If this was the case, I usually went alone with the rifle; but if one or two other men were at the ranch, and we wanted a morning's fun, we would often summon the dogs, mount our horses, and go trooping out to the antelope-ground. As there was good deer-country between the ranch bottom and the plains where we found the prongbuck, it not infrequently happened that we had a chase after blacktail or whitetail on the way. Moreover, when we got out to the ground, before sighting antelope, it frequently happened that the dogs would jump a jack-rabbit or a fox, and away the whole set would go after it, streaking through the short grass, sometimes catching their prey in a few hundred yards, and sometimes having to run a mile or so. In consequence, by the time we reached the regular hunting-ground the dogs were apt to have lost a good deal of their freshness. We would get them in behind the horses and creep cautiously along, trying to find some solitary prongbuck in a suitable place, where we could bring up the dogs from behind a hillock and give them a fair start. Usually we failed to get the dogs near enough for a good start; and in most cases their chases after unwounded prongbuck resulted in the quarry running clean away from them. Thus the odds were greatly against them; but, on the other hand, we helped them wherever possible with the rifle. We usually rode well scattered out, and if one of us put up an antelope, or had a chance at one when driven by the dogs, he always fired, and the pack were saved from the ill effects of total discouragement by so often getting these wounded beasts. It was astonishing to see how fast an antelope with a broken leg could run. If such a beast had a good start, and especially if the dogs were tired, it would often lead them a hard chase, and the dogs would be utterly exhausted after it had been killed; so that we would have to let them lie where they were for a long time before trying to lead them down to some stream-bed. If possible, we carried water for them in canteens.

There were red-letter days, however, on which our dogs fairly ran down and killed unwounded antelope— days when the weather was cool, and when it happened that we got our dogs out to the ground without their being tired by previous runs, and found our quarry soon, and in favorable places for slipping the hounds. I remember one such chase in particular. We had at the time a mixed pack, in which there was only one dog of my own, the others being contributed from various sources. It included two greyhounds, a rough-coated deerhound, a foxhound, and the fawn-colored cross-bred mentioned above.

We rode out in the early morning, the dogs trotting behind us; and, coming to a low tract of rolling hills, just at the edge of the great prairie, we separated and rode over the crest of the nearest ridge. Just as we topped it, a fine buck leaped up from a hollow a hundred yards off, and turned to look at us for a moment. All the dogs were instantly spinning toward him down the grassy slope. He apparently saw those at the right, and, turning, raced away from us in a diagonal line, so that the left-hand greyhound, which ran cunning and tried to cut him off, was very soon almost alongside. He saw her, however—she was a very fast bitch—just in time, and, wheeling, altered his course to the right. As he reached the edge of the prairie, this alteration nearly brought him in contact with the cross-bred, which had obtained a rather poor start, on the extreme right of the line. Around went the buck again, evidently panic-struck and puzzled to the last degree, and started straight off across the prairie, the dogs literally at his heels, and we, urging our horses with whip and spur, but a couple of hundred yards behind. For half a mile the pace was tremendous, when one of the greyhounds made a spring at his ear, but failing to make good his hold, was thrown off. However, it halted the buck for a moment, and made him turn quarter round, and in a second the deerhound had seized him by the flank and thrown him, and all the dogs piled on top, never allowing him to rise.

Later we again put up a buck not far off. At first it went slowly, and the dogs hauled up on it; but when they got pretty close, it seemed to see them, and letting itself out, went clean away from them almost without effort.

Once or twice we came upon bands of antelope, and the hounds would immediately take after them. I was always rather sorry for this, however, because the frightened animals, as is generally the case when beasts are in a herd, seemed to impede one another, and the chase usually ended by the dogs seizing a doe, for it was of course impossible to direct them to any particular beast.

It will be seen that with us coursing was a homely sport. Nevertheless we had good fun, and I shall always have enjoyable memories of the rapid gallops across the prairie, on the trail of a flying prongbuck.

Usually my pronghorn hunting has been done while I have been off with a wagon on a trip intended primarily for the chase, or else while travelling for some other purpose.

All life in the wilderness is so pleasant that the temptation is to consider each particular variety, while one is enjoying it, as better than any other. A canoe trip through the great forests, a trip with a pack-train among the mountains, a trip on snow-shoes through the silent, mysterious fairyland of the woods in winter—each has its peculiar charm. To some men the sunny monotony

CAMPING ON THE ANTELOPE GROUNDS

of the great plains is wearisome; personally there are few things I have enjoyed more than journeying over them where the game was at all plentiful. Sometimes I have gone off for three or four days alone on horseback, with a slicker or oilskin coat behind the saddle, and some salt and hardtack as my sole provisions. But for comfort on a trip of any length it was always desirable to have a wagon. My regular outfit consisted of a wagon and team driven by one man who cooked, together with another man and four riding ponies, two of which we rode, while the other two were driven loose or led behind the wagon. While it is eminently desirable that a hunter should be able to rough it, and should be entirely willing to put up with the bare minimum of necessities, and to undergo great fatigue and hardship, it is yet not at all necessary that he should refrain from comfort of a wholesome sort when it is obtainable. By taking the wagon we could carry a tent to put up if there was foul weather. I had a change of clothes to put on if I was wet, two or three books to read—and nothing adds more to the enjoyment of a hunting trip—as well as plenty of food; while having two men made me entirely foot-loose as regards camp, so that I could hunt whenever I pleased, and, if I came in tired, I simply rested, instead of spending two or three hours in pitching camp, cooking, tethering horses, and doing the innumerable other little things which in the aggregate amount to so much.

On such a trip, when we got into unknown country, it was of course very necessary to stay near the wagon, especially if we had to hunt for water. But if we knew the country at all, we would decide in the morning about where the camp was to be made in the afternoon, and then I would lope off on my own account, while the wagon lumbered slowly across the rough prairie sward straight toward its destination. Sometimes I took the spare man with me, and sometimes not. It was convenient to have him, for there are continually small emergencies in which it is well to be with a companion. For instance, if one jumps off for a sudden shot, there is always a slight possibility that any but a thoroughly trained horse will get frightened and gallop away. On some of my horses I could absolutely depend, but there were others, and very good ones too, which would on rare occasions fail me; and few things are more disheartening than a long stern chase after one's steed under such circumstances, with the unpleasant possibility of seeing him leave the country entirely and strike out for the ranch fifty or sixty miles distant. If there is a companion with one, all danger of this is over. Moreover, in galloping at full speed after the game it is impossible now and then to avoid a tumble, as the horse may put his leg into a prairie-dog hole or badger burrow; and on such occasions a companion may come in very handily. On the other hand, there is so great a charm in absolute solitude, in the wild, lonely freedom of the great plains, that often I would make some excuse and go off entirely by myself.

Such rides had a fascination of their own. Hour after hour the wiry pony shuffled onward across the sea of short, matted grass. On every side the plains stretched seemingly limitless. Sometimes there would be no object to break the horizon; sometimes across a score of miles there would loom through the clear air the fantastic outlines of a chain of buttes, rising grim and barren. Occasionally there might be a slightly marked watercourse, every drop of moisture long dried; and usually there would not be as much as the smallest sage brush anywhere in sight. As the sun rose higher and higher the shadows of horse and rider shortened, and the beams were reflected from the short, bleached blades until in the hot air all the landscape afar off seemed to dance and waver. Often on such trips days went by without our coming across another human being, and the loneliness and vastness of the country seemed as unbroken as if the old vanished days had returned—the days of the wild wilderness wanderers, and the teeming myriads of game they followed, and the scarcely wilder savages against whom they warred.

Now and then prongbuck would appear, singly or in bands; and their sharp bark of alarm or curiosity would come to me through the still, hot air over great distances, as they stood with head erect looking at me, the white patches on their rumps shining in the sun, and the bands and markings on their heads and necks showing as if they were in livery. Scan the country as carefully as I would, they were far more apt to see me than I was them, and once they had seen me, it was normally hopeless to expect to get them. But their strange freakishness of nature frequently offsets the keenness of their senses. At least half of the prongbucks which I shot were obtained, not by stalking, but by coming across them purely through their own fault. Though the prairie seemed level, there was really a constant series of undulations, shallow and of varying width. Now and then as I topped some slight rise I would catch a glimpse of a little band,of pronghorns feeding, and would slip off my horse before they could see me. A hasty determination as to where the best chance of approaching them lay would be followed by a half-hour's laborious crawl, a good part of the time flat on my face. They might discover me when I was still too far for a shot; or by taking advantage of every little inequality I might get within long range before they got a glimpse of me, and then in a reasonable proportion of cases I would bag my buck. At other times the buck would come to me. Perhaps one would suddenly appear over a divide himself, and his curiosity would cause him to stand motionless long enough to give me a shot; while on other occasions I have known one which was out of range to linger around, shifting his position as I shifted mine, until by some sudden gallop or twist I was able to get close enough to empty my magazine at him.

When the shadows had lengthened, but before any coolness had come into the air, I would head for the appointed camping-place. Sometimes this would be on the brink of some desolate little pool under a low, treeless butte, or out on the open prairie where the only wood was what we had brought with us. At other times I would find the wagon drawn up on the edge of some shrunken plains river, under a line of great cottonwoods with splintered branches and glossy leaves that rustled all day long. Such a camp was always comfortable, for there was an abundance of wood for the fire, plenty of water, and thick feed in which the horses grazed—one or two being picketed and the others feeding loose until night came on. If I had killed a prongbuck, steaks were speedily sizzling in the frying-pan over the hot coals. If I had failed to get anything, I would often walk a mile or two down or up the river to see if I could not kill a couple of prairie-chickens or ducks. If the evening was at all cool, we built a fire as darkness fell, and sat around it, while the leaping flames lit up the trunks of the cottonwoods and gleamed on the pools of water in the half-dry river bed. Then I would wrap myself in my blanket and lie looking up at the brilliant stars until I fell asleep.

In both 1893 and 1894 I made trips to a vast tract of rolling prairie land, some fifty miles from my ranch, where I had for many years enjoyed the keen pleasure of hunting the prongbuck. In 1893 the pronghorned bands were as plentiful in this district as I have ever seen them anywhere. Lambert was with me; and in a week's trip, including the journey out and back, we easily shot all the antelope we felt we had any right to kill; for we only shot to get meat, or an unusually fine head. Lambert did most of the shooting; and I have never seen a professional hunter do better in stalking antelope on the open prairie. I myself fired at only two antelope, both of which had already been missed. In each case a hard run and much firing at long ranges, together with in one case some skilful manœuvring, got me my game; yet one buck cost ten cartridges and the other eight. In 1894 I had exactly the reverse experience. I killed five antelope for thirty-six shots, but each one that I killed was killed with the first bullet, and in not one case where I missed the first time did I hit with any subsequent shot. These five antelope were killed at an average distance of about 150 yards. Those that I missed were, of course, much farther off on an average, and I usually emptied my magazine at each. The number of cartridges spent would seem extraordinary to a tyro; and an unusually skilful shot, or else a very timid shot who fears to take risks, will of course make a better showing per head killed; but I doubt if men with experience in antelope hunting, who keep an accurate account of the cartridges they expend, will see anything much out of the way in the performance.

During the years I have hunted in the West I have always, where possible, kept a record of the number of cartridges expended for every head of game killed, and of the distances at which it was shot. I have found that with bison, bear, moose, elk, caribou, bighorn and white goat, where the animals shot at were mostly of large size and usually stationary, and where the mountainous or wooded country gave chance for a close approach, the average distance at which I have killed the game has been eighty yards, and the average number of cartridges expended per head slain, three; one of these representing the death-shot, and the others standing either for misses outright, of which there were not many, or else for wounding game which escaped, or which I afterward overtook, or for stopping cripples or charging beasts. I have killed but two peccaries, using but one cartridge for each; they were close up. My experiences with cougar have already been narrated. At wolves and coyotes I have generally had to take running shots at very long range, and I have shot but two—one of each—for fifty cartridges. Blacktail deer I have generally shot at about ninety yards, at an expenditure of about four cartridges apiece. Whitetail I have killed at shorter range; but the shots were generally running, often taken under difficult circumstances, so that my expenditure of cartridges was rather larger. Antelope, on the other hand, I have on the average shot at a little short of 150 yards, and they have cost me about nine cartridges apiece. This, of course, as I have explained above, does not mean that I have missed eight out of nine antelope, for often the entire nine cartridges would be spent at an antelope which I eventually got. It merely means that, counting all the shots of every description fired at antelope, I had one head to show for each nine cartridges expended.

Thus, the first antelope I shot in 1893 cost me ten cartridges, of which three hit him, while the seven that missed were fired at over 400 yards' distance while he was running. We saw him while we were with the wagon. As we had many miles to go before sunset, we cared nothing about frightening other game, and, as we had no fresh meat, it was worth while to take some chances to procure it. When I first fired, the prongbuck had already been shot at and was in full flight. He was beyond all reasonable range, but some of our bullets went over him and he began to turn. By running to one side I got a shot at him at a little over 400 paces, as he slowed to a walk, bewildered by the firing, and the bullet broke his hip. I missed him two or three times as he plunged off, and then by hard running down a watercourse got a shot at 180 paces and broke his shoulder, and broke his neck with another bullet when I came up.

This one was shot while going out to the hunting-ground. While there Lambert killed four others. I did not fire again until on our return, when I killed another buck one day while we were riding with the wagon. The day was gray and overcast. There were slight flurries of snow, and the cold wind chilled us as it blew across the endless reaches of sad-colored prairie. Behind us loomed Sentinel Butte, and all around the rolling surface was broken by chains of hills, by patches of bad lands, or by isolated, saddle-shaped mounds. The ranch wagon jolted over the uneven sward, and plunged in and out of the dry beds of the occasional water courses; for we were following no road, but merely striking northward across the prairie toward the P. K. ranch. We went at a good pace, for the afternoon was bleak, the wagon was lightly loaded, and the Sheriff of the county, whose deputy I had been, and who was serving for the nonce as our teamster and cook, kept the two gaunt, wild-looking horses trotting steadily. Lambert and I rode to one side on our unkempt cow-ponies, our rifles slung across the saddle bows.

Our stock of fresh meat was getting low and we were anxious to shoot something; but in the early hours of the afternoon we saw no game. Small parties of horned larks ran along the ground ahead of the wagon, twittering plaintively as they rose, and now and then flocks of long-spurs flew hither and thither; but of larger life we saw nothing, save occasional bands of range horses. The drought had been severe and we were far from the river, so that we saw no horned stock. Horses can travel much farther to water than cattle, and, when the springs dry up, they stay much farther out on the prairie.

At last we did see a band of four antelope, lying in the middle of a wide plain, but they saw us before we saw them, and the ground was so barren of cover that it was impossible to get near them. Moreover, they were very shy and ran almost as soon as we got our eyes on them. For an hour or two after this we jogged along without seeing anything, while the gray clouds piled up in the west and the afternoon began to darken; then, just after passing Saddle Butte, we struck a rough prairie road, which we knew led to the P. K. ranch—a road very faint in places, while in others the wheels had sunk deep in the ground and made long, parallel ruts.

Almost immediately after striking this road, on top-ping a small rise, we discovered a young prongbuck standing off a couple of hundred yards to one side, gazing at the wagon with that absorbed curiosity which in this game so often conquers its extreme wariness and timidity, to a certain extent offsetting the advantage conferred upon it by its marvellous vision. The little antelope stood broadside on, gazing at us out of its great bulging eyes, the sharply contrasted browns and whites of its coat showing plainly. Lambert and I leaped off our horses immediately, and I knelt and pulled trigger; but the cartridge snapped, and the little buck, wheeling round, cantered off, the white hairs on its rump standing erect. There was a strong cross-wind, almost a gale, blowing, and Lambert's bullet went just behind him; off he went at a canter, which changed to a breakneck gallop, as we again fired; and he went out of sight unharmed, over the crest of the rising ground in front. We ran after him as hard as we could pelt up the hill, into a slight valley, and then up another rise, and again got a glimpse of him standing, but this time farther off than before; and again our shots went wild.

However, the antelope changed its racing gallop to a canter while still in sight, going slower and slower, and, what was rather curious, it did not seem much frightened. We were naturally a good deal chagrined at our shooting and wished to retrieve ourselves, if possible; so we ran back to the wagon, got our horses and rode after the buck. He had continued his flight in a straight line, gradually slackening his pace, and a mile's brisk gallop enabled us to catch a glimpse of him, far ahead and merely walking. The wind was bad, and we decided to sweep off and try to circle round ahead of him. Accordingly, we dropped back, turned into a slight hollow to the right, and galloped hard until we came to the foot of a series of low buttes, when we turned more to the left; and, when we judged that we were about across the antelope's line of march, leaped from our horses, threw the reins over their heads, and left them standing, while we stole up the nearest rise; and, when close to the top, took off our caps and pushed ourselves forward, flat on our faces to peep over. We had judged the distance well, for we saw the antelope at once, now stopping to graze. Drawing back, we ran along some little distance nearer, then drew up over the same rise. He was only about 125 yards off, and this time there was no excuse for my failing to get him; but fail I did, and away the buck raced again, with both of us shooting. My first two shots were misses, but I kept correcting my aim and holding farther in front of the flying beast. My last shot was taken just as the antelope reached the edge of the broken country, in which he would have been safe; and almost as I pulled the trigger I had the satisfaction of seeing him pitch forward and, after turning a complete somerset, lie motionless. I had broken his neck. He had cost us a good many cartridges, and, though my last shot was well aimed, there was doubtless considerable chance in my hitting him, while there was no excuse at all for at least one of my previous misses. Nevertheless, all old hunters know that there is no other kind of shooting in which so many cartridges are expended for every head of game bagged.

As we knelt down to butcher the antelope, the clouds broke and the rain fell. Hastily we took off the saddle and hams, and, packing them behind us on our horses, loped to the wagon in the teeth of the cold storm. When we overtook it, after some sharp riding, we threw in the meat, and not very much later, when the day was growing dusky, caught sight of the group of low ranch buildings toward which we had been headed. We were received with warm hospitality, as one always is in a ranch country. We dried our streaming clothes inside the warm ranch house and had a good supper, and that night we rolled up in our blankets and tarpaulins, and slept soundly in the lee of a big haystack. The ranch house stood in the winding bottom of a creek; the flanking hills were covered with stunted cedar, while dwarf cotton-wood and box elder grew by the pools in the half-dried creek bed.

Next morning we had risen by dawn. The storm was over, and it was clear and cold. Before sunrise we had started. We were only some thirty miles away from my ranch, and I directed the Sheriff how to go there, by strik-ing east until he came to the main divide, and then fol-lowing that down till he got past a certain big plateau, when a turn to the right down any of the coulees would bring him into the river bottom near the ranch house. We wished ourselves to ride off to one side and try to pick up another antelope. However, the Sheriff took the wrong turn after getting to the divide, and struck the river bottom some fifteen miles out of his way, so that we reached the ranch a good many hours before he did.

When we left the wagon we galloped straight across country, looking out from the divide across the great roll-ing landscape, every feature standing clear through the frosty air. Hour after hour we paced and loped on and on over the grassy seas in the glorious morning. Once we stopped, and I held the horses while Lambert stalked and shot a fine prongbuck; then we tied his head and hams to our saddles and again pressed forward along the divide. We had hoped to get lunch at a spring that I knew of some twelve miles from my ranch, but when we reached it we found it dry and went on without halting. Early in the afternoon we came out on the broad, tree-clad bottom on which the ranch house stands, and, threading our way along the cattle trails soon drew up in front of the gray empty buildings.

Just as we were leaving the hunting-grounds on this trip, after having killed all the game we felt we had a right to kill, we encountered bands of Sioux Indians from the Standing Rock and Cheyenne River reservations coming in to hunt, and I at once felt that the chances for much future sport in that particular district were small. Indians are not good shots, but they hunt in large numbers, killing everything, does, fawns and bucks alike, and they follow the wounded animals with the utmost perseverance, so that they cause much destruction of game.

Accordingly, in 1894, when I started for these same grounds, it was with some misgivings; but I had time only to make a few days' hunt, and I knew of no other accessible grounds where prongbuck were plentiful. My foreman was with me, and, as usual, we took the ranch wagon, driven this time by a cowboy who had just come up over the trail with cattle from Colorado. On reaching our happy hunting-grounds of the previous season, I found my fears sadly verified; and one unforeseen circumstance also told against me. Not only had the Indians made a great killing of antelope the season before, but in the spring one or two sheep men had moved into the country. We found that the big flocks had been mov-

ing from one spring pool to another, eating the pasturage
bare, while the shepherds whom we met—wild-looking
men on rough horses, each accompanied by a pair of furtive sheep dogs—had taken every opportunity to get a
shot at antelope, so as to provide themselves with fresh
meat. Two days of fruitless hunting in this sheep-ridden
region was sufficient to show that the antelope were too
scarce and shy to give us hope for sport, and we shifted
quarters, a long day's journey, to the head of another
creek; and we had to go to yet another before we found
much game. As so often happens on such a trip, when
we started to have bad luck we had plenty. One night
two of the three saddle horses stampeded and went
straight as the crow flies back to the home range, so that
we did not get them until on our return from the trip.
On another occasion the team succeeded in breaking the
wagon pole; and as there was an entire absence of wood
where we were at the time, we had to make a splice for
it with the two tent poles and the picket ropes. Nevertheless, it was very enjoyable out on the great grassy
plains. Although we had a tent with us, I always slept
in the open in my buffalo bag, with the tarpaulin to pull
over me if it rained. On each night before going to sleep,
I lay for many minutes gazing at the stars above, or
watching the rising of the red moon, which was just at
or past the full.

We had plenty of fresh meat—prairie fowl and young
sage fowl at first, and antelope venison afterward. We
camped by little pools, generally getting fair water; and
from the camps where there was plenty of wood we took

enough to build the fires at those where there was none. The nights were frosty, and the days cool and pleasant, and from sunrise to sunset we were off riding or walking among the low hills and over the uplands, so that we slept well and ate well, and felt the beat of hardy life in our veins.

Much of the time we were on a high divide between two creek systems, from which we could see the great landmarks of all the regions roundabout, Sentinel Butte, Square Butte and Middle Butte, far to the north and east of us. Nothing could be more lonely and nothing more beautiful than the view at nightfall across the prairies to these huge hill masses, when the lengthening shadows had at last merged into one and the faint afterglow of the red sunset filled the west. The endless waves of rolling prairie, sweeping, vast and dim, to the feet of the great hills, grew purple as the evening darkened, and the buttes loomed into vague, mysterious beauty as their sharp outlines softened in the twilight.

Even when we got out of reach of the sheep men we never found antelope very plentiful, and they were shy, and the country was flat, so that the stalking was extremely difficult; yet I had pretty good sport. The first animal I killed was a doe, shot for meat, because I had twice failed to get bucks at which I emptied my magazine at long range, and we were all feeling hungry for venison. After that I killed nothing but bucks. Of the five antelope killed, one I got by a headlong gallop to cut off his line of flight. As sometimes happens with this queer, erratic animal, when the buck saw that I was trying to cut off his flight he simply raced ahead just as hard as he knew how, and, as my pony was not fast, he got to the little pass for which he was headed 200 yards ahead of me. I then jumped off, and his curiosity made him commit the fatal mistake of halting for a moment to look round at me. He was standing end on, and offered a very small mark at 200 yards; but I made a good line shot, and, though I held a trifle too high, I hit him in the head, and down he came. Another buck I shot from under the wagon early one morning as he was passing just beyond the picketed horses. I have several times shot antelope which unexpectedly came into camp in this fashion. The other three I got after much manœuvring and long, tedious stalks.

In some of the stalks, after infinite labor, and perhaps after crawling on all-fours for an hour, or pulling myself flat on my face among some small sage-brush for ten or fifteen minutes, the game took alarm and went off. Too often, also, when I finally did get a shot, it was under such circumstances that I missed. Sometimes the game was too far; sometimes it had taken alarm and was already in motion; sometimes the trouble could only be ascribed to lack of straight powder, and I was covered with shame as with a garment. Once in the afternoon I had to spend so much time waiting for the antelope to get into a favorable place that, when I got up close, I found the light already so bad that my front sight glimmered indistinctly, and the bullet went wild. Another time I met with one of those misadventures which are especially irritating. It was at midday, and I made out at a long distance a band of antelope lying for their noon rest in a slight hollow. A careful stalk brought me up within fifty yards of them. I was crawling flat on my face, for the crest of the hillock sloped so gently that this was the only way to get near them. At last, peering through the grass, I saw the head of a doe. In a moment she saw me and jumped to her feet, and up stood the whole band, including the buck. I immediately tried to draw a bead on the latter, and to my horror found that, lying flat as I was, and leaning on my elbows, I could not bring the rifle above the tall shaking grass, and was utterly unable to get a sight. In another second away tore all the antelope. I jumped to my feet, took a snap shot at the buck as he raced round a low-cut bank and missed, and then walked drearily home, chewing the cud of my ill-luck. Yet again in more than one instance, after making a good stalk upon a band seen at some distance, I found it contained only does and fawns, and would not shoot at them.

Three times, however, the stalk was successful. Twice I was out alone; the other time my foreman was with me, and held my horse while I manœuvred hither and thither, and finally succeeded in getting into range. In both the first instances I got a standing shot, but on this last occasion, when my foreman was with me, two of the watchful does which were in the band saw me before I could get a shot at the old buck. I was creeping up a low washout, and, by ducking hastily down again and running back and up a side coulee, I managed to get within long range of the band as they cantered off, not yet thoroughly alarmed. The buck was behind, and I held just ahead of him. He plunged to the shot, but went off over the hill-crest. When I had panted up to the ridge I found him dead just beyond.

One of the antelope I killed while I was out on foot toward nightfall, a couple of miles from the wagon. I saw the prongbuck quite half a mile off, and though I dropped at once I was uncertain whether he had seen me. He was in a little hollow or valley. A long, smoothly sloping plateau led up to one edge of it. Across this plateau I crawled, and when I thought I was near the run I ventured slowly to look up, and almost immediately saw vaguely through the tops of the long grasses what I took to be the head and horns of the buck, looking in my direction. There was no use in going back, and I dropped flat on my face again and crawled another hundred yards, until it was evident that I was on the rise from which the plateau sank into the shallow valley beyond. Raising my head inch by inch, I caught sight of the object toward which I had been crawling, and after a moment's hesitation recognized it as a dead sunflower, the stalks and blossoms so arranged as to be in a **V** shape. Completely puzzled, I started to sit up, when by sheer good luck I caught sight of the real prongbuck, still feeding, some three hundred yards off, and evidently unaware of my presence. It was feeding toward a slight hill to my left. I crept off until behind this, and then walked up until I was in line with a big bunch of weeds on its shoulder. Crawling on all-fours to the weeds, I peeped through and saw the prongbuck still slowly feeding my way. When he was but seventy yards off, I sat up and shot him; and trudged back to the wagon, carrying the saddle and hams.

In packing an antelope or deer behind the saddle, I cut slashes through the sinews of the legs just above the joints; then I put the buck behind the saddle, run the picket rope from the horn of the saddle, under the belly of the horse, through the slashes in the legs on the other side, bring the end back, swaying well down on it, and fasten it to the horn; then I repeat the same feat for the other side. Packed in this way, the carcass always rides steady, and cannot shake loose, no matter what antics the horse may perform.

In the fall of 1896 I spent a fortnight on the range with the ranch wagon. I was using for the first time one of the new small-calibre, smokeless-powder rifles, with the usual soft-nosed bullet. While travelling to and fro across the range we usually moved camp each day, not putting up the tent at all during the trip; but at one spot we spent three nights. It was in a creek bottom, bounded on either side by rows of grassy hills, beyond which stretched the rolling prairie. The creek bed, which at this season was of course dry in most places, wound in **S**-shaped curves, with here and there a pool and here and there a fringe of stunted wind-beaten timber. We were camped near a little grove of ash, box-elder, and willow, which gave us shade at noonday; and there were two or three pools of good water in the creek bed—one so deep that I made it my swimming-bath.

The first day that I was able to make a hunt I rode out with my foreman, Sylvane Ferris. I was mounted on Muley. Twelve years before, when Muley was my favorite cutting pony on the round-up, he never seemed to tire or lose his dash, but Muley was now sixteen years old, and on ordinary occasions he liked to go as soberly as possible; yet the good old pony still had the fire latent in his blood, and at the sight of game—or, indeed, of cattle or horses—he seemed to regain for the time being all the headlong courage of his vigorous and supple youth.

On the morning in question it was two or three hours before Sylvane and I saw any game. Our two ponies went steadily forward at a single-foot or shack, as the cow-punchers term what Easterners call a " fox trot." Most of the time we were passing over immense grassy flats, where the mat of short curled blades lay brown and parched under the bright sunlight. Occasionally we came to ranges of low barren hills, which sent off gently rounded spurs into the plain.

It was on one of these ranges that we first saw our game. As we were travelling along the divide we spied eight antelope far ahead of us. They saw us as soon as we saw them, and the chance of getting to them seemed small; but it was worth an effort, for by humoring them when they started, so as to let them wheel and zigzag before they became really frightened, and then, when they had settled into their run, by galloping toward them at an angle oblique to their line of flight, there was always some little chance of getting a shot. Sylvane was on a light buckskin horse, and I left him on the ridge crest to occupy their attention while I cantered off to one side. The pronghorns became uneasy as I galloped away, and ran off the ridge crest in a line nearly parallel to mine. They did not go very fast, and I held in Muley, who was all on fire at the sight of the game. After crossing two or three spurs, the antelope going at half speed, they found I had come closer to them, and turning, they ran up one of the valleys between two spurs. Now was my chance, and wheeling at right angles to my former course, I galloped Muley as hard as I knew how up the valley nearest and parallel to where the antelope had gone. The good old fellow ran like a quarter-horse, and when we were almost at the main ridge crest I leaped off, and ran ahead with my rifle at the ready, crouching down as I came to the sky-line. Usually on such occasions I find that the antelope have gone on, and merely catch a glimpse of them half a mile distant, but on this occasion everything went right. The band had just reached the ridge crest about 220 yards from me across the head of the valley, and had halted for a moment to look around. They were starting as I raised my rifle, but the trajectory is very flat with these small-bore smokeless-powder weapons, and taking a coarse front sight I fired at a young buck which was broadside to me. There was no smoke, and as the band raced away I saw him sink backward, the ball having broken his hips.

We packed him bodily behind Sylvane on the buckskin and continued our ride, as there was no fresh meat in camp, and we wished to bring in a couple of bucks if possible. For two or three hours we saw nothing. The unshod feet of the horses made hardly any noise on the stretches of sun-cured grass, but now and then we passed through patches of thin weeds, their dry stalks rattling curiously, making a sound like that of a rattlesnake. At last, coming over a gentle rise of ground, we spied two more prongbucks, half a mile ahead of us and to our right.

Again there seemed small chance of bagging our quarry, but again fortune favored us. I at once cantered Muley ahead, not toward them, but so as to pass them well on one side. After some hesitation they started, not straight away, but at an angle to my own course. For some moments I kept at a hand gallop, until they got thoroughly settled in their line of flight; then I touched Muley, and he went as hard as he knew how. Immediately the two panic-stricken and foolish beasts seemed to feel that I was cutting off their line of retreat, and raced forward at mad speed. They went much faster than I did, but I had the shorter course, and when they crossed me they were not fifty yards ahead—by which time I had come nearly a mile. At the pull of the rein Muley stopped short, like the trained cow-pony he is; I leaped off, and held well ahead of the rearmost and largest buck. At the crack of the little rifle down he went with his neck broken. In a minute or two he was packed behind me on Muley, and we bent our steps toward camp.

During the remainder of my trip we were never out of fresh meat, for I shot three other bucks—one after a smart chase on horseback, and the other two after careful stalks; and I missed two running shots.

The game being both scarce and shy, I had to exercise much care, and after sighting a band I would sometimes have to wait and crawl round for two or three hours before they would get into a position where I had any chance of approaching. Even then they were more apt to see me and go off than I was to get near them.

Antelope are the only game that can be hunted as well at noonday as in the morning or evening, for their times for sleeping and feeding are irregular. They never seek shelter from the sun, and when they lie down for a noonday nap they are apt to choose a hollow, so as to be out of the wind; in consequence, if the band is seen at all at this time, it is easier to approach them than when they are up and feeding. They sometimes come down to water in the middle of the day, sometimes in the morning or evening. On this trip I came across bands feeding and resting at almost every hour of the day. They seemed usually to rest for a couple of hours, then began feeding again.

The last shot I got was when I was out with Joe Ferris, in whose company I had killed my first buffalo, just thirteen years before, and not very far from this same spot. We had seen two or three bands that morning, and in each case, after a couple of hours of useless effort, I failed to get near enough. At last, toward midday, after riding and tramping over a vast extent of broken sun-scorched country, we got within range of a small band lying down in a little cup-shaped hollow in the middle of a great flat. I did not have a close shot, for they were running about 180 yards off. The buck was rearmost, and at him I aimed; the bullet struck him in the flank, coming out of the opposite shoulder, and he fell in his next bound. As we stood over him, Joe shook his head, and said, " I guess that little rifle is the ace; " and I told him I guessed so too.

CHAPTER V

A SHOT AT A MOUNTAIN SHEEP

IN the fall of 1893 I was camped on the Little Missouri, some ten miles below my ranch. The bottoms were broad and grassy, and were walled in by curving rows of high, steep bluffs. Back of them lay a mass of broken country, in many places almost impassable for horses. The wagon was drawn up on the edge of the fringe of tall cottonwoods which stretched along the brink of the shrunken river. The weather had grown cold, and at night the frost gathered thickly on our sleeping-bags. Great flocks of sandhill cranes passed overhead from time to time, the air resounding with their strange, musical, guttural clangor.

For several days we had hunted perseveringly, but without success, through the broken country. We had come across tracks of mountain sheep, but not the animals themselves, and the few blacktail which we had seen had seen us first and escaped before we could get within shot. The only thing killed had been a young whitetail, which Lambert, who was with me, had knocked over by a very pretty shot as we were riding through a long, heavily-timbered bottom. Four men in stalwart health and taking much out-door exercise have large appetites, and the flesh of the whitetail was almost gone.

One evening Lambert and I hunted nearly to the head of one of the creeks which opened close to our camp, and, in turning to descend what we thought was one of the side coulees leading into it, we contrived to get over the divide into the coulees of an entirely different creek system, and did not discover our error until it was too late to remedy it. We struck the river about nightfall, and were not quite sure where, and had six miles' tramp in the dark along the sandy river bed and through the dense timber bottoms, wading the stream a dozen times before we finally struck camp, tired and hungry, and able to appreciate to the full the stew of hot venison and potatoes, and afterward the comfort of our buffalo and caribou hide sleeping-bags. The next morning the Sheriff's remark of " Look alive, you fellows, if you want any breakfast," awoke the other members of the party shortly after dawn. It was bitterly cold as we scrambled out of our bedding, and, after a hasty wash, huddled around the fire, where the venison was sizzling and the coffee-pot boiling, while the bread was kept warm in the Dutch oven. About a third of a mile away to the west the bluffs, which rose abruptly from the river bottom, were crowned by a high plateau, where the grass was so good that overnight the horses had been led up and picketed on it, and the man who had led them up had stated the previous evening that he had seen what he took to be fresh footprints of a mountain sheep crossing the surface of a bluff fronting our camp. From the footprints it appeared that the animal had been there since the camp was pitched. The face of the bluff on this side was very sheer, the path

RANCH WAGON RETURNING FROM HUNT

by which the horses scrambled to the top being around a shoulder and out of sight of camp.

While sitting close around the fire finishing breakfast, and just as the first level sunbeams struck the top of the plateau, we saw on this cliff crest something moving, and at first supposed it to be one of the horses which had broken loose from its picket pin. Soon the thing, whatever it was, raised its head, and we were all on our feet in a moment, exclaiming that it was a deer or a sheep. It was feeding in plain sight of us only about a third of a mile distant, and the horses, as I afterward found, were but a few rods beyond it on the plateau. The instant I realized that it was game of some kind I seized my rifle, buckled on my cartridge-belt, and slunk off toward the river bed. As soon as I was under the protection of the line of cottonwoods, I trotted briskly toward the cliff, and when I got up to where it impinged on the river I ran a little to the left, and, selecting what I deemed to be a favorable place, began to make the ascent. The animal was on a grassy bench, some eight or ten feet below the crest, when I last saw it; but it was evidently moving hither and thither, sometimes on this bench and sometimes on the crest itself, cropping the short grass and browsing on the young shrubs. The cliff was divided by several shoulders or ridges, there being hollows like vertical gullies between them, and up one of these I scrambled, using the utmost caution not to dislodge earth or stones. Finally I reached the bench just below the skyline, and then, turning to the left, wriggled cautiously along it, hat in hand. The cliff was so steep and bulged

so in the middle, and, moreover, the shoulders or projecting ridges in the surface spoken of above were so pronounced, that I knew it was out of the question for the
animal to have seen me, but I was afraid it might have
heard me. The air was absolutely still, and so I had no
fear of its sharp nose. Twice in succession I peered with
the utmost caution around shoulders of the cliff, merely
to see nothing beyond save another shoulder some forty
or fifty yards distant. Then I crept up to the edge and
looked over the level plateau. Nothing was in sight excepting the horses, and these were close up to me, and, of
course, they all raised their heads to look. I nervously
turned half round, sure that if the animal, whatever it
was, was in sight, it would promptly take the alarm.
However, by good luck, it appeared that at this time it
was below the crest on the terrace or bench already mentioned, and, on creeping to the next shoulder, I at last
saw it—a yearling mountain sheep—walking slowly away
from me, and evidently utterly unsuspicious of any danger. I straightened up, bringing my rifle to my shoulder,
and as it wheeled I fired, and the sheep made two or three
blind jumps in my direction. So close was I to the camp,
and so still was the cold morning, that I distinctly heard
one of the three men, who had remained clustered about
the fire eagerly watching my movements, call, " By
George, he's missed! I saw the bullet strike the cliff."
I had fired behind the shoulders, and the bullet, going
through, had buried itself in the bluff beyond. The
wound was almost instantaneously fatal, and the sheep,
after striving in vain to keep its balance, fell heels over

head down a crevice, where it jammed. I descended, released the carcass, and pitched it on ahead of me, only to have it jam again near the foot of the cliff. Before I got it loose I was joined by my three companions, who had been running headlong toward me through the brush ever since the time they had seen the animal fall.

I never obtained another sheep under circumstances which seemed to me quite so remarkable as these; for sheep are, on the whole, the wariest of game. Nevertheless, with all game there is an immense amount of chance in the chase, and it is perhaps not wholly uncharacteristic of a hunter's luck that, after having hunted faithfully in vain and with much hard labor for several days through a good sheep country, we should at last have obtained one within sight and earshot of camp. Incidentally I may mention that I have never tasted better mutton, or meat of any kind, than that furnished by this tender yearling.

The nomenclature and exact specific relationships of American sheep, deer and antelope offer difficulties not only to the hunter but to the naturalist. As regards the nomenclature, we share the trouble encountered by all peoples of European descent who have gone into strange lands. The incomers are almost invariably men who are not accustomed to scientific precision of expression. Like other people, they do not like to invent names if they can by any possibility make use of those already in existence, and so in a large number of cases they call the new birds and animals by names applied to entirely different birds and animals of the Old World to which, in

the eyes of the settlers, they bear some resemblance.   In
South America the Spaniards, for instance, christened
" lion " and " tiger " the great cats which are .properly
known as cougar and jaguar.   In South Africa the Dutch
settlers, who came from a land where all big game had
long been exterminated, gave fairly grotesque names to
the great antelopes, calling them after the European elk,
stag, and chamois.   The French did but little better in
Canada.   Even in Ceylon the English, although belong-
ing for the most part to the educated classes, did no better
than the ordinary pioneer settlers, miscalling the sambur
stag an elk, and the leopard a cheetah.   Our own pioneers
behaved in the same way.   Hence it is that we have no
distinctive name at all for the group of peculiarly American game birds of which the bobwhite is the typical rep-
resentative; and that, when we could not use the words
quail, partridge, or pheasant, we went for our terminology to the barn-yard, and called our fine grouse, fool-
hens, sage-hens, and prairie-chickens.   The bear and wolf
our people recognized at once.   The bison they called a
buffalo, which was no worse than the way in which in
Europe the Old World bison was called an aurochs.
The American true elk and reindeer were rechristened
moose and caribou—excellent names, by the way, derived from the Indian.   The huge stag was called an elk.
The extraordinary antelope of the high Western peaks
was christened the white goat; not unnaturally, as it has
a most goatlike look.   The prongbuck of the plains, an
animal standing entirely alone among ruminants, was
simply called antelope.   Even when we invented names

for ourselves, we applied them loosely. The ordinary deer is sometimes known as the red deer, sometimes as the Virginia deer, and sometimes as the whitetail deer— the last being by far the best and most distinctive term.

In the present condition of zoological research it is not possible to state accurately how many " species " of deer and sheep there are in North America, both because mammalogists have not at hand a sufficient amount of material in the way of large series of specimens from different localities, and because they are not agreed among themselves as to the value of " species," or indeed as to exactly what is denoted by the term. Of course, if we had a complete series of specimens of extinct and fossil deer before us, there would be a perfect intergradation among all the existing forms through their long-vanished ancestral types, as the existing gaps have been created by the extinction and transformation of those former types. Where the gap is very broad and well marked no difficulty exists in using terms which shall express the difference. Thus the gap separating the moose, the caribou, and the wapiti from one another, and from the smaller American deer, is so wide, and there is so complete a lack of transitional forms, that the differences among them are expressed by naturalists by the use of different generic terms. The gap between the whitetail and the different forms of blacktail, though much less, is also clearly marked. But when we come to consider the blacktail among themselves, we find two very distinct types which yet show a certain tendency to intergrade; and with the whitetail very wide differences exist, even in the United

States, both individually among the deer of certain localities, and also as between all the deer of one locality when
compared with all the deer of another. Our present
knowledge of the various forms hardly justifies us in dog-
matizing as to their exact relative worth; and even if our
knowledge was more complete, naturalists are as yet
wholly at variance as to the laws which should govern
specific nomenclature. However, the hunter, the mere
field naturalist, and the lover of out-door life, are only
secondarily interested in the niceness of these distinc-
tions.

In addition to being a true sportsman and not a game
butcher, in addition to being a humane man as well as
keen-eyed, strong-limbed, and stout-hearted, the big
game hunter should be a field naturalist. If possible,
he should be an adept with the camera; and hunting with
the camera will tax his skill far more than hunting with
the rifle, while the results in the long run give much
greater satisfaction. Wherever possible he should keep
a note-book, and should carefully study and record the
habits of the wild creatures, especially when in some
remote regions to which trained scientific observers but
rarely have access. If we could only produce a hunter
who would do for American big game what John Burroughs has done for the smaller wild life of hedgerow
and orchard, farm and garden and grove, we should indeed be fortunate. Yet even though a man does not
possess the literary faculty and the powers of trained
observation necessary for such a task, he can do his part
toward adding to our information by keeping careful

notes of all the important facts which he comes across. Such note-books would show the changed habits of game with the changed seasons, their abundance at different times and different places, the melancholy data of their disappearance, the pleasanter facts as to their change of habits which enable them to continue to exist in the land, and, in short, all their traits. A real and lasting service would thereby be rendered not only to naturalists, but to all who care for nature.

Along the Little Missouri there have been several curious changes in the fauna within my own knowledge. Thus magpies have greatly decreased in numbers. This is, I believe, owing to the wolf hunters, for magpies often come around carcasses and pick up poisoned baits. I have seen as many as seven lying dead around a bait. They are much less plentiful than they formerly were. In 1894 I was rather surprised at meeting a porcupine, usually a beast of the timber, at least twenty miles from trees. He was grubbing after sage-brush roots on the edge of a cut bank by a half-dried creek. I was stalking an antelope at the time, and stopped to watch him for about five minutes. He paid no heed to me, though I was within three or four paces of him. Porcupines are easily exterminated; and they have diminished in numbers in this neighborhood. Both the lucivee, or northern lynx, and the wolverene have been found on the Little Missouri, near the Kildeer Mountains, but I do not know of a specimen of either that has been killed there for some years past. Bobcats are still not uncommon. The blackfooted ferret was always rare, and is rare now. But few beaver are left; they were very abundant in 1880, but were speedily trapped out when the Indians vanished and the Northern Pacific Railroad was built. While this railroad was building, the beaver frequently caused much trouble by industriously damming the culverts.

With us the first animal to disappear was the buffalo. In the old days, say from 1870 to 1880, the buffalo were probably the most abundant of all animals along the Little Missouri in the region that I know, ranging, say, from Pretty Buttes to the Kildeer Mountains. They were migratory, and at times almost all of them might leave; but, on the whole, they were the most abundant of the game animals. In 1881 they were still almost as numerous as ever. In 1883 all were killed but a few stragglers, and the last of these stragglers that I heard of as seen in our immediate neighborhood was in 1885. The second game animal in point of abundance was the blacktail. It did not go out on the prairies, but in the broken country adjoining the river it was far more plentiful than any other kind of game. Blacktail were not much slaughtered until the buffalo began to give out, say in 1882; but by 1896 they were not a twentieth—probably not a fiftieth—as plentiful as they had been in 1882. A few are still found in out-of-the-way places, where the ground is very rough. Elk were plentiful in 1880, though never anything like as abundant as the buffalo and the blacktail. Only straggling parties or individuals have been seen since 1883. The last I shot near my ranch was in 1886; but two or three have been shot since, and a cow and calf were seen, chased and almost roped by the riders on the round-up in the fall of 1893. Whitetail were never as numerous as the other game, but they held their own better, and a few can be shot yet. In 1883 probably twenty blacktail were killed for every one whitetail; in 1896 the numbers were about equal. Antelope were plentiful in the old days, though not nearly so much so as the buffalo and blacktail. The hunters did not molest them while the buffalo and elk lasted, and they then turned their attention to the blacktail. For some years after 1889 I think the pronghorn in our neighborhood positively increased in numbers. In 1886 I thought them more plentiful than I had ever known them before. Then they decreased; after 1894 the decrease was rapid. A few still remain. Mountain sheep were never very plentiful, and decreased proportionately with less rapidity than any other game; but they are now almost exterminated. Bears likewise were never plentiful, and cougars were always scarce.

There were two stages of hunting in this country, as in almost all other countries similarly situated. In 1880 the Northern Pacific Railroad was built nearly to the edge of the Bad Lands, and the danger of Indian war was totally eliminated. A great inrush of hunters followed. In 1881, 1882 and 1883 buffalo, elk and blacktail were slaughtered in enormous numbers, and a good many whitetail and prongbuck were killed too. By 1884 the game had been so thinned out that hide-hunting and meat-hunting ceased to pay. A few professional hunters remained, but most of them moved elsewhere, or were obliged to go into other business. From that time the hunting has chiefly been done by ranchers and occasional small grangers. In consequence, for six or eight years the game about held its own—the antelope, as I have said above, at one time increasing; but the gradual growth in the number of actual settlers then began to tell, and the game became scarce. Nowadays settlers along the Little Missouri can kill an occasional deer or antelope; but it can hardly be called a game country.

CHAPTER VI

THE WHITETAIL DEER

THE whitetail deer is now, as it always has been, the most plentiful and most widely distributed of American big game. It holds its own in the land better than any other species, because it is by choice a dweller in the thick forests and swamps, the places around which the tide of civilization flows, leaving them as islets of refuge for the wild creatures which formerly haunted all the country. The range of the whitetail is from the Atlantic to the Pacific, and from the Canadian to the Mexican borders, and somewhat to the north and far to the south of these limits. The animal shows a wide variability, both individually and locally, within these confines; from the hunter's standpoint it is not necessary to try to determine exactly the weight that attaches to these local variations.

There is also a very considerable variation in habits. As compared with the mule-deer, the whitetail is not a lover of the mountains. As compared with the prongbuck, it is not a lover of the treeless plains. Yet in the Alleghanies and the Adirondacks, at certain seasons especially, and in some places at all seasons, it dwells high among the densely wooded mountains, wandering over their crests and sheer sides, and through the deep ravines;

while in the old days there were parts of Texas and the Indian Territory where it was found in great herds far out on the prairie. Moreover, the peculiar nature of its chosen habitat, while generally enabling it to resist the onslaught of man longer than any of its fellows, sometimes exposes it to speedy extermination. To the westward of the rich bottom-lands and low prairies of the Mississippi Valley proper, when the dry plains country is reached, the natural conditions are much less favorable for whitetail than for other big game. The black bear, which in the East has almost precisely the same habitat as the whitetail, disappears entirely on the great plains, and reappears in the Rockies in regions which the whitetail does not reach. All over the great plains, into the foothills of the Rockies, the whitetail is found, but only in the thick timber of the river bottoms. Throughout the regions of the Upper Missouri and Upper Platte, the Big Horn, Powder, Yellowstone, and Cheyenne, over all of which I have hunted, the whitetail lives among the cottonwood groves and dense brush growth that fringe the river beds and here and there extend some distance up the mouths of the large creeks. In these places the whitetail and the mule-deer may exist in close proximity; but normally neither invades the haunts of the other.

Along the ordinary plains river, such as the Little Missouri, where I ranched for many years, there are three entirely different types of country through which a man passes as he travels away from the bed of the river. There is first the alluvial river bottom covered with cottonwood and box-elder, together with thick brush.

These bottoms may be a mile or two across, or they may shrink to but a few score yards. After the extermination of the wapiti, which roamed everywhere, the only big game animal found in them was the whitetail deer. Beyond this level alluvial bottom the ground changes abruptly to bare, rugged hills or fantastically carved and shaped Bad Lands rising on either side of the river, the ravines, coulees, creeks, and canyons twisting through them in every direction. Here there are patches of ash, cedar, pine, and occasionally other trees, but the country is very rugged, and the cover very scanty. This is the home of the mule-deer, and, in the roughest and wildest parts, of the bighorn. The absolutely clear and sharply defined line of demarkation between this rough, hilly country, flanking the river, and the alluvial river bottom, serves as an equally clearly marked line of demarkation between the ranges of the whitetail and the mule-deer. This belt of broken country may be only a few hundred yards in width; or it may extend for a score of miles before it changes into the open prairies, the high plains proper. As soon as these are reached, the prongbuck's domain begins.

As the plains country is passed, and the vast stretches of mountainous region entered, the river bottoms become narrower, and the plains on which the prongbuck is found become of very limited extent, shrinking to high valleys and plateaus, while the mass of rugged foothills and mountains add immensely to the area of the mule-deer's habitat.

Given equal areas of country, of the three different

types alluded to above, that in which the mule-deer is found offers the greatest chance of success to the rifle-bearing hunter, because there is enough cover to shield him and not enough to allow his quarry to escape by stealth and hiding. On the other hand, the thick river bottoms offer him the greatest difficulty. In consequence, where the areas of distribution of the different game animals are about equal, the mule-deer disappears first before the hunter, the prongbuck next, while the whitetail holds out the best of all. I saw this frequently on the Yellowstone, the Powder, and the Little Missouri. When the ranchmen first came into this country the mule-deer swarmed, and yielded a far more certain harvest to the hunter than did either the prongbuck or the whitetail. They were the first to be thinned out, the prongbuck lasting much better. The cowboys and small ranchmen, most of whom did not at the time have hounds, then followed the prongbuck; and this, in its turn, was killed out before the whitetail. But in other places a slight change in the conditions completely reversed the order of destruction. In parts of Wyoming and Montana the mountainous region where the mule-deer dwelt was of such vast extent, and the few river bottoms on which the whitetail were found were so easily hunted, that the whitetail was completely exterminated throughout large districts where the mule-deer continued to abound. Moreover, in these regions the table-lands and plains upon which the prongbuck was found were limited in extent, and although the prongbuck outlasted the whitetail, it vanished long before the herds of the mule-deer had been destroyed from among the neighboring mountains.

The whitetail was originally far less common in the forests of northern New England than was the moose, for in the deep snows the moose had a much better chance to escape from its brute foes and to withstand cold and starvation. But when man appeared upon the scene he followed the moose so much more eagerly than he followed the deer that the conditions were reversed and the moose was killed out. The moose thus vanished entirely from the Adirondacks, and almost entirely from Maine; but the excellent game laws of the latter State, and the honesty and efficiency with which they have been executed during the last twenty years, have resulted in an increase of moose during that time. During the same period the whitetail deer has increased to an even greater extent. It is doubtless now more plentiful in New York and New England than it was a quarter of a century ago. Stragglers are found in Connecticut, and, what is still more extraordinary, even occasionally come into wild parts of densely populated little Rhode Island—my authority for the last statement being Mr. C. Grant La Farge. Of all our wild game, the whitetail responds most quickly to the efforts for its protection, and except the wapiti, it thrives best in semi-domestication; in consequence, it has proved easy to preserve it, even in such places as Cape Cod in Massachusetts and Long Island in New York; while it has increased greatly in Vermont, New Hampshire, and Maine, and has more than held its own in the Adirondacks. Mr. James R. Sheffield, of New York City, in the summer of 1899, spent several weeks on a fishing trip through northern Maine. He kept count of the moose and deer he saw, and came across no less than thirty-five of the former and over five hundred and sixty of the latter. In the most lonely parts of the forest deer were found by the score, feeding in broad daylight on the edges of the ponds. Deer are still plentiful in many parts of the Alleghany Mountains, from Pennsylvania southward, and also in the swamps and canebrakes of the South Atlantic and Gulf States.

Where the differences in habitat and climate are so great there are many changes of habits, and some of them of a noteworthy kind. Mr. John A. McIlhenny, of Avery's Island, Louisiana, formerly a lieutenant in my regiment, lives in what is still a fine game country. His plantation is in the delta of the Mississippi, among the vast marshes, north of which lie the wooded swamps. Both the marshes and the swamps were formerly literally thronged with whitetail deer, and the animals are still plentiful in them. Mr. McIlhenny has done much deer-hunting, always using hounds. He informs me that the breeding times are unexpectedly different from those of the northern deer. In the North, in different localities, the rut takes place in October or November, and the fawns are dropped in May or June. In the Louisiana marshes around Avery's Island the rut begins early in July and the fawns are dropped in February. In the swamps immediately north of these marshes the dates are fully a month later. The marshes are covered with tall reeds and grass and broken by bayous, while there are scattered over them what are called " islands " of firmer ground overgrown with timber. In this locality the deer live in the same neighborhood all the year round, just as, for instance, they do on Long Island. So on the Little Missouri, in the neighborhood of my ranch, they lived in exactly the same localities throughout the entire year. Occasionally they would shift from one river bottom to another, or go a few miles up or down stream because of scarcity of food. But there was no general shifting.

On the Little Missouri, in one place where they were not molested, I knew a particular doe and fawn with whose habits I became quite intimately acquainted. When the moon was full they fed chiefly by night, and spent most of the day lying in the thick brush. When there was little or no moon they would begin to feed early in the morning, then take a siesta, and then—what struck me as most curious of all—would go to a little willow-bordered pool about noon to drink, feeding for some time both before and after drinking. After another siesta they would come out late in the afternoon and feed until dark.

In the Adirondacks the deer often completely alter their habits at different seasons. Soon after the fawns are born they come down to the water's edge, preferring the neighborhood of the lakes, but also haunting the stream banks. The next three months, during the hot weather, they keep very close to the water, and get a large proportion of their food by wading in after the lilies and other aquatic plants. Where they are much hunted, they only come to the water's edge after dark, but in regions where they are little disturbed they are quite as often diurnal in their habits. I have seen dozens feeding in the neighborhood of a lake, some of them two or three hundred yards out in shallow places, up to their bellies; and this after sunrise, or two or three hours before sunset. Before September the deer cease coming to the water, and go back among the dense forests and on the mountains. There is no genuine migration, as in the case of the mule-deer, from one big tract to another, and no entire desertion of any locality. But the food supply which drew the animals to the water's edge during the summer months shows signs of exhaustion toward fall; the delicate water-plants have vanished, the marsh-grass is dying, and the lilies are less succulent. An occasional deer still wanders along the shores or out into the lake, but most of them begin to roam the woods, eating the berries and the leaves and twig ends of the deciduous trees, and even of some of the conifers—although a whitetail is fond of grazing, especially upon the tips of the grass. I have seen moose feeding on the tough old lily stems and wading after them when the ice had skimmed the edges of the pool. But the whitetail has usually gone back into the woods long before freezing-time.

From Long Island south there is not enough snow to make the deer alter their habits in the winter. As soon as the rut is over, which in different localities may be from October to December, whitetail are apt to band together—more apt than at any other season, although even then they are often found singly or in small parties. While nursing, the does have been thin, and at the end of the rut the bucks are gaunt, with their necks swollen and distended. From that time on bucks and does alike put on flesh very rapidly in preparation for the winter. Where there is no snow, or not enough to interfere with their travelling, they continue to roam anywhere through the woods and across the natural pastures and meadows, eating twigs, buds, nuts, and the natural hay which is cured on the stalk.

In the Northern woods they form yards during the winter. These yards are generally found in a hardwood growth which offers a supply of winter food, and consist simply of a tangle of winding trails beaten out through the snow by the incessant passing and repassing of the animal. The yard merely enables the deer to move along the various paths in order to obtain food. If there are many deer together, the yards may connect by interlacing paths, so that a deer can run a considerable distance through them. Often, however, each deer will yard by itself, as food is the prime consideration, and a given locality may only have enough to support a single animal. When the snows grow deep the deer is wholly unable to move, once the yard is left, and hence it is absolutely at the mercy of a man on snow-shoes, or of a cougar or a wolf, if found at such times. The man on snow-shoes can move very comfortably; and the cougar and the wolf, although hampered by the snow, are not rendered help-less like the deer. I have myself scared a deer out of a yard, and seen it flounder helplessly in a great drift be-fore it had gone thirty rods. When I came up close it ploughed its way a very short distance through the drifts, making tremendous leaps. But as the snow was over six

feet deep, so that the deer sank below the level of the surface at each jump, and yet could not get its feet on the
solid ground, it became so exhausted that it fell over on
its side and bleated in terror as I came up. After looking
at it I passed on. Hide-hunters and frontier settlers sometimes go out after the deer on snow-shoes when there is
a crust, and hence this method of killing is called crusting. It is simple butchery, for the deer cannot, as the
moose does, cause its pursuer a chase which may last
days. No self-respecting man would follow this method
of hunting save from the necessity of having meat.

In very wild localities deer sometimes yard on the ice
along the edges of lakes, eating off all the twigs and
branches, whether of hardwood trees or of conifers,
which they can reach.

At the beginning of the rut the does flee from the
bucks, which follow them by scent at full speed. The
whitetail buck rarely tries to form a herd of does, though
he will sometimes gather two or three. The mere fact
that his tactics necessitate a long and arduous chase after
each individual doe prevents his organizing herds as the
wapiti bull does. Sometimes two or three bucks will be
found strung out one behind the other, following the
same doe. The bucks wage desperate battle among themselves during this season, coming together with a clash,
and then pushing and straining for an hour or two at a
time, with their mouths open, until the weakest gives way.
As soon as one abandons the fight he flees with all possible
speed, and usually escapes unscathed. While head to
head there is no opportunity for a disabling thrust, but

if, in the effort to retreat, the beaten buck gets caught, he may be killed. Owing to the character of the antlers, whitetail bucks are peculiarly apt to get them interlocked in such a fight, and if the efforts of the two beasts fail to disentangle them, both ultimately perish by starvation. I have several times come across a pair of skulls with interlocked antlers. The same thing occurs, though far less frequently, to the mule-deer and even the wapiti.

The whitetail is the most beautiful and graceful of all our game animals when in motion. I have never been able to agree with Judge Caton that the mule-deer is clumsy and awkward in his gait. I suppose all such terms are relative. Compared to the moose or caribou the mule-deer is light and quick in his movements, and to me there is something very attractive in the poise and power with which one of the great bucks bounds off, all four legs striking the earth together and shooting the body upward and forward as if they were steel springs. But there can be no question as to the infinitely superior grace and beauty of the whitetail when he either trots or runs. The mule-deer and blacktail bound, as already described. The prongbuck gallops with an even gait, and so does the bighorn, when it happens to be caught on a flat; but the whitetail moves with an indescribable spring and buoyancy. If surprised close up, and much terrified, it simply runs away as hard as it can, at a gait not materially different from that of any other game animal under like circumstances, while its head is thrust forward and held down, and the tail is raised perpendicularly. But normally its mode of progression, whether it trots or gallops, is entirely unique. In trotting, the head and tail are both held erect, and the animal throws out its legs with a singularly proud and free motion, bringing the feet well up, while at every step there is an indescribable spring. In the canter or gallop the head and tail are also held erect, the flashing white brush being very conspicuous. Three or four low, long, marvellously springy bounds are taken, and then a great leap is made high in the air, which is succeeded by three or four low bounds, and then by another high leap. A whitetail going through the brush in this manner is a singularly beautiful sight. It has been my experience that they are not usually very much frightened by an ordinary slow trackhound, and I have seen a buck play along in front of one, alternately trotting and cantering, head and flag up, and evidently feeling very little fear.

To my mind the chase of the whitetail, as it must usually be carried on, offers less attraction than the chase of any other kind of our large game. But this is a mere matter of taste, and such men as Judge Caton and Mr. George Bird Grinnell have placed it above all others as a game animal. Personally I feel that the chase of any animal has in it two chief elements of attraction. The first is the chance given to be in the wilderness; to see the sights and hear the sounds of wild nature. The second is the demand made by the particular kind of chase upon the qualities of manliness and hardihood. As regards the first, some kinds of game, of course, lead the hunter into particularly remote and wild localities; and the farther one gets into the wilderness, the greater is the

attraction of its lonely freedom. Yet to camp out at all
implies some measure of this delight. The keen, fresh
air, the breath of the pine forests, the glassy stillness of
the lake at sunset, the glory of sunrise among the mountains, the shimmer of the endless prairies, the ceaseless
rustle of the cottonwood leaves where the wagon is drawn
up on the low bluff of the shrunken river—all these appeal intensely to any man, no matter what may be the
game he happens to be following. But there is a wide
variation, and indeed contrast, in the qualities called for
in the chase itself, according as one quarry or another
is sought.

The qualities that make a good soldier are, in large
part, the qualities that make a good hunter. Most important of all is the ability to shift for one's self, the mixture
of hardihood and resourcefulness which enables a man
to tramp all day in the right direction, and, when night
comes, to make the best of whatever opportunities for
shelter and warmth may be at hand. Skill in the use
of the rifle is another trait; quickness in seeing game,
another; ability to take advantage of cover, yet another;
while patience, endurance, keenness of observation, resolution, good nerves, and instant readiness in an emer-
gency, are all indispensable to a really good hunter.

If a man lives on a ranch, or is passing some weeks
in a lodge in a game country, and starts out for two or
three days, he will often do well to carry nothing whatever but a blanket, a frying-pan, some salt pork, and some
hardtack. If the hunting-ground is such that he can use
a wagon or a canoe, and the trip is not to be too long,

he can carry about anything he chooses, including a tent, any amount of bedding, and if it is very cold, a small, portable stove, not to speak of elaborate cooking apparatus. If he goes with a pack-train, he will also be able to carry a good deal; but in such a case he must rely on the judgment of the trained packers, unless he is himself an expert in the diamond hitch. If it becomes necessary to go on foot for any length of time, he must be prepared to do genuine roughing, and must get along with the minimum of absolute necessities.

It is hardly necessary to point out that the hunter worthy of the name should be prepared to shift for himself in emergencies. A ranchman, or any other man whose business takes him much in the mountains and out on the great plains or among the forests, ought to be able to get along entirely on his own account. But this cannot usually be done by those whose existence is habitually more artificial. When a man who normally lives a rather over-civilized life, an over-luxurious life—especially in the great cities—gets off for a few weeks' hunting, he cannot expect to accomplish much in the way of getting game without calling upon the services of a trained guide, woodsman, plainsman, or mountain man, whose life-work it has been to make himself an adept in all the craft of the wilderness. Until a man unused to wilderness life, even though a good sportsman, has actually tried it, he has no idea of the difficulties and hardships of shifting absolutely for himself, even for only two or three days. Not only will the local guide have the necessary knowledge as to precisely which one of two seemingly similar places is most apt to contain game; not only will he possess the skill in packing horses, or handling a canoe in rough water, or finding his way through the wilderness, which the amateur must lack; but even the things which the amateur does, the professional will do so much more easily and rapidly, as in the one case to leave, and in the other case not to leave, ample time for the hunting proper. Therefore the ordinary amateur sportsman, especially if he lives in a city, must count upon the services of trained men, possibly to help him in hunting, certainly to help him in travelling, cooking, pitching camp, and the like; and this he must do, if he expects to get good sport, no matter how hardy he may be, and no matter how just may be the pride he ought to take in his own craft, skill, and capacity to undergo fatigue and exposure. But while normally he must take advantage of the powers of others, he should certainly make a point of being able to shift for himself whenever the need arises; and he can only be sure of possessing this capacity by occasionally exercising it. It ought to be unnecessary to point out that the wilderness is not a place for those who are dependent upon luxuries, and above all for those who make a camping trip an excuse for debauchery. Neither the man who wants to take a French cook and champagne on a hunting trip, nor his equally objectionable though less wealthy brother who is chiefly concerned with filling and emptying a large whiskey jug, has any place whatever in the real life of the wilderness.

The chase of an animal should rank according as it

calls for the exercise in a high degree of a large number of these qualities. The grizzly is almost our only dangerous game, and under certain conditions shooting the grizzly calls for considerable courage on the part of the hunter. Disregarding these comparatively rare occasions, the chase of mountain game, especially the bighorn, demands more hardihood, power of endurance, and moral and physical soundness than any other kind of sport, and so must come first. The wapiti and mule-deer rank next, for they too must be killed by stalking as a result of long tramps over very rough ground. To kill a moose by still hunting is a feat requiring a high degree of skill, and entailing severe fatigue. When game is followed on horseback, it means that the successful hunter must ride well and boldly.

The whitetail is occasionally found where it yields a very high quality of sport. But normally it lives in regions where it is extremely difficult to kill it legitimately, as the wapiti and mule-deer are killed, and yet comparatively easy to kill it under circumstances which make no demand for any particular prowess on the part of the hunter. It is far more difficult to still hunt successfully in the dense brushy timber frequented by the whitetail than in the open glades, the mountains, and the rocky hills, through which the wapiti and mule-deer wander. The difficulty arises, however, because the chief requirement is stealth, noiselessness. The man who goes out into the hills for a mule-deer must walk hard and far, must be able to bear fatigue, and possibly thirst and hunger, must have keen eyes, and be a good shot. He does not need to display the extraordinary power of stealthy advance which is necessary to the man who would creep up to and kill a whitetail in thick timber. Now, the qualities of hardihood and endurance are better than the quality of stealth, and though all three are necessary in both kinds of chase, yet it is the chase of the mule-deer which most develops the former, and the chase of the whitetail which most develops the latter. When the woods are bare and there is some snow on the ground, however, still hunting the whitetail becomes not only possible, but a singularly manly and attractive kind of sport. Where the whitetail can be followed with horse and hound, the sport is also of a very high order. To be able to ride through woods and over rough country at full speed, rifle or shotgun in hand, and then to leap off and shoot at a running object, is to show that one has the qualities which made the cavalry of Forrest so formidable in the Civil War. There could be no better training for the mounted rifleman, the most efficient type of modern soldier.

By far the easiest way to kill the whitetail is in one or other of certain methods which entail very little work or skill on the part of the hunter. The most noxious of these, crusting in the deep snows, has already been spoken of. No sportsman worthy of the name would ever follow so butcherly a method. Fire hunting must also normally be ruled out. It is always mere murder if carried on by a man who sits up at a lick, and is not much better where the hunter walks through the fields—not to mention the fact that on such a walk he is quite as apt to kill stock as to kill a deer. But fire hunting from a boat, or jacking, as it is called, though it entails absolutely no skill in the hunter, and though it is, and ought to be, forbidden, as it can best be carried on at the season when nursing does are particularly apt to be the victims, nevertheless has a certain charm of its own. The first deer I ever killed, when a boy, was obtained in this way, and I have always been glad to have had the experience, though I have never been willing to repeat it. I was at the time camped out in the Adirondacks.

Two or three of us, all boys of fifteen or sixteen, had been enjoying what was practically our first experience in camping out, having gone out with two guides, Hank Martin and Mose Sawyer, from Paul Smith's on Lake St. Regis. My brother and cousin were fond of fishing and I was not, so I was deputed to try to bring in a deer. I had a double-barrelled 12-bore gun, French pin-fire, with which I had industriously collected " specimens " on a trip to Egypt and Palestine and on Long Island; except for three or four enthralling but not over-successful days after woodcock and quail, I had done no game shooting. As to every healthy boy with a taste for out-door life, the Northern forests were to me a veritable land of enchantment. We were encamped by a stream among the tall pines, and I had enjoyed everything; poling and paddling the boat, tramping through the woods, the cries of chickaree and chipmunk, of jay, woodpecker, chickadee, nuthatch, and cross-bill, which broke the forest stillness; and, above all, the great reaches of sombre woodland themselves. The heart-shaped footprints which showed where the deer had come down to drink and feed on the marshy edges of the water made my veins thrill; and the nights around the flickering camp-fire seemed filled with romance.

My first experiment in jacking was a failure. The jack, a bark lantern, was placed upon a stick in the bow of the boat, and I sat in a cramped huddle behind it, while Mose Sawyer plied the paddle with noiseless strength and skill in the stern. I proved unable to respond even to the very small demand made upon me, for when we actually did come upon a deer I failed to see it until it ran, when I missed it; and on the way back capped my misfortune by shooting a large owl which perched on a log projecting into the water, looking at the lantern with two glaring eyes.

All next day I was miserably conscious of the smothered disfavor of my associates, and when night fell was told I would have another chance to redeem myself. This time we started across a carry, the guide carrying the light boat, and launched it in a quiet little pond about a mile off. Dusk was just turning into darkness when we reached the edge of the little lake, which was perhaps a mile long by three-quarters of a mile across, with indented shores. We did not push off for half an hour or so, until it was entirely dark; and then for a couple of hours we saw no deer. Nevertheless, I thoroughly enjoyed the ghostly, mysterious, absolutely silent night ride over the water. Not the faintest splash betrayed the work of the paddler. The boat glided stealth-

ily alongshore, the glare of the lantern bringing out for
one moment every detail of the forest growth on the
banks, which the next second vanished into absolute
blackness. Several times we saw muskrats swimming
across the lane of light cut by the lantern through the
darkness, and two or three times their sudden plunging
and splashing caused my heart to leap. Once when we
crossed the lake we came upon a loon floating buoyantly
right out in the middle of it. It stayed until we were
within ten yards, so that I could see the minute outlines
of the feathers and every movement of the eye. Then
it swam off, but made no cry. At last, while crossing
the mouth of a bay we heard a splashing sound among
the lilies inshore, which even my untrained ears recognized as different from any of the other noises we had
yet heard, and a jarring motion of the paddle showed
that the paddler wished me to be on the alert. Without any warning, the course of the boat was suddenly
changed, and I was aware that we were moving stern
foremost. Then we swung around, and I could soon
make out that we were going down the little bay. The
forest-covered banks narrowed; then the marsh at the
end was lighted up, and on its hither edge, knee-deep
among the water-lilies, appeared the figure of a yearling
buck still in the red. It stood motionless, gazing at the
light with a curiosity wholly unmixed with alarm, and
at the shot wheeled and fell at the water's edge. We
made up our mind to return to camp that night, as it was
before midnight. I carried the buck and the torch, and
the guide the boat, and the mile walk over the dim trail,

occasionally pitching forward across a stump or root, was a thing to be remembered. It was my first deer, and I was very glad to get it; but although only a boy, I had sense enough to realize that it was not an experience worth repeating. The paddler in such a case deserves considerable credit, but the shooter not a particle, even aside from the fact to which I have already alluded, that in too many cases such shooting results in the killing of nursing does. No matter how young a sportsman is, if he has a healthy mind, he will not long take pleasure in any method of hunting in which somebody else shows the skill and does the work so that his share is only nominal. The minute that sport is carried on on these terms it becomes a sham, and a sham is always detrimental to all who take part in it.

Whitetail are comparatively easily killed with hounds, and there are very many places where this is almost the only way they can be killed at all. Formerly in the Adirondacks this method of hunting was carried on under circumstances which rendered those who took part in it objects of deserved contempt. The sportsman stood in a boat while his guides put out one or two hounds in the chosen forest side. After a longer or shorter run the deer took to the water; for whitetail are excellent swimmers, and when pursued by hounds try to shake them off by wading up or down stream or by swimming across a pond, and, if tired, come to bay in some pool or rapid. Once the unfortunate deer was in the water, the guide rowed the boat after it. If it was yet early in the season, and the deer was still in the red summer coat, it would sink when shot, and therefore the guide would usually take hold of its tail before the would-be Nimrod butchered it. If the deer was in the blue, the carcass would float, so it was not necessary to do anything quite so palpably absurd. But such sport, so far as the man who did the shooting was concerned, had not one redeeming feature. The use of hounds has now been prohibited by law.

In regions where there are no lakes, and where the woods are thick, the shooters are stationed at runways by which it is supposed the deer may pass when the hounds are after them. Under such circumstances the man has to show the skill requisite to hit the running quarry, and if he uses the rifle, this means that he must possess a certain amount of address in handling the weapon. But no other quality is called for, and so even this method, though often the only possible one (and it may be necessary to return to it in the Adirondacks), can never rank high in the eyes of men who properly appreciate what big game hunting should be. It is the usual method of killing deer on Long Island, during the three or four days of each year when they can be legally hunted. The deer are found along the south and centre of the eastern half of the island; they were nearly exterminated a dozen years ago, but under good laws they have recently increased greatly. The extensive grounds of the various sportsmen's clubs, and the forests of scrub-oak in the sparsely settled inland region, give them good harbors and sanctuaries. On the days when it is legal to shoot them, hundreds of hunters turn out from the neighborhood, and indeed from all the island and from New York. On such a day it is almost impossible to get any work done; for the sport is most democratic, and is shared by everybody. The hunters choose their position before dawn, lying in lines wherever deer are likely to pass, while the hounds are turned into every patch of thick cover. A most lively day follows, the fusillade being terrific; some men are invariably shot, and a goodly number of deer are killed, mostly by wily old hunters who kill ducks and quail for a living in the fall.

When the horse is used together with the hounds the conditions are changed. To ride a horse over rough country after game always implies hardihood and good horsemanship, and therefore makes the sport a worthy one. In very open country—in such country, for instance, as the whitetail formerly frequented both in Texas and the Indian Territory—the horseman could ride at the tail of the pack until the deer was fairly run down. But nowadays I know of no place where this is possible, for the whitetail's haunts are such as to make it impracticable for any rider to keep directly behind the hounds. What he must do is to try to cut the game off by riding from point to point. He then leaps off the horse and watches his chance for a shot. This is the way in which Mr. McIlhenny has done most of his deer-hunting, in the neighborhood of his Louisiana plantation.

Around my ranch I very rarely tried to still-hunt whitetail, because it was always easier to get mule-deer or prongbuck, if I had time to go off for an all-day's hunt. Occasionally, however, we would have at the ranch hounds, usually of the old black-and-tan Southern type, and then if we needed meat, and there was not time for a hunt back in the hills, we would turn out and hunt one or two of the river bottoms with these hounds. If I rode off to the prairies or the hills I went alone, but if the quarry was a whitetail, our chance of success depended upon our having a sufficient number of guns to watch the different passes and runways. Accordingly, my own share of the chase was usually limited to the fun of listening to the hounds, and of galloping at headlong speed from one point where I thought the deer would not pass to some other, which, as a matter of fact, it did not pass either. The redeeming feature of the situation was that if I did get a shot, I almost always got my deer. Under ordinary circumstances to merely wound a deer is worse than not hitting it; but when there are hounds along they are certain to bring the wounded animal to bay, and so on these hunts we usually got venison.

Of course, I occasionally got a whitetail when I was alone, whether with the hounds or without them. There were whitetail on the very bottom on which the ranch house stood, as well as on the bottom opposite, and on those to the right and left up and down stream. Occasionally I have taken the hounds out alone, and then as they chevied the whitetail around the bottom, have endeavored by rapid running on foot or on horseback to get to some place from which I could obtain a shot. The deer knew perfectly well that the hounds could not overtake them, and they would usually do a

ELKHORN RANCH

great deal of sneaking round and round through the underbrush and cottonwoods before they finally made up their minds to leave the bottom. On one occasion a buck came sneaking down a game trail through the buck brush where I stood, going so low that I could just see the tips of his antlers, and though I made desperate efforts I was not able to get into a position from which I could obtain a shot. On another occasion, while I was looking intently into a wood through which I was certain a deer would pass, it deliberately took to the open ground behind me, and I did not see it until it was just vanishing. Normally, the end of my efforts was that the deer went off and the hounds disappeared after it, not to return for six or eight hours. Once or twice things favored me; I happened to take the right turn or go in the right direction, and the deer happened to blunder past me; and then I returned with venison for supper. Two or three times I shot deer about nightfall or at dawn, in the immediate neighborhood of the ranch, obtaining them by sneaking as noiselessly as possible along the cattle trails through the brush and timber, or by slipping along the edge of the river bank. Several times I saw deer while I was sitting on the piazza or on the doorstep of the ranch, and on one occasion I stepped back into the house, got the rifle, and dropped the animal from where I stood.

On yet other occasions I obtained whitetail which lived not on the river bottoms but among the big patches of brush and timber in the larger creeks. When they were found in such country I hunted them very much as I hunted the mule-deer, and usually shot one when

I was expecting as much to see a mule-deer as a white-tail. When the game was plentiful I would often stay on my horse until the moment of obtaining the shot, especially if it was in the early morning or late evening. My method then was to ride slowly and quietly down the winding valleys and across the spurs, hugging the bank, so that, if deer were feeding in the open, I would get close up before either of us saw the other. Sometimes the deer would halt for a moment when it saw me, and sometimes it would bound instantly away. In either case my chance lay in the speed with which I could jump off the horse and take my shot. Even in favorable localities this method was of less avail with whitetail than mule-deer, because the former were so much more apt to skulk.

As soon as game became less plentiful my hunting had to be done on foot. My object was to be on the hunting-ground by dawn, or else to stay out there until it grew too dark to see the sights of my rifle. Often all I did was to keep moving as quietly as possible through likely ground, ever on the alert for the least trace of game; sometimes I would select a lookout and carefully scan a likely country to see if I could not detect something moving. On one occasion I obtained an old whitetail buck by the simple exercise of patience. I had twice found him in a broad basin, composed of several coulees, all running down to form the head of a big creek, and all of them well timbered. He dodged me on both occasions, and I made up my mind that I would spend a whole day in watching for him from a little natural ambush of sage-bush and cedar on a high point which overlooked the entire basin. I crept up to my ambush with the utmost caution early in the morning, and there I spent the entire day, with my lunch and a water-bottle, continually scanning the whole region most carefully with the glasses. The day passed less monotonously than it sounds, for every now and then I would catch a glimpse of wild life; once a fox, once a coyote, and once a badger; while the little chipmunks had a fine time playing all around me. At last, about mid-afternoon, I suddenly saw the buck come quietly out of the dense thicket in which he had made his midday bed, and deliberately walk up a hillside and lie down in a thin clump of ash where the sun could get at him—for it was in September, just before the rut began. There was no chance of stalking him in the place he had chosen, and all I could do was to wait. It was nearly sunset before he moved again, except that I occasionally saw him turn his head. Then he got up, and after carefully scrutinizing all the neighborhood, moved down into a patch of fairly thick brush, where I could see him standing and occasionally feeding, all the time moving slowly up the valley. I now slipped most cautiously back and trotted nearly a mile until I could come up behind one of the ridges bounding the valley in which he was. The wind had dropped and it was almost absolutely still when I crawled flat on my face to the crest, my hat in my left hand, my rifle in my right. There was a big sage-bush conveniently near, and under this I peered. There was a good deal of brush in the valley below, and if I had not known that the buck was there, I would never have discovered him. As it was, I watched for a quarter of an hour, and had about made up my mind that he must have gone somewhere else, when a slight movement nearly below me attracted my attention, and I caught a glimpse of him nearly three hundred yards off, moving quietly along by the side of a little dry watercourse which was right in the middle of the brush. I waited until he was well past, and then again slipped back with the utmost care, and ran on until I was nearly opposite the head of the coulee, when I again approached the ridge-line. Here there was no sage-bush, only tufts of tall grass, which were stirring in the little breeze which had just sprung up, fortunately in the right direction. Taking advantage of a slight inequality in the soil, I managed to get behind one of these tufts, and almost immediately saw the buck. Toward the head of the coulee the brush had become scanty and low, and he was now walking straight forward, evidently keeping a sharp lookout. The sun had just set. His course took him past me at a distance of eighty yards. When directly opposite I raised myself on my elbows, drawing up the rifle, which I had shoved ahead of me. The movement of course caught his eye at once; he halted for one second to look around and see what it was, and during that second I pulled the trigger. Away he went, his white flag switching desperately, and though he galloped over the hill, I felt he was mine. However, when I got to the top of the rise over which he had gone, I could not see him, and as there was a deep though narrow coulee filled with brush on the other side, I had a very ugly feeling that I might have lost him, in spite of the quantity of blood he had left along his trail. It was getting dark, and I plunged quickly into the coulee. Usually a wounded deer should not be followed until it has had time to grow stiff, but this was just one of the cases where the rule would have worked badly; in the first place, because darkness was coming on, and in the next place, because the animal was certain to die shortly, and all that I wanted was to see where he was. I followed his trail into the coulee, and expected to find that he had turned down it, but a hurried examination in the fading light showed me that he had taken the opposite course, and I scrambled hastily out on the other side, and trotted along, staring into the brush, and now and then shouting or throwing in a clod of earth. When nearly at the head there was a crackling in the brush, and out burst the wounded buck. He disappeared behind a clump of elms, but he had a hard hill to go up, and the effort was too much for him. When I next saw him he had halted, and before I could fire again down he came.

On another occasion I spied a whole herd of whitetail feeding in a natural meadow, right out in the open, in mid-afternoon, and was able to get up so close that when I finally shot a yearling buck (which was one of the deer farthest away from me, there being no big buck in the outfit), the remaining deer, all does and fawns, scattered in every direction, some galloping right past me in their panic. Once or twice I was able to perform a feat of which I had read, but in which I scarcely believed. This was, to creep up to a deer while feeding in the open, by watching when it shook its tail, and then remaining motionless. I cannot say whether the habit is a universal one, but on two occasions at least I was able thus to creep up to the feeding deer, because before lifting its head it invariably shook its tail, thereby warning me to stay without moving until it had lifted its head, scrutinized the landscape, and again lowered its head to graze. The eyesight of the whitetail, as compared with that of the pronghorn antelope, is poor. It notes whatever is in motion, but it seems unable to distinguish clearly anything that is not in motion. On the occasions in question no antelope that I have ever seen would have failed to notice me at once and to take alarm. But the whitetail, although it scrutinized me narrowly, while I lay motionless with my head toward it, seemed in each case to think that I must be harmless, and after a while it would go on feeding. In one instance the animal fed over a ridge and walked off before I could get a shot; in the other instance I killed it.

In 1894, on the last day I spent at the ranch, and with the last bullet I fired from my rifle, I killed a fine whitetail buck. I left the ranch house early in the afternoon on my favorite pony, Muley, my foreman, Sylvane Ferris, riding with me. We forded the shallow river and rode up a long winding coulee, with belts of timber running down its bottom. After going a couple of miles, by sheer good luck we stumbled on three whitetail—a buck, a doe and a fawn. When we saw them they were trying to sneak off, and immediately my foreman galloped toward one end of the belt of timber in which they were, and started to ride down through it, while I ran Muley to the other end to intercept them. They were, of course, quite likely to break off to one side; but this happened to be one of the occasions when everything went right. When I reached the spot from which I covered the exits from the timber, I leaped off, and immediately afterward heard a shout from my foreman that told me the deer were on foot. Muley was a pet horse, and enjoyed immensely the gallop after game; but his nerves invariably failed him at the shot. On this occasion he stood snorting beside me, and finally, as the deer came in sight, away he tore—only to go about 200 yards, however, and stand and watch us, snorting, with his ears pricked forward until, when I needed him, I went for him. At the moment, however, I paid no heed to Muley, for a cracking in the brush told me the game was close, and I caught the shadowy outlines of the doe and the fawn as they scudded through the timber. By good luck, the buck, evidently flurried, came right on the edge of the woods next to me, and as he passed, running like a quarter-horse, I held well ahead of him and pulled trigger. The bullet broke his neck and down he went— a fine fellow with a handsome ten-point head, and fat as a prize sheep; for it was just before the rut. Then we rode home, and I sat in a rocking-chair on the ranch-house veranda, looking across the wide, sandy river bed at the strangely shaped buttes and the groves of shimmering cottonwoods until the sun went down and the frosty air bade me go in.

CHAPTER VII

THE MULE-DEER, OR ROCKY MOUNTAIN BLACKTAIL

THIS is the largest and finest of our three smaller deer. Throughout its range it is known as the blacktail deer, and it has as good a historic claim to the title as its Pacific coast kinsman, the coast or true blacktail. In writing purely of this species, it seems like pedantry to call it by its book name of mule-deer, a name which conveys little or no meaning to the people who live in its haunts and who hunt it; but it is certainly very confusing to know two distinct types of deer by one name, and as both the Rocky Mountain blacktail and Coast blacktail are thus known, and as the former is occasionally known as mule-deer, I shall, for convenience' sake, speak of it un- der this name—a name given it because of its great ears, which rather detract from its otherwise very handsome appearance.

The mule-deer is a striking and beautiful animal. As is the case with our other species, it varies greatly in size, but is on the average heavier than either the white-tail or the true blacktail. The horns also average longer and heavier, and in exceptional heads are really note-worthy trophies. Ordinarily a full-grown buck has a head of ten distinct and well-developed points, eight of which consist of the bifurcations of the two main prongs into which each antler divides, while in addition there are two shorter basal or frontal points. But the latter are very irregular, being sometimes missing; while sometimes there are two or three of them on each antler. When missing it usually means that the antlers are of young animals that have not attained their full growth. A yearling will sometimes have merely a pair of spikes, and sometimes each spike will be bifurcated so as to make two points. A two-year-old may develop antlers which, though small, possess the normal four points. Occasionally, where unusually big heads are developed, there are a number of extra points. If these are due to deformity, they simply take away from the beauty of the head; but where they are symmetrical, while at the same time the antlers are massive, they add greatly to the beauty. All the handsomest and largest heads show this symmetrical development of extra points. It is rather hard to lay down a hard-and-fast rule for counting them. The largest and finest antlers are usually rough, and it is not easy to say when a particular point in roughness has developed so that it may legitimately be called a prong. The largest head I ever got to my own rifle had twenty-eight points, symmetrically arranged, the antlers being rough and very massive as well as very long. The buck was an immense fellow, but no bigger than other bucks I have shot which possessed ordinary heads.

The mule-deer is found from the rough country which begins along the eastern edges of the great plains, across the Rocky Mountains to the eastern slopes of the coast ranges, and into southern California. It extends into Canada on the north and Mexico on the south. On the west it touches, and here and there crosses, the boundaries of the Coast blacktail. The whitetail is found in places throughout its habitat from east to west and from north to south. But there are great regions in this territory which are peculiarly fitted for the mule-deer, but in which the whitetail is never found, as the habits of the two are entirely different. In the mountains of western Colorado and Wyoming, for instance, the mule-deer swarms, but the whole region is unfit for the whitetail, which is accordingly only found in a very few narrowly restricted localities.

The mule-deer does not hold its own as well as the whitetail in the presence of man, but it is by no means as quickly exterminated as the wapiti. The outside limits of its range have not shrunk materially in the century during which it has been known to white hunters. It was never found until the fertile, moist country of the Mississippi Valley was passed and the dry plains region to the west of it reached, and it still exists in some numbers here and there in this country, as, for instance, in the Bad Lands along the Little Missouri, and in the Black Hills. But although its limits of distribution have not very sensibly diminished, there are large portions of the range within these limits from which it has practically vanished, and in most places its numbers have been woefully thinned. It holds its own best among the more inaccessible mountain masses of the Rockies, and from Chihuahua to Alberta there are tracts where it is still abundant. Yet even in these places the numbers are diminishing, and this process can be arrested only by better laws, and above all, by a better administration of the law. The national Government could do much by establishing its forest reserves as game reserves, and putting on a sufficient number of forest rangers who should be empowered to prevent all hunting on the reserves. The State governments can do still more. Colorado has good laws, but they are not well enforced. The easy method of accounting for this fact is to say that it is due to the politicians; but in reality the politicians merely represent the wishes, or more commonly the indifference, of the people. As long as the good citizens of a State are indifferent to game protection, or take but a tepid interest in it, the politicians, through their agents, will leave the game laws unenforced. But if the people of Colorado, Wyoming, and Montana come to feel the genuine interest in the enforcement of these laws that the people of Maine and Vermont have grown to take during the past twenty years, that the people of Montana and Wyoming who dwell alongside the Yellowstone Park are already taking —then not only will the mule-deer cease to diminish, but it will positively increase. It is a mistake to suppose that such a change would only be to the advantage of well-to-do sportsmen. Men who are interested in hunting for hunting's sake, men who come from the great cities remote from the mountains in order to get three or four weeks' healthy, manly holiday, would undoubtedly be benefited; but the greatest benefit would be to the people of the localities, of the neighborhoods round about. The presence of the game would attract outsiders who would leave in the country money, or its equivalent, which would many times surpass in value the game they actually killed; and furthermore, the preservation of the game would mean that the ranchmen and grangers who live near its haunts would have in perpetuity the chance of following the pleasantest and healthiest of all out-of-door pastimes; whereas, if through their short-sightedness they destroy, or permit to be destroyed, the game, they are themselves responsible for the fact that their children and children's children will find themselves forever debarred from a pursuit which must under such circumstances become the amusement only of the very rich. If we are really alive to our opportunities under our democratic social and political system, we can keep for ourselves—and by " ourselves " I mean the enormous bulk of men whose means range from moderate to very small—ample opportunity for the enjoyment of hunting and shooting, of vigorous and blood-stirring out-of-doors sport. If we fail to take advantage of our possibilities, if we fail to pass, in the interest of all, wise game laws, and to see that these game laws are properly enforced, we shall then have to thank ourselves if in the future the game is only found in the game preserves of the wealthy; and under such circumstances only these same wealthy people will have the chance to hunt it.

The mule-deer differs widely from the whitetail in its habits, and especially in its gait, and in the kind of country which it frequents. Although in many parts of its range it is found side by side with its whitetail cousin, the two do not actually associate together, and their propinquity is due simply to the fact, that the river bottoms being a favorite haunt of the whitetail, long tongues of the distribution area of this species are thrust into the domain of its bolder, less stealthy and less crafty kinsman. Throughout the plains country the whitetail is the deer of the river bottoms, where the rank growth gives it secure hiding-places, as well as ample food. The mule-deer, on the contrary, never comes down into the dense growths of the river bottoms. Throughout the plains country it is the deer of the broken Bad Lands which fringe these river bottoms on either side, and of the rough ravines which wind their way through the Bad Lands to the edge of the prairie country which lies back of them. The broken hills, their gorges filled with patches of ash, buck brush, cedar, and dwarf pine, form a country in which the mule-deer revels. The whitetail will, at times, wander far out on the prairies where the grass is tall and rank; but it is not nearly so bold or fond of the open as the mule-deer. The latter is frequently found in hilly country where the covering is so scanty that the animal must be perpetually on the watch, as if it were a bighorn or prongbuck, in order to spy its foes at a distance and escape before they can come near; whereas the whitetail usually seeks to elude observation by hiding—by its crouching, stealthy habits.

It must be remembered, however, that with the mule-deer, as with all other species of animals, there is a wide variability in habits under different conditions. This is often forgotten even by trained naturalists, who accept the observations made in one locality as if they applied throughout the range of the species. Thus in the generally good account of the habits of this species in Mr. Lydeker's book on the " Deer of All Lands " it is asserted that mule-deer never dwell permanently in the forest, and feed almost exclusively on grass. The first statement is entirely, the second only partly, true of the mule-deer of the plains from the Little Missouri westward to the head-waters of the Platte, the Yellowstone, and the Big Horn; but there are large parts of the Rockies in which neither statement applies at all. In the course of several hunt-ing trips among the densely wooded mountains of western Montana, along the water-shed separating the streams that flow into Clarke's Fork of the Columbia from those that ultimately empty into Kootenay Lake, I found the mule-deer plentiful in many places where practically the whole country was covered by dense forest, and where the opportunities for grazing were small indeed, as we found to our cost in connection with our pack-train. In this region the mule-deer lived the entire time among the timber, and subsisted for the most part on browse. Occasionally they would find an open glade and graze; but the stomachs of those killed contained not grass, but blueberries and the leaves and delicate tips of bushes. I was not in this country in winter, but it was evident that even at that season the deer must spend their time in the thick timber. There was no chance for them to go above the timber line, because the mountains were densely wooded to their summits, and the white goats of the local-ity also lived permanently in the timber.[1] It was far

[1] I call particular attention to this fact concerning the white goat, as certain recent writers, including Mr. Madison Grant, have erroneously denied it.

harder to get the mule-deer than it was to get the white goats, for the latter were infinitely more conspicuous, were slower in their movements, and bolder and less shy. Almost the only way we succeeded in killing the deer was by finding one of their well-trodden paths and lying in wait beside it very early in the morning or quite late in the afternoon. The season was August and September, and the deer were astir long before sunset. They usually, but not always, lay high up on the mountain-sides, and while they sometimes wandered to and fro browsing on the mountains, they often came down to feed in the valleys, where the berries were thicker. Their paths were well beaten, although, like all game trails, after being as plainly marked as a pony track for a quarter of a mile or so, they would suddenly grow faint and vanish. The paths ran nearly straight up and down hill, and even when entirely undisturbed, the deer often came down them at a great rate, bouncing along in a way that showed that they had no fear of developing the sprung knees which we should fear for a domestic animal which habitually tried the same experiment.

In other habits also the deer vary widely in different localities. For instance, there is an absolute contrast as regards their migratory habits between the mule-deer which live in the Bad Lands along the Little Missouri, and those which live in northwestern Colorado; and this difference is characteristic generally of the deer which in the summer dwell in the high mountains, as contrasted with those which bear and rear their young in the low, broken hill-country. Along the Little Missouri there was no regular or clearly defined migration of the mule-deer in a mass. Some individuals, or groups of individuals, shifted their quarters for a few miles, so that in the spring, for instance, a particular district of a few square miles, in which they had been abundant before, might be wholly without them. But there were other districts, which happened to afford at all times sufficient food and shelter, in which they were to be found the year round; and the animals did not band and migrate as the prong-bucks did in the same region. In the immediate neighborhood of my ranch there were groups of high hills containing springs of water, good grass, and an abundance of cedar, ash, and all kinds of brush in which the mule-deer were permanent residents. There were big dry creeks, with well-wooded bottoms, lying among rugged hills, in which I have found whitetail and mule-deer literally within a stone's throw of one another. I once started from two adjoining pockets in this particular creek two does, each with a fawn, one being a mule-deer and the other a whitetail. On another occasion, on an early spring afternoon, just before the fawns were born, I came upon a herd of twenty whitetails, does, and young of the preceding year, grazing greedily on the young grass; and half a mile up the creek, in an almost exactly similar locality, I came upon just such a herd of mule-deer. In each case the animals were so absorbed in the feasting, which was to make up for their winter privations, that I was able to stalk to within fifty yards, though of course I did not shoot.

In northwestern Colorado the conditions are entirely

different. Throughout this region there are no whitetail and never have been, although in the winter range of the mule-deer there are a few prongbuck; and the wapiti once abounded. The mule-deer are still plentiful. They make a complete migration summer and winter, so that in neither season is a single individual to be found in the haunts they frequent during the other season. In the summer they live and bring forth their young high up in the main chain of the mountains, in a beautiful country of northern forest growth, dotted with trout-filled brooks and clear lakes. The snowfall is so deep in these wooded mountains that the deer would run great risk of perishing if they stayed therein, and indeed could only winter there at all in very small numbers. Accordingly, when the storms begin in the fall, usually about the first of October, just before the rut, the deer assemble in bands and move west and south to the lower, drier country, where the rugged hills are here and there clothed with an open growth of pinyon and cedar, instead of the tall spruces and pines of the summer range. The migrating bands follow one another along definite trails over mountains, through passes and valleys, and across streams; and their winter range swarms with them a few days after the forerunners have put in their appearance in what has been, during the summer, an absolutely deerless country.

In January and February, 1901, I spent five weeks north of the White River, in northwestern Colorado. It was in the heart of the wintering ground of the great Colorado mule-deer herd. Forty miles away to the east, extending north, lay the high mountains in which these deer had spent the summer. The winter range, in which I was at the time hunting cougars, is a region of comparatively light snowfall, though the cold is bitter. On several occasions during my stay the thermometer went down to twenty degrees below zero. The hills, or low mountains, for it was difficult to know which to call them, were steep and broken, and separated by narrow flats covered with sage-brush. The ordinary trees were the pinyon and cedar, which were scattered in rather open groves over the mountain-sides and the spurs between the ravines. There were also patches of quaking asp, scrub oak, and brush. The entire country was thinly covered with ranches, and there were huge pastures enclosed by wire fences. I have never seen the mule-deer so numerous anywhere as they were in this country at this time; although in 1883, on the Little Missouri, they were almost as plentiful. There was not a day we did not see scores, and on some days we saw hundreds. Frequently they were found in small parties of two or three, or a dozen individuals, but on occasions we saw bands of thirty or forty. Only rarely were they found singly. The fawns were of course well grown, being eight or nine months old, and long out of the spotted coat. They were still accompanying their mothers. Ordinarily a herd would consist of does, fawns, and yearlings, the latter carrying their first antlers. But it was not possible to lay down a universal rule. Again and again I saw herds in which there were one or two full-grown bucks associating with the females and younger deer. At other times we came across small bands of full-grown bucks by themselves, and occasionally a solitary buck. Considering the extent to which these deer must have been persecuted, I did not think them shy. We were hunting on horseback, and had hounds with us, so we made no especial attempt to avoid noise. Yet very frequently we would come close on the deer before they took alarm; and even when alarmed they would sometimes trot slowly off, halting and looking back. On one occasion, in some bad lands, we came upon four bucks which had been sunning themselves on the face of a clay wall. They jumped up and went off one at a time, very slowly, passing diagonally by us, certainly not over seventy yards off. All four could have been shot without effort, and as they had fine antlers I should certainly have killed one, had it been the open season.

When we came on these Colorado mule-deer suddenly, they generally behaved exactly as their brethren used to in the old days on the Little Missouri; that is, they would run off at a good speed for a hundred yards or so, then slow up, halt, gaze inquisitively at us for some seconds, and again take to flight. While the sun was strong they liked to lie out in the low brush on slopes where they would get the full benefit of the heat. During the heavy snowstorms they usually retreated into some ravine where the trees grew thicker than usual, not stirring until the weight of the storm was over. Most of the night, especially if it was moonlight, they fed; but they were not at all regular about this. I frequently saw them standing up and grazing, or more rarely browsing, in the middle of the day, and in the late afternoon they often came down to graze on the flats within view of the different ranch-houses where I happened to stop. The hours for feeding and resting, however, always vary accordingly as the deer are or are not persecuted. In wild localities I have again and again found these deer grazing at all hours of the day, and coming to water at high noon; whereas, where they have been much persecuted, they only begin to feed after dusk, and come to water after dark. Of course during this winter weather they could get no water, snow supplying its place.

I was immensely interested with the way they got through the wire fences. A mule-deer is a great jumper; I have known them to clear with ease high timber corral fences surrounding hayricks. If the animals had chosen, they could have jumped any of the wire fences I saw; yet never in a single instance did I see one of them so jump a fence, nor did I ever find in the tell-tale snow tracks which indicated their having done so. They paid no heed whatever to the fences, so far as I could see, and went through them at will; but they always got between the wires, or went under the lowest wire. The dexterity with which they did this was extraordinary. When alarmed they would run full speed toward a wire fence, would pass through it, often hardly altering their stride, and never making any marks in the snow which looked as though they had crawled. Twice I saw bands thus go through a wire fence, once at speed, the other time when they were not alarmed. On both occasions they were too far off to allow me to see exactly their mode of procedure, but on examining the snow where they had passed, there was not the slightest mark of their bodies, and the alteration in their gait, as shown by the footprints, was hardly perceptible. In one instance, however, where I scared a young buck which ran over a hill and through a wire fence on the other side, I found one of his antlers lying beside the fence, it having evidently been knocked off by the wire. Their antlers were getting very loose, and toward the end of our stay they had begun to shed them.

The deer were preyed on by many foes. Sportsmen and hide-hunters had been busy during the fall migrations, and the ranchmen of the neighborhood were shooting them occasionally for food, even when we were out there. The cougars at this season were preying upon them practically to the exclusion of everything else. We came upon one large fawn which had been killed by a bobcat. The gray wolves were also preying upon them. A party of these wolves can sometimes run down even an unwounded blacktail; I have myself known of their performing this feat. Twice on this very hunt we came across the carcasses of blacktail which had thus been killed by wolves, and one of the cow-punchers at a ranch where we were staying came in and reported to us that while riding among the cattle that afternoon he had seen two coyotes run a young mule-deer to a standstill, and they would without doubt have killed it had they not been frightened by his approach. Still the wolf is very much less successful than the cougar in killing these deer, and even the cougar continually fails in his stalks. But the deer were so plentiful that at this time all the cougars we killed were very fat, and evidently had no difficulty in getting as much venison as they needed. The wolves were not as well off, and now and then made forays on the young stock of the ranchmen, which at this season the cougar let alone, reserving his attention to them for the summer season when the deer had vanished.

In the Big Horn Mountains, where I also saw a good deal of the mule-deer, their habits were intermediate between those of the species that dwell on the plains and those that dwell in the densely timbered regions of the Rockies farther to the northwest. In the summer time they lived high up on the plateaus of the Big Horn, sometimes feeding in the open glades and sometimes in the pine forests. In the fall they browsed on certain of the bushes almost exclusively. In winter they came down into the low country. South of the Yellowstone Park, where the wapiti swarmed, the mule-deer were not numerous. I believe that by choice they prefer rugged, open country, and they certainly care comparatively little for bad weather, as they will often visit bleak, wind-swept ridges in midwinter, as being places where they can best get food at that season, when the snow lies deep in the sheltered places. Nevertheless, many of the species pass their whole life in thick timber.

My chief opportunities for observing the mule-deer were in the eighties, when I spent much of my time on my ranch on the Little Missouri. Mule-deer were then very plentiful, and I killed more of them than of all other game put together. At that time in the cattle country no ranchman ever thought of killing beef, and if

THE RANCH HOUSE

we had fresh meat at all it was ordinarily venison. In the fall we usually tried to kill enough deer to last out the winter. Until the settlers came in, the Little Missouri country was an ideal range for mule-deer, and they fairly swarmed; while elk were also plentiful, and the restless herds of the buffalo surged at intervals through the land. After 1882 and 1883 the buffalo and elk were killed out, the former completely, and the latter practically, and by that time the skin-hunters, and then the ranchers, turned their attention chiefly to the mule-deer. It lived in open country where there was cover for the stalker, and so it was much easier to kill than either the whitetail, which was found in the dense cover of the river bottoms, or the prongbuck, which was found far back from the river, on the flat prairies where there was no cover at all. I have been informed of other localities in which the antelope has disappeared long before the mule-deer, and I believe that in the Rockies the mule-deer has a far better chance of survival than the antelope has on the plains; but on the Little Missouri the antelope continued plentiful long after the mule-deer had become decidedly scarce. In 1886 I think the antelope were fully as abundant as ever they were, while the mule-deer had wofully diminished. In the early nineties there were still regions within thirty or forty miles of my ranch where the antelope were very plentiful—far more so than the mule-deer were at that time. Now they are both scarce along the Little Missouri, and which will outlast the other I cannot say.

In the old days, as I have already said, it was by no

means infrequent to see both the whitetail and the mule-deer close together, and when, under such circumstances, they were alarmed, one got a clear idea of the extraordinary gait which is the mule-deer's most striking characteristic. It trots well, gallops if hard pressed, and is a good climber, though much inferior to the mountain sheep. But its normal gait consists of a series of stiff-legged bounds, all four feet leaving and striking the ground at the same time. This gait differs more from the gait of bighorn, prongbuck, whitetail, and wapiti than the gaits of these latter animals differ among themselves. The wapiti, for instance, rarely gallops, but when he does, it is a gallop of the ordinary type. The prong-buck runs with a singularly even gait; whereas the white-tail makes great bounds, some much higher than others. But fundamentally in all cases the action is the same, and has no resemblance to the stiff-legged buck jumping which is the ordinary means of progression of the mule-deer. These jumps carry it not only on the level, but up and down hill at a great speed. It is said to be a tire-some gait for the animal, if hunted for any length of time on the level; but of this I cannot speak with full knowledge.

Compared to the wapiti, the mule-deer, like our other small deer, is a very silent animal. For a long time I believed it uttered no sound beyond the snort of alarm and the rare bleat of the doe to her fawn; but one after-noon I heard two bucks grunting or barking at one an-other in a ravine back of the ranch-house, and crept up and shot them. I was still uncertain whether this was an indication of a regular habit; but a couple of years later, on a moonlight night just after sunset, I heard a big buck travelling down a ravine and continually barking, evidently as a love challenge. I have been informed by some hunters that the bucks at the time of the rut not infrequently thus grunt and bark; but most hunters are ignorant of this habit; and it is certainly not a common practice.

The species is not nearly as gregarious as the wapiti or caribou. During the winter the bucks are generally found singly, or in small parties by themselves, although occasionally one will associate with a party of does and of young deer. When in May or June—for the exact time varies with the locality—the doe brings forth her young, she retires to some lonely thicket. Sometimes one and sometimes two fawns are brought forth. They lie very close for the first few days. I have picked them up and handled them without their making the slightest effort to escape, while the mother hung about a few hundred yards off. On one occasion I by accident surprised a doe in the very act of giving birth to two fawns. One had just been born and the other was born as the doe made her first leap away. She ran off with as much speed and unconcern as if nothing whatever had happened. I passed on immediately, lest she should be so frightened as not to come back to the fawns. It has happened that where I have found the newly born fawns I have invariably found the doe to be entirely alone, but her young of the previous year must sometimes at least be in the neighborhood, for a little later I have frequently seen the doe and her fawn or fawns, and either one or two young of the previous year, together. Often, however, these young deer will be alone, or associated with an older doe which is barren. The bucks at the same time go to secluded places; sometimes singly, while sometimes an old buck will be accompanied by a younger one, or a couple of old bucks will lie together. They move about as little as possible while their horns are growing, and if a hunter comes by, they will lie far closer than at any other time of the year, squatting in the dense thickets as if they were whitetails.

When in the Bad Lands of the Western Dakotas the late September breezes grow cold, then the bucks, their horns already clean of velvet which they have thrashed off on the bushes and saplings, feel their necks begin to swell; and early in October—sometimes not until November— they seek the does. The latter, especially the younger ones, at first flee in frantic haste. As the rut goes on the bucks become ever bolder and more ardent. Not only do they chase the does by night, but also by day. I have sat on the side of a ravine in the Bad Lands at noon and seen a young doe race past me as if followed by a wolf. When she was out of sight a big buck appeared on her trail, following it by scent, also at speed. When he had passed I got up, and the motion frightened a younger buck which was following two or three hundred yards in the rear of the big one. After a while the doe yields, and the buck then accompanies her. If, however, it is early in the season, he may leave her entirely in order to run after another doe. Later in the season he will have a better chance of adding the second doe to his harem, or of robbing another buck of the doe or does which he has accumulated. I have often seen merely one doe and one buck together, and I have often seen a single doe which for several days was accompanied by several bucks, one keeping off the others. But generally the biggest bucks collect each for himself several does, yearlings also being allowed in the band. The exact amount of companionship with the does allowed these young bucks depends somewhat upon the temper of the master buck. In books by imperfectly informed writers we often see allusions to the buck as protecting the doe, or even taking care of the fawn. Charles Dudley Warner, for instance, in describing with great skill and pathos an imaginary deer hunt, after portraying the death of the doe, portrays the young fawn as following the buck when the latter comes back to it in the evening.[1] As a matter of fact, while the fawn is so young as to be wholly dependent upon the doe, the buck never comes near either. Moreover, during the period when the buck and the doe are together, the buck's attitude is merely that of a brutal, greedy, and selfish tyrant. He will unhesitatingly rob the doe of any choice bit of food, and though he will fight to keep her if another buck approaches, the moment that a dangerous foe appears his one thought is for his own preservation. He will not only desert the doe, but if he is an old and cunning buck, he will try his

[1] While the situation thus described was an impossible one, the purpose of Mr. Warner's article was excellent, it being intended as a protest against hunting deer while the fawns are young, and against killing them in the water.

best to sacrifice her by diverting the attention of the pursuer to her and away from him.

By the end of the rut the old bucks are often exhausted, their sides are thin, their necks swollen; though they are never as gaunt as wapiti bulls at this time. They then rest as much as possible, feeding all the time to put on fat before winter arrives, and rapidly attaining a very high condition.

Except in dire need no one would kill a deer after the hard weather of winter begins or before the antlers of the buck are full-grown and the fawns are out of the spotted coat. Even in the old days we, who lived in the ranch country, always tried to avoid killing deer in the spring or early summer, though we often shot buck antelope at those times. The close season for deer varies in different States, and now there is generally a limit set to the number any one hunter can kill; for the old days of wasteful plenty are gone forever.

To my mind there is a peculiar fascination in hunting the mule-deer. By the time the hunting season has arrived the buck is no longer the slinking beast of the thicket, but a bold and yet wary dweller in the uplands. Frequently he can be found clear of all cover, often at midday, and his habits at this season are, from the hunter's standpoint, rather more like those of the wapiti than of the whitetail; but each band, though continually shifting its exact position, stays permanently in the same tract of country, whereas wapiti are apt to wander.

In the old days, when mule-deer were plentiful in

country through which a horse could go at a fair rate
of speed, it was common for the hunter to go on horseback, and not to dismount save at the moment of the
shot. In the early eighties, while on my ranch on the
Little Missouri, this was the way in which I usually
hunted. When I first established my ranch I often went
out, in the fall, after the day's work was over, and killed
a deer before dark. If it was in September, I would
sometimes start after supper. Later in the year I would
take supper when I got back. Under such circumstances
my mode of procedure was simple. Deer were plentiful.
Every big tangle of hills, every set of grassy coulees winding down to a big creek bottom, was sure to contain them.
The time being short, with at most only an hour or two
of light, I made no effort to find the tracks of a deer
or to spy one afar off. I simply rode through the likely
places, across the heads of the ravines or down the winding valleys, until I jumped a deer close enough up to give
me a shot. The unshod hoofs of the horse made but little noise as he shuffled along at the regular cow-pony
fox trot, and I kept him close into the bank or behind
cover, so as to come around each successive point without warning. If the ground was broken and rugged, I
made no attempt to go fast. If, on the other hand, I
struck a smooth ravine with gentle curves, I would often
put the pony to a sharp canter or gallop, so as to come
quickly on any deer before it could quite make up its
mind what course was best to follow. Sooner or later,
as I passed a thick clump of young ash or buck brush,
or came abruptly around a sharp bend, there would be

a snort, and then the thud, thud, thud, of four hoofs striking the ground exactly in unison, and away would go a
mule-deer with the peculiar bounding motion of its kind.
The pony, well accustomed to the work, stopped short,
and I was off its back in an instant. If the deer had
not made out exactly what I was, it would often show
by its gait that it was not yet prepared to run straight
out of sight. Under such circumstances I would wait
until it stopped and turned round to look back. If it
was going very fast, I took the shot running. Once I
put up a young buck from some thick brush in the bottom of a winding washout. I leaped off the pony, standing within ten yards of the washout. The buck went up
a hill on my left, and as he reached the top and paused
for a second on the sky-line, I fired. At the shot there
was a great scrambling and crashing in the washout below me, and another and larger buck came out and tore
off in frantic haste. I fired several shots at him, finally
bringing him down. Meanwhile, the other buck had
disappeared, but there was blood on his trail, and I found
him lying down in the next coulee, and finished him.
This was not much over a mile from the ranch-house,
and after dressing the deer, I put one behind the saddle
and one on it, and led the pony home.

Such hunting, though great fun, does not imply any
particular skill either in horsemanship, marksmanship, or
plainscraft and knowledge of the animal's habits; and
it can of course be followed only where the game is very
plentiful. Ordinarily the mule-deer must be killed by
long tramping among the hills, skilful stalking, and good

shooting. The successful hunter should possess good eyes, good wind, and good muscles. He should know how to take cover and how to use his rifle. The work is sufficiently rough to test any man's endurance, and yet there is no such severe and intense toil as in following true mountain game, like the bighorn or white goat. As the hunter's one aim is to see the deer before it sees him, he can only use the horse to take him to the hunting-ground. Then he must go through the most likely ground and from every point of vantage scan with minute care the landscape round about, while himself unseen. If the country is wild and the deer have not been much molested, he will be apt to come across a band that is feeding. Under such circumstances it is easy to see them at once. But if lying down, it is astonishing how the gray of their winter coats fits in with the color of their surroundings. Too often I have looked carefully over a valley with my glasses until, thinking I had searched every nook, I have risen and gone forward, only to see a deer rise and gallop off out of range from some spot which I certainly thought I had examined with all possible precaution. If the hunter is not himself hidden, he will have his labor for his pains. Neither the mule-deer nor the whitetail is by any means as keen-sighted as the pronghorn antelope, and men accustomed chiefly to antelope shooting are quite right in speaking of the sight of deer as poor by comparison. But this is only by comparison. A motionless object does not attract the deer's gaze as it attracts the telescopic eye of a prongbuck; but any motion is seen at once, and as soon as this has occurred, the chances of the hunter are usually at an end. On the other hand, from the nature of its haunts the mule-deer usually offers fairly good opportunities for stalking. It is not as big or as valuable as the elk, and therefore it is not as readily seen or as eagerly followed, and in consequence holds its own better. But though the sport it yields calls normally for a greater amount of hardihood and endurance in the hunter than is the case with the sport yielded by the prongbuck, and especially by the whitetail, yet when existing in like numbers it is easier to kill than either of these two animals.

Sometimes in the early fall, when hunting from the ranch, I have spent the night in some likely locality, sleeping rolled up in a blanket on the ground so as to be ready to start at the first streak of dawn. On one such occasion a couple of mule-deer came to where my horse was picketed just before I got up. I heard them snort or whistle, and very slowly unwrapped myself from the blanket, turned over, and crawled out, rifle in hand. Overhead the stars were paling in the faint gray light, but the ravine in which the deer were was still so black that, watch as I would, I could not see them. I feared to move around lest I might disturb them, but after wiggling toward a little jutting shoulder I lay still to wait for the light. They went off, however, while it was still too dusk to catch more than their dim and formless outlines, and though I followed them as rapidly and cautiously as possible, I never got a shot at them. On other occasions fortune has favored me, and before the sun rose I have spied some buck leisurely seeking his day bed,

THE RANCH VERANDAH

and have been able either to waylay him or make a running stalk on him from behind.

In the old days it was the regular thing with most ranchmen to take a trip in the fall for the purpose of laying in the winter's supply of venison. I frequently took such trips myself, and though occasionally we killed wapiti, bighorn, prongbuck, and whitetail, our ordinary game was the mule-deer. Around my ranch it was not necessary to go very far. A day's journey with the wagon would usually take us to where a week's hunting would enable us to return with a dozen deer or over. If there was need of more, I would repeat the hunt later on. I have several times killed three of these deer in a day, but I do not now recall ever killing a greater number. It is perhaps unnecessary to say that every scrap of flesh was used.

These hunts were always made late in the fall, usually after the close of the rut. The deer were then banded, and were commonly found in parties of from three or four to a score, although the big bucks might be lying by themselves. The weather was apt to be cold, and the deer evidently liked to sun themselves, so that at midday they could be found lying sometimes in thin brush and sometimes boldly out on the face of a cliff or hill. If they were unmolested, they would feed at intervals throughout the day, and not until the bands had been decimated by excessive hunting did they ever spend the hours of daylight in hiding.

On such a hunt our proceedings were simple. The nights were longer than the days, and therefore we were away from camp at the first streak of dawn, and might not return until long after darkness. All the time between was spent in climbing and walking through the rugged hills, keeping a sharp lookout for our game. Only too often we were seen before we ourselves saw the quarry, and even when this was not the case the stalks were sometimes failures. Still blank days were not very common. Probably every hunter remembers with pride some particular stalk. I recall now outwitting a big buck which I had seen and failed to get on two successive days. He was hanging about a knot of hills with brush on their shoulders, and was not only very watchful, but when he lay down always made his bed at the lower end of a brush patch, whence he could see into the valley below, while it was impossible to approach him from above, through the brush, without giving the alarm. On the third day I saw him early in the morning, while he was feeding. He was very watchful, and I made no attempt to get near him, simply peeping at him until he finally went into a patch of thin brush and lay down. As I knew what he was I could distinctly make him out. If I had not seen him go in, I certainly never would have imagined that he was a deer, even had my eyes been able to pick him out at all among the gray shadows and small dead tree-tops. Having waited until he was well settled down, I made a very long turn and came up behind him, only to find that the direction of the wind and the slope of the hill rendered it an absolute impossibility to approach him unperceived. After careful study of the ground I abandoned the effort, and returned to my former position, having spent several hours of considerable labor in vain. It was now about noon, and I thought I would lie still to see what he would do when he got up, and accordingly I ate my lunch stretched at full length in the long grass which sheltered me from the wind. From time to time I peered cautiously between two stones toward where the buck lay. It was nearly mid-afternoon before he moved. Sometimes mule-deer rise with a single motion, all four legs unbending like springs, so that the four hoofs touch the ground at once. This old buck, however, got up very slowly, looked about for certainly five minutes, and then came directly down the hill and toward me. When he had nearly reached the bottom of the valley between us he turned to the right and sauntered rapidly down it. I slipped back and trotted as fast as I could without losing my breath along the hither side of the spur which lay between me and the buck. While I was out of sight he had for some reason made up his mind to hurry, and when I was still fifty yards from the end of the spur he came in sight just beyond it, passing at a swinging trot. I dropped on one knee so quickly that for a moment he evidently could not tell what I was—my buckskin shirt and gray slouch-hat fading into the color of the background—and halted, looking sharply around. Before he could break into flight my bullet went through his shoulders.

Twice I have killed two of these deer at a shot; once two bucks, and once a doe and a buck.

It has proved difficult to keep the mule-deer in captivity, even in large private parks or roomy zoological gardens. I think this is because hitherto the experiment has been tried east of the Mississippi in an alien habitat. The wapiti and whitetail are species that are at home over most of the United States, East and West, in rank, wet prairies, dense woodland, and dry mountain regions alike; but the mule-deer has a far more sharply localized distribution. In the Bronx Zoological Gardens, in New York, Mr. Hornaday informs me that he has comparatively little difficulty in keeping up the stock alike of wapiti and whitetail by breeding—as indeed any visitor can see for himself. The same is true in the game preserves in the wilder regions of New York and New England; but hitherto the mule-deer has offered an even more difficult problem in captivity than the pronghorn antelope. Doubtless the difficulty would be minimized if the effort at domestication were made in the neighborhood of the Rocky Mountains.

The true way to preserve the mule-deer, however, as well as our other game, is to establish on the nation's property great nurseries and wintering grounds, such as the Yellowstone Park, and then to secure fair play for the deer outside these grounds by a wisely planned and faithfully executed series of game laws. This is the really democratic method of solving the problem. Occasionally even yet some one will assert that the game " belongs to the people, and should be given over to them "—meaning, thereby, that there should be no game laws, and that every man should be at liberty indiscriminately to kill every kind of wild animal, harmless, useless, or noxious, until the day when our woods become wholly bereft of all the forms of higher animal life. Such an argument can only be made from the standpoint of those big game dealers in the cities who care nothing for the future, and desire to make money at the present day by a slaughter which in the last analysis only benefits the wealthy people who are able to pay for the game; for once the game has been destroyed, the livelihood of the professional gunner will be taken away. Most emphatically wild game not on private property *does* belong to the people, and the only way in which the people can secure their ownership is by protecting it in the interest of all against the vandal few. As we grow older I think most of us become less keen about that part of the hunt which consists in the killing. I know that as far as I am concerned I have long gone past the stage when the chief end of a hunting trip was the bag. One or two bucks, or enough grouse and trout to keep the camp supplied, will furnish all the sport necessary to give zest and point to a trip in the wilderness. When hunters proceed on such a plan they do practically no damage to the game. Those who are not willing to act along these lines of their own free will, should be made to by the State. The people of Montana, Wyoming, and Colorado, and of the States near by, can do a real service, primarily to themselves, but secondarily to others also, by framing and executing laws which will keep these noble deer as permanent denizens of their lofty mountains and beautiful valleys. There are other things much more important than game laws; but it will be a great mistake to imagine, because until recently in Europe game laws have been administered in the selfish interest of one class and against the interest of the people as a whole, that here in this country, and under our institutions, they would not be beneficial to all of our people. So far from game laws being in the interest of the few, they are emphatically in the interest of the many. The very rich man can stock a private game preserve, or journey afar off to where game is still plentiful; but it is only where the game is carefully preserved by the State that the man of small means has any chance to enjoy the keen delight of the chase.

There are many sides to the charm of big game hunting; nor should it be regarded as being without its solid advantages from the standpoint of national character. Always in our modern life, the life of a highly complex industrialism, there is a tendency to softening of fibre. This is true of our enjoyments; and it is no less true of very many of our business occupations. It is not true of such work as railroading, a purely modern development, nor yet of work like that of those who man the fishing fleets; but it is preeminently true of all occupations which cause men to lead sedentary lives in great cities. For these men it is especially necessary to provide hard and rough play. Of course, if such play is made a serious business, the result is very bad; but this does not in the least affect the fact that within proper limits the play itself is good. Vigorous athletic sports carried on in a sane spirit are healthy. The hardy out-of-door sports of the wilderness are even healthier. It is a mere truism to say that the qualities developed by the hunter are the qualities needed by the soldier; and a curious feature of the changed conditions of modern warfare is that they call, to a much greater extent than during the two or three centuries immediately past, for the very qualities of individual initiative, ability to live and work in the open, and personal skill in the management of horse and weapons, which are fostered by a hunter's life. No training in the barracks or on the parade-ground is as good as the training given by a hard hunting trip in which a man really does the work for himself, learns to face emergencies, to study country, to perform feats of hardihood, to face exposure and undergo severe labor. It is an excellent thing for any man to be a good horseman and a good marksman, to be bold and hardy, and wonted to feats of strength and endurance, to be able to live in the open, and to feel a self-reliant readiness in any crisis. Big game hunting tends to produce or develop exactly these physical and moral traits. To say that it may be pursued in a manner or to an extent which is demoralizing, is but to say what can likewise be said of all other pastimes and of almost all kinds of serious business. That it can be abused either in the way in which it is done, or the extent to which it is carried, does not alter the fact that it is in itself a sane and healthy recreation.

CHAPTER VIII

THE WAPITI, OR ROUND-HORNED ELK

THE wapiti is the largest and stateliest deer in the world. A full-grown bull is as big as a steer. The antlers are the most magnificent trophies yielded by any game animal of America, save the giant Alaskan moose. When full grown they are normally of twelve tines; frequently the tines are more numerous, but the increase in their number has no necessary accompaniment in increase in the size of the antlers. The length, massiveness, roughness, spread, and symmetry of the antlers must all be taken into account in rating the value of a head. Antlers over fifty inches in length are large; if over sixty, they are gigantic. Good heads are getting steadily rarer under the persecution which has thinned out the herds.

Next to the bison the wapiti is of all the big game animals of North America the one whose range has most decreased. Originally it was found from the Pacific coast east across the Alleghanies, through New York to the Adirondacks, through Pennsylvania into western New Jersey, and far down into the mid-country of Virginia and the Carolinas. It extended northward into Canada, from the Great Lakes to Vancouver; and southward into Mexico, along the Rockies. Its range thus corresponded roughly with that of the bison, except that it went farther west and not so far north. In the early colonial days so little heed was paid by writers to the teeming myriads of game that it is difficult to trace the wapiti's distribution in the Atlantic coast region. It was certainly killed out of the Adirondacks long before the period when the backwoodsmen were settling the valleys of the Alleghany Mountains; there they found the elk abundant, and the stately creatures roamed in great bands over Tennessee, Kentucky, Ohio, and Indiana when the first settlers made their way into what are now these States, at the outbreak of the Revolution. These first settlers were all hunters, and they followed the wapiti (or, as they always called it, the elk) with peculiar eagerness. In consequence its numbers were soon greatly thinned, and about the beginning of the present century it disappeared from that portion of its former range lying south of the Great Lakes and between the Alleghanies and the Mississippi. In the northern Alleghanies it held its own much longer, the last individual of which I have been able to get record having been killed in Pennsylvania in 1869. In the forests of northern Wisconsin, northern Michigan, and Minnesota wapiti existed still longer, and a very few individuals may still be found. A few are left in Manitoba. When Lewis and Clark and Pike became the pioneers among the explorers, army officers, hunters, and trappers who won for our people the great West, they found countless herds of wapiti throughout the high plains country from the Mississippi River to the Rocky Mountains. Throughout this region it was exterminated almost as rapidly as the bison, and by the early eighties there only remained a few scattered individuals, in bits of rough country such as the Black Hills, the sand-hills of Nebraska, and certain patches of Bad Lands along the Little Missouri. Doubtless stragglers exist even yet in one or two of these localities. But by the time the great buffalo herds of the plains were completely exterminated, in 1883, the wapiti had likewise ceased to be a plains animal; the peculiar Californian form had also been well-nigh exterminated.

The nature of its favorite haunts was the chief factor in causing it to suffer more than any other game in America, save the bison, from the persecution of hunters and settlers. The boundaries of its range have shrunk in far greater proportion than in the case of any of our other game animals, save only the great wild ox, with which it was once so commonly associated. The moose, a beast of the forest, and the caribou, which, save in the far North, is also a beast of the forest, have in most places greatly diminished in numbers, and have here and there been exterminated altogether from outlying portions of their range; but the wapiti, which, when free to choose, preferred to frequent the plains and open woods, has completely vanished from nine-tenths of the territory over which it roamed a century and a quarter ago. Although it was never found in any one place in such enormous numbers as the bison and the caribou, it nevertheless went in herds far larger than the herds of any other American game save the two mentioned, and was formerly very much more abundant within the area of its distribution than was the moose within the area of its distribution.

This splendid deer affords a good instance of the difficulty of deciding what name to use in treating of our American game. On the one hand, it is entirely undesirable to be pedantic; and on the other hand, it seems a pity, at a time when speech is written almost as much as spoken, to use terms which perpetually require explanation in order to avoid confusion. The wapiti is not properly an elk at all; the term wapiti is unexceptionable, and it is greatly to be desired that it should be generally adopted. But unfortunately it has not been generally adopted. From the time when our backwoodsmen first began to hunt the animal among the foothills of the Appalachian chains to the present day, it has been universally known as elk wherever it has been found. In ordinary speech it is never known as anything else, and only an occasional settler or hunter would understand what the word wapiti referred to. The book name is a great deal better than the common name; but after all, it is only a book name. The case is almost exactly parallel to that of the buffalo, which was really a bison, but which lived as the buffalo, died as the buffalo, and left its name imprinted on our landscape as the buffalo. There is little use in trying to upset a name which is imprinted in our geography in hundreds of such titles as Elk Ridge, Elk Mountain, Elkhorn River. Yet in the books it is often necessary to call it the wapiti in order to distinguish it both from its differently named close kinsfolk of the Old World, and from its more distant relatives with which it shares the name of elk.

Disregarding the Pacific coast form of Vancouver

and the Olympian Mountains, the wapiti is now a beast of the Rocky Mountain region proper, especially in western Montana, Wyoming, and Colorado. Throughout these mountains its extermination, though less rapid than on the plains, has nevertheless gone on with melancholy steadiness. In the early nineties it was still as abundant as ever in large regions in western Wyoming and Montana and northwestern Colorado. In northwestern Colorado the herds are now represented by only a few hundred individuals. In western Montana they are scattered over a wider region and are protected by the denser timber, but are nowhere plentiful. They have nearly vanished from the Big Horn Mountains. They are still abundant in and around their great nursery and breeding-ground, the Yellowstone National Park. If this park could be extended so as to take in part of the winter range to the south, it would help to preserve them, to the delight of all lovers of nature, and to the great pecuniary benefit of the people of Wyoming and Montana. But at present the winter range south of the park is filling up with settlers, and unless the conditions change, those among the Yellowstone wapiti which would normally go south will more and more be compelled to winter among the mountains, which will mean such immense losses from starvation and deep snow that the southern herds will be wofully thinned.[1] Surely all men who care for nature, no less than all men who care for big game hunting, should combine to try to see that not merely the States but the Federal authorities make every effort, and are given every

[1] Steps in the direction indicated are now being taken by the Federal authorities.

power, to prevent the extermination of this stately and beautiful animal, the lordliest of the deer kind in the entire world.

The wapiti, like the bison, and even more than the whitetail deer, can thrive in widely varying surroundings. It is at home among the high mountains, in the deep forests, and on the treeless, level plains. It is rather omnivorous in its tastes, browsing and grazing on all kinds of trees, shrubs and grasses. These traits, and its hardihood, make it comparatively easy to perpetuate in big parks and forest preserves in a semi-wild condition; and it has thriven in such preserves and parks in many of the Eastern States. As it does not, by preference, dwell in such tangled forests as are the delight of the moose and the whitetail deer, it vanishes much quicker than either when settlers appear in the land. In the mountains and foothills its habitat is much the same as that of the mule-deer, the two animals being often found in the immediate neighborhood of each other. In such places the superior size and value of the wapiti put it at a disadvantage in the keen struggle for life, and when the rifle-bearing hunter appears upon the scene, it is killed out long before its smaller kinsman.

Moreover, the wapiti is undoubtedly subject to queer freaks of panic stupidity, or what seems like a mixture of tameness and of puzzled terror. At these times a herd will remain almost motionless, the individuals walking undecidedly to and fro, and neither flinching nor giving any other sign even when hit with a bullet. In the old days it was not uncommon for a professional hunter to destroy an entire herd of wapiti when one of these fits of confusion was on them. Even nowadays they sometimes behave in this way. In 1897, Mr. Ansley Wilcox, of Buffalo, was hunting in the Teton basin. He came across a small herd of wapiti, the first he had ever seen, and opened fire when a hundred and fifty yards distant. They paid no heed to the shots, and after taking three or four at one bull, with seemingly no effect, he ran in closer and emptied his magazine at another, also seemingly without effect, before the herd slowly disappeared. After a few rods, both bulls fell; and on examination it was found that all nine bullets had hit them.

To my mind, the venison of the wapiti is, on the whole, better than that of any other wild game, though its fat, when cooled, at once hardens, like mutton tallow.

In its life habits the wapiti differs somewhat from its smaller relatives. It is far more gregarious, and is highly polygamous. During the spring, while the bulls are growing their great antlers, and while the cows have very young calves, both bulls and cows live alone, each individual for itself. At such time each seeks the most secluded situation, often going very high up on the mountains. Occasionally a couple of bulls lie together, moving around as little as possible. The cow at this time realizes that her calf's chance of life depends upon her absolute seclusion, and avoids all observation.

As the horns begin to harden the bulls thrash the velvet off against quaking asp, or ash, or even young spruce, splintering and battering the bushes and small trees. The cows and calves begin to assemble; the bulls seek them. But the bulls do not run the cows as among the smaller deer the bucks run the does. The time of the beginning of the rut varies in different places, but it usually takes place in September, about a month earlier than that of the deer in the same locality. The necks of the bulls swell and they challenge incessantly, for, unlike the smaller deer, they are very noisy. Their love and war calls, when heard at a little distance amid the mountains, have a most musical sound. Frontiersmen usually speak of their call as " whistling," which is not an appropriate term. The call may be given in a treble or in a bass, but usually consists of two or three bars, first rising and then falling, followed by a succession of grunts. The grunts can only be heard when close up. There can be no grander or more attractive chorus than the challenging of a number of wapiti bulls when two great herds happen to approach one another under the moonlight or in the early dawn. The pealing notes echo through the dark valleys as if from silver bugles, and the air is filled with the wild music. Where little molested the wapiti challenge all day long.

They can be easiest hunted during the rut, the hunter placing them, and working up to them, by the sound alone. The bulls are excessively truculent and pugnacious. Each big one gathers a herd of cows about him and drives all possible rivals away from his immediate neighborhood, although sometimes spike bulls are allowed to remain with the herd. Where wapiti are very abundant, however, many of these herds may join together and become partially welded into a mass that may contain thousands of animals. In the old days such huge herds were far from uncommon, especially during the migrations; but nowadays there only remain one or two localities in which wapiti are sufficiently plentiful ever to come together in bands of any size. The bulls are incessantly challenging and fighting one another, and driving around the cows and calves. Each keeps the most jealous watch over his own harem, treating its members with great brutality, and is selfishly indifferent to their fate the instant he thinks his own life in jeopardy. During the rut the erotic manifestations of the bull are extraordinary.

One or two fawns are born about May. In the mountains the cow usually goes high up to bring forth her fawn. Personally I have only had a chance to observe the wapiti in spring in the neighborhood of my ranch in the Bad Lands of the Little Missouri. Here the cow invariably selected some wild, lonely bit of very broken country in which there were dense thickets and some water. There was one such patch some fifteen miles from my ranch, in which for many years wapiti regularly bred. The breeding cow lay by herself, although sometimes the young of the preceding year would lurk in the neighborhood. For the first few days the calf hardly left the bed, and would not move even when handled. Then it began to follow the mother. In this particular region the grass was coarse and rank, save for a few patches in the immediate neighborhood of little alkali springs. Accordingly, it was not much visited by the cattle or by the cowboys. Doubtless in the happier days of the past,

THE PACK TRAIN

when man was merely an infrequent interloper, the wapiti cows had made their nurseries in pleasanter and more fruitful valleys. But in my time the hunted creatures had learned that their only chance was to escape observation. I have known not only cows with young calves, but cows when the calves were out of the spotted coat, and even yearlings, to try to escape by hiding—the great beasts lying like rabbits in some patch of thick brush, while I rode close by. The best hunting horse I ever had, old Manitou, in addition to his other useful qualities, would serve as a guard on such occasions. I would leave him on a little hillock to one side of such a patch of brush, and as he walked slowly about, grazing and rattling his bridle chains, he would prevent the wapiti breaking cover on that side, and give me an additional chance of slipping around toward them—although if the animal was a cow, I never molested it unless in dire need of meat.

Most of my elk-hunting was done among the stupendous mountain masses of the Rockies, which I usually reached after a long journey, with wagon or pack-train, over the desolate plains. Ordinarily I planned to get to the hunting-ground by the end of August, so as to have ample time. By that date the calves were out of the spotted coat, the cows and the young of the preceding year had banded, and the big bulls had come down to join them from the remote recesses in which they had been lying, solitary or in couples, while their antlers were growing. Many bulls were found alone, or, if young, in small parties; but the normal arrangement was for each big bull to have his own harem, around the out-skirts of which there were to be found lurking occasional spike bulls or two-year-olds who were always venturing too near and being chased off by the master bull. Fre-quently several such herds joined together into a great band. Before the season was fairly on, when the bulls had not been worked into actual frenzy, there was not much fighting in these bands. Later they were the scenes of desperate combats. Each master bull strove to keep his harem under his own eyes, and was always threaten-ing and fighting the other master bulls, as well as those bulls whose prowess had proved insufficient hitherto to gain them a band, or who, after having gained one, had been so exhausted and weakened as to succumb to some new aspirant for the leadership. The bulls were calling and challenging all the time, and there was ceaseless tur-moil, owing to their fights and their driving the cows around. The cows were more wary than the bulls, and there were so many keen noses and fairly good eyes that it was difficult to approach a herd; whereas the single bulls were so noisy, careless, and excited that it was com-paratively easy to stalk them. A rutting wapiti bull is as wicked-looking a creature as can be imagined, swagger-ing among the cows and threatening the young bulls, his jaws mouthing and working in a kind of ugly leer.

The bulls fight desperately with one another. The two combatants come together with a resounding clash of antlers, and then push and strain with their mouths open. The skin on their necks and shoulders is so thick and tough that the great prongs cannot get through or

do more than inflict bruises. The only danger comes
when the beaten party turns to flee. The victor pursues
at full speed. Usually the beaten one gets off; but if by
accident he is caught where he cannot escape, he is very
apt to be gored in the flank and killed. Mr. Baillie-
Grohman has given a very interesting description of one
such fatal duel of which he was an eye-witness on a moonlight night in the mountains. I have never known of the
bull trying to protect the cow from any enemy. He
battles for her against rivals with intense ferocity; but
his attitude toward her, once she is gained, is either that
of brutality or of indifference. She will fight for her
calf against any enemy which she thinks she has a chance
of conquering, although of course not against man. But
the bull leaves his family to their fate the minute he
thinks there is any real danger. During the rut he is
greatly excited, and does not fear a dog or a single wolf,
and may join with the rest of the herd of both sexes in
trying to chase off one or the other, should he become
aware of its approach. But if there is serious danger,
his only thought is for himself, and he has no compunc-
tions about sacrificing any of his family. When on the
move a cow almost always goes first, while the bull brings
up the rear.

In domestication the bulls are very dangerous to
human beings, and will kill a man at once if they can
get him at a disadvantage; but in a state of nature they
rarely indeed overcome their abject terror of humanity,
even when wounded and cornered. Of course, if the man
comes straight up to him where he cannot get away, a

wapiti will fight as, under like circumstances, a blacktail or whitetail will fight, and equally, of course, he is then far more dangerous than his smaller kinsfolk; but he is not nearly so apt to charge as a bull moose. I have never known but two authentic instances of their thus charging. One happened to a hunter named Bennett, on the Little Missouri; the other to a gentleman I met, a doctor, in Meeker, Colorado. The doctor had wounded his wapiti, and as it was in the late fall, followed him easily in the snow. Finally he came upon the wapiti standing where the snow was very deep at the bottom of a small valley, and on his approach the wapiti deliberately started to break his way through the snow toward him, and had almost reached him when he was killed. But for every one such instance of a wapiti's charging there are a hundred in which a bull moose has charged. Senator Redfield Proctor was charged most resolutely by a mortally hurt bull moose which fell in the death throes just before reaching him; and I could cite case after case of the kind.

The wapiti's natural gaits are a walk and a trot. It walks very fast indeed, especially if travelling to reach some given point. More than once I have sought to overtake a travelling bull, and have found myself absolutely unable to do so, although it never broke its walk. Of course, if I had not been obliged to pay any heed to cover or wind, I could have run up on it; but the necessity for paying heed to both handicapped me so that I was actually unable to come up to the quarry as it swung steadily on through woodland and open, over rough ground and smooth. Wapiti have a slashing trot, which they can keep up for an indefinite time and over any kind of country. Only a good pony can overtake them when they have had any start and have settled into this trot. If much startled they break into a gallop—the young being always much more willing to gallop than the old. Their gallop is very fast, especially downhill. But they speedily tire under it. A yearling or a two-year-old can keep it up for a couple of miles. A heavy old bull will be done out after a few hundred yards. I once saw a band of wapiti frightened into a gallop down a steep incline where there were also a couple of mule-deer. I had not supposed that wapiti ran as fast as mule-deer, but this particular band actually passed the deer, though the latter were evidently doing their best; the wapiti were well ahead, when, after thundering down the steep, broken incline, they all disappeared into a belt of woodland. In spite of their size, wapiti climb well and go sure-footedly over difficult and dangerous ground. They have a habit of coming out to the edges of cliffs, or on mountain spurs, and looking over the landscape beneath, almost as though they enjoyed the scenery. What their real object is on such occasions I do not know.

The nose of the wapiti is very keen. Its sight is much inferior to that of the antelope, but about as good as a deer's. Its hearing is also much like that of a deer. When in country where it is little molested, it feeds and moves about freely by day, lying down to rest at intervals, like cattle. Wapiti offer especial attractions to the hunter, and next to the bison are more quickly exterminated than any other kind of game. Only the fact that they possessed a far wider range of habitat than either the mule-deer, the prongbuck, or the moose, has enabled them still to exist. Their gregariousness is also against them. Even after the rut the herds continue together until in midspring the bulls shed their antlers—for they keep their antlers at least two months longer than deer. During the fall, winter, and early spring wapiti are roving, restless creatures. Their habit of migration varies with locality, as among mule-deer. Along the little Missouri, as in the plains country generally, there was no well-defined migration. Up to the early eighties, when wapiti were still plentiful, the bands wandered far and wide, but fitfully and irregularly, wholly without regard to the season, save that they were stationary from May to August. After 1883 there were but a few individuals left, although as late as 1886 I once came across a herd of nine. These surviving individuals had learned caution. The bulls only called by night, and not very frequently then, and they spent the entire year in the roughest and most out-of-the-way places, having the same range both winter and summer. They selected tracts where the ground was very broken and there was much shrubbery and patches of small trees. This tree and bush growth gave them both shelter and food; for they are particularly fond of browsing on the leaves and tender twig ends, though they also eat weeds and grass.

Wherever wapiti dwell among the mountains they make regular seasonal migrations. In northwestern

Wyoming they spend the summer in the Yellowstone National Park, but in winter some go south to Jackson's Hole, while others winter in the park to the northeast. In northwestern Colorado their migrations followed much the same line as those of the mule-deer. In different localities the length of the migration, and even the time, differed. There were some places where the shift was simply from the high mountains down to their foothills. In other places great herds travelled a couple of hundred miles, so that localities absolutely barren one month would be swarming with wapiti the next. In some places the shift took place as early as the month of August; in others not until after the rut, in October or even November; and in some places the rut took place during the migration.

No chase is more fascinating than that of the wapiti. In the old days, when the mighty antlered beasts were found upon the open plains, they could be followed upon horseback, with or without hounds. Nowadays, when they dwell in the mountains, they are to be killed only by the rifle-bearing still-hunter. Needless butchery of any kind of animal is repulsive, but in the case of the wapiti it is little short of criminal. He is the grandest of the deer kind throughout the world, and he has already vanished from most of the places where he once dwelt in his pride. Every true sportsman should feel it incumbent upon him to do all in his power to preserve so noble a beast of the chase from extinction. No harm whatever comes to the species from killing a certain number of bulls; but an excessive number should never be killed, and no cow or calf should under any circumstances be touched. Formerly, when wapiti were plentiful, it would have been folly for hunters and settlers in the unexplored wilderness not to kill wild game for their meat, and occasionally a cow or a calf had to be thus slain; but there is no excuse nowadays for a hunting party killing anything but a full-grown bull.

In a civilized and cultivated country wild animals only continue to exist at all when preserved by sportsmen. The excellent people who protest against all hunting, and consider sportsmen as enemies of wild life, are ignorant of the fact that in reality the genuine sportsman is by all odds the most important factor in keeping the larger and more valuable wild creatures from total extermination. Of course, if wild animals were allowed to breed unchecked, they would, in an incredibly short space of time, render any country uninhabitable by man —a fact which ought to be a matter of elementary knowledge in any community where the average intelligence is above that of certain portions of Hindoostan. Equally, of course, in a purely utilitarian community all wild animals are exterminated out of hand. In order to preserve the wild life of the wilderness at all, some middle ground must be found between brutal and senseless slaughter and the unhealthy sentimentalism which would just as surely defeat its own end by bringing about the eventual total extinction of the game. It is impossible to preserve the larger wild animals in regions thoroughly fit for agriculture; and it is perhaps too much to hope that the larger carnivores can be preserved for merely æsthetic reasons. But throughout our country there are large regions entirely unsuited for agriculture, where, if the people only have foresight, they can, through the power of the State, keep the game in perpetuity. There is no hope of preserving the bison permanently, save in large private parks; but all other game, including not merely deer, but the pronghorn, the splendid bighorn, and the stately and beautiful wapiti, can be kept on the public lands, if only the proper laws are passed, and if only these laws are properly enforced.

Most of us, as we grow older, grow to care relatively less for sport than for the splendid freedom and abounding health of outdoor life in the woods, on the plains, and among the great mountains; and to the true nature lover it is melancholy to see the wilderness stripped of the wild creatures which gave it no small part of its peculiar charm. It is inevitable, and probably necessary, that the wolf and the cougar should go; but the bighorn and white goat among the rocks, the blacktail and wapiti grouped on the mountain side, the whitetail and moose feeding in the sedgy ponds—these add beyond measure to the wilderness landscape, and if they are taken away they leave a lack which nothing else can quite make good. So it is of those true birds of the wilderness, the eagle and the raven, and, indeed, of all the wild things, furred, feathered, and finned.

A peculiar charm in the chase of the wapiti comes from the wild beauty of the country in which it dwells. The moose lives in marshy forests; if one would seek the white goat or caribou of the northern Rockies, he

must travel on foot, pack on back; while the successful
chase of the bighorn, perhaps on the whole the manliest
of all our sports, means heart-breaking fatigue for any
but the strongest and hardiest. The prongbuck, again,
must be followed on the desolate, sun-scorched plains.
But the wapiti now dwells amid lofty, pine-clad mountains, in a region of lakes and streams. A man can travel
in comfort while hunting it, because he can almost always take a pack-train with him, and the country is usually sufficiently open to enable the hunter to enjoy all
the charm of distant landscapes. Where the wapiti lives
the spotted trout swarm in the brooks, and the wood-
grouse fly upward to perch among the tree-tops as the
hunter passes them. When hunting him there is always
sweet cold water to be drunk at night, and beds of aro-
matic fir boughs on which to sleep, with the blankets
drawn over one to keep out the touch of the frost. He
must be followed on foot, and the man who follows him
must be sound in limb and wind. But his pursuit does
not normally mean such wearing exhaustion as is en-
tailed by climbing cliffs all day long after the white
goat. Whoever has hunted the wapiti, as he looks at his
trophies will always think of the great mountains with
the snow lying in the rifts in their sides; of the splashing
murmur of rock-choked torrents; of the odorous breath
of the pine branches; of tents pitched in open glades;
of long walks through cool, open forests; and of great
camp-fires, where the pitchy stumps flame like giant
torches in the darkness.

In the old days, of course, much of the hunting was

done on the open plains or among low, rugged hills. The wapiti that I shot when living at my Little Missouri ranch were killed under exactly the same conditions as mule-deer. When I built my ranch-house, wapiti were still not uncommon, and their shed antlers were very numerous both on the bottoms and in places among the hills. There was one such place a couple of miles from my ranch in a stretch of comparatively barren but very broken hill-country in which there were many score of these shed antlers. Evidently a few years before this had been a great gathering-place for wapiti toward the end of winter. My ranch itself derived its name, " The Elkhorn," from the fact that on the ground where we built it were found the skulls and interlocked antlers of two wapiti bulls who had perished from getting their antlers fastened in a battle. I never, however, killed a wapiti while on a day's hunt from the ranch itself. Those that I killed were obtained on regular expeditions, when I took the wagon and drove off to spend a night or two on ground too far for me to hunt it through in a single day from the ranch. Moreover, the wapiti on the Little Missouri had been so hunted that they had entirely abandoned the diurnal habits of their kind, and it was a great advantage to get on the ground early. This hunting was not carried on amid the glorious mountain scenery which marks the home of the wapiti in the Rockies; but the surroundings had a charm of their own. All really wild scenery is attractive. The true hunter, the true lover of the wilderness, loves all parts of the wilderness, just as the true lover of nature loves all seasons. There is no season of the year when the country is not more attractive than the city; and there is no portion of the wilderness, where game is found, in which it is not a keen pleasure to hunt. Perhaps no other kind of country quite equals that where snow lies on the lofty mountain peaks, where there are many open glades in the pine forests, and clear mountain lakes and rushing trout-filled torrents. But the fantastic desolation of the Bad Lands, and the endless sweep of the brown prairies, alike have their fascination for the true lover of nature and lover of the wilderness who goes through them on foot or on horseback. As for the broken hill-country in which I followed the wapiti and the mule-deer along the Little Missouri, it would be strange indeed if any one found it otherwise than attractive in the bright, sharp fall weather. Long, grassy valleys wound among the boldly shaped hills. The basins were filled with wind-beaten trees and brush, which generally also ran alongside of the dry watercourses down the middle of each valley. Cedars clustered in the sheer ravines, and here and there groups of elm and ash grew to a considerable height in the more sheltered places. At the first touch of the frost the foliage turned russet or yellow—the Virginia creepers crimson. Under the cloudless blue sky the air was fresh and cool, and as we lay by the camp-fire at night the stars shone with extraordinary brilliancy. Under such conditions the actual chase of the wapiti was much like that of the mule-deer. They had been so hunted that they showed none of the foolish traits which they are prone to exhibit when bands are found in regions where they have been

TROPHIES OF A SUCCESSFUL HUNT

little persecuted; and they were easier to kill than mule-deer simply because they were more readily tracked and more readily seen, and offered a larger, and on the whole a steadier, mark at which to shoot. When a small band had visited a pool their tracks could be identified at once, because in the soft ground the flexible feet spread and yielded so as to leave the marks of the false hoofs. On ordinary ground it was difficult to tell their footprints from those of the yearling and two-year-old ranch cattle.

But the mountains are the true ground for the wapiti. Here he must be hunted on foot, and nowadays, since he has grown wiser, skill and patience, and the capacity to endure fatigue and exposure, must be shown by the successful hunter. My own wapiti-hunting has been done in September and early October during the height of the rut, and therefore at a time when the conditions were most favorable for the hunter. I have hunted them in many places throughout the Rockies, from the Big Horn in western Wyoming to the Big Hole Basin in western Montana, close to the Idaho line. Where I hunted, the wapiti were always very noisy both by day and by night, and at least half of the bulls that I killed attracted my attention by their calling before I saw either them or their tracks. At night they frequently passed close to camp, or came nearly up to the picketed horses, challenging all the time. More than once I slipped out, hoping to kill one by moonlight, but I never succeeded. Occasionally, when they were plentiful, and were restless and always roving about, I simply sat still on a log, until one gave me a chance. Sometimes I came across them while hunting through likely localities, going up or across wind, keeping the sharpest lookout, and moving with great care and caution, until I happened to strike the animals I was after. More than once I took the trail of a band, when out with some first-class woodsman, and after much running, dodging, and slipping through the timber, overtook the animals—though usually when thus merely following the trail I failed to come up with them. On two different occasions I followed and came up to bands, attracted by their scent. Wapiti have a strong, and, on the whole, pleasing scent, like that of Alderney cattle, although in old bulls it becomes offensively strong. This scent is very penetrating. I once smelt a herd which was lying quite still taking its noonday siesta, certainly half a mile to the windward of me; and creeping up I shot a good bull as he lay. On another occasion, while working through the tangled trees and underbrush at the bottom of a little winding valley, I suddenly smelt wapiti ahead, and without paying any further attention to the search for tracks, I hunted cautiously up the valley, and when it forked was able to decide by the smell alone which way the wapiti had gone. He was going up wind ahead of me, and his ground-covering walk kept me at a trot in order to overtake him. Finally I saw him, before he saw me, and then, by making a run to one side, got a shot at him when he broke cover, and dropped him.

It is exciting to creep up to a calling wapiti. If it is a solitary bull, he is apt to be travelling, seeking the cows, or on the lookout for some rival of weaker thews.

Under such circumstances only hard running will enable the hunter to overtake him, unless there is a chance to cut him off. If, however, he hears another bull, or has a herd under him, the chances are that he is nearly stationary, or at least is moving slowly, and the hunter has every opportunity to approach. In a herd the bull himself is usually so absorbed both with his cows and with his rivals that he is not at all apt to discover the approaching hunter. The cows, however, are thoroughly awake, and it is their eyes and keen noses for which the hunter must look out. A solitary bull which is answering the challenge of another is the easiest of all to approach. Of course, if there has been much hunting, even such a bull is wary and is on the lookout for harm. But in remote localities he becomes so absorbed in finding out the whereabouts of his rival, and is so busy answering the latter's challenges and going through motions of defiance, that with proper care it is comparatively easy to approach him. Once, when within seventy yards of such a bull, he partly made me out and started toward me. Evidently he could not tell exactly what I was— my buckskin shirt probably helping to puzzle him—and in his anger and eagerness he did not think of danger until it was too late. On another occasion I got up to two bulls that were fighting, and killed both. In the fights, weight of body seems to count for more than size of antlers.

Once I spent the better part of a day in following a wapiti bull before I finally got him. Generally when hunting wapiti I have been with either one of my men from the ranch or a hunter like Tazewell Woody, or John Willis. On this particular occasion, however, I happened to be alone; and though I have rarely been as successful alone as when in the company of some thoroughly trained and experienced plainsman or mountainman, yet when success does come under such circumstances it is always a matter of peculiar pride.

At the time, I was camped in a beautiful valley high among the mountains which divide southwestern Montana from Idaho. The weather was cold, and there were a couple of inches of snow on the ground, so that the conditions were favorable for tracking and stalking. The country was well wooded, but the forest was not dense, and there were many open glades. Early one morning, just about dawn, the cook, who had been up for a few minutes, waked me, to say that a bull wapiti was calling not far off. I rolled out of my bed and was dressed in short order. The bull had by this time passed the camp, and was travelling toward a range of mountains on the other side of the stream which ran down the valley bottom. He was evidently not alarmed, for he was still challenging. I gulped down a cup of hot coffee, munched a piece of hardtack, and thrust four or five other pieces and a cold elk tongue into my hunting-shirt, and then, as it had grown light enough to travel, started after the wapiti. I supposed that in a few minutes I should either have overtaken him or abandoned the pursuit, and I took the food with me simply because in the wilderness it never pays to be unprepared for emergencies. The wisdom of such a course was shown in this instance by the fact that I did not see camp again until long after dark.

I at first tried to cut off the wapiti by trotting through the woods toward the pass for which I supposed he was headed. The morning was cold, and, as always happens at the outset when one starts to take violent exercise under such circumstances, the running caused me to break into a perspiration; so that the first time I stopped to listen for the wapiti a regular fog rose over my glasses and then froze on them. I could not see a thing, and after wiping them found I had to keep gently moving in order to prevent them from clouding over again. It is on such cold mornings, or else in very rainy weather, that the man who has not been gifted with good eyes is most sensible of his limitations. I once lost a caribou which I had been following at speed over the snow because when I came into sight and halted the moisture instantly formed and froze on my glasses so that I could not see anything, and before I got them clear the game had vanished. Whatever happened, I was bound that I should not lose this wapiti from a similar accident.

However, when I next heard him he had evidently changed his course and was going straight away from me. The sun had now risen, and following after him I soon found his tracks. He was walking forward with the regular wapiti stride, and I made up my mind I had a long chase ahead of me. We were going up hill, and though I walked hard, I did not trot until we topped the crest. Then I jogged along at a good gait, and as I had on moccasins, and the woods were open, I did not have to exercise much caution. Accordingly I gained, and felt I was about to come up with him, when the wind brought down from very far off another challenge. My bull heard it before I did, and instantly started toward the spot at a trot. There was not the slightest use of my attempting to keep up with this, and I settled down into a walk. Half an hour afterward I came over a slight crest, and immediately saw a herd of wapiti ahead of me, across the valley and on an open hillside. The herd was in commotion, the master bull whistling vigorously and rounding up his cows, evidently much excited at the new bull's approach. There were two or three yearlings and two-year-old bulls on the outskirts of the herd, and the master bull, whose temper had evidently not been improved by the coming of the stranger, occasionally charged these and sent them rattling off through the bushes. The ground was so open between me and them that I dared not venture across it, and I was forced to lie still and await developments. The bull I had been following and the herd bull kept challenging vigorously, but the former probably recognized in the latter a heavier animal, and could not rouse his courage to the point of actually approaching and doing battle. It by no means follows that the animal with the heaviest body has the best antlers, but the hesitation thus shown by the bull I was following made me feel that the other would probably yield the more valuable trophies, and after a couple of hours I made up my mind to try to get near the herd, abandoning the animal I had been after.

The herd showed but little symptoms of moving, the

cows when let alone scattering out to graze, and some of them even lying down. Accordingly I did not hurry myself, and spent considerably over an hour in slipping off to the right and approaching through a belt of small firs. Unfortunately, however, the wind had slightly shifted, and while I was out of sight of the herd they had also come down toward the spot from whence I had been watching them. Accordingly, just as I was beginning to creep forward with the utmost caution, expecting to see them at any moment, I heard a thumping and cracking of branches that showed they were on the run. With wapiti there is always a chance of overtaking them after they have first started, because they tack and veer and halt to look around. Therefore I ran forward as fast as I could through the woods; but when I came to the edge of the fir belt I saw that the herd were several hundred yards off. They were clustered together and looking back, and saw me at once.

Off they started again. The old bull, however, had neither seen me nor smelt me, and when I heard his whistle of rage I knew he had misinterpreted the reason for the departure of his cows, and in another moment he came in sight, evidently bent on rounding them up. On his way he attacked and drove off one of the yearlings, and then took after the cows, while the yearling ran toward the outlying bull. The latter evidently failed to understand what had happened; at least he showed no signs of alarm. Neither, however, did he attempt to follow the fleeing herd, but started off again on his own line.

I was sure the herd would not stop for some miles,

and accordingly I resumed my chase of the single bull. He walked for certainly three miles before he again halted, and I was then half a mile behind him. On this occasion he struck a small belt of woodland and began to travel to and fro through it, probably with an idea of lying down. I was able to get up fairly close by crawling on all-fours through the snow for part of the distance; but just as I was about to fire he moved slightly, and though my shot hit him, it went a little too far back. He plunged over the hill crest and was off at a gallop, and after running forward and failing to overtake him in the first rush, I sat down to consider matters. The snow had begun to melt under the sun, and my knees and the lower parts of my sleeves were wet from my crawl, and I was tired and hungry and very angry at having failed to kill the wapiti. It was, however, early in the afternoon, and I thought that if I let the wapiti alone for an hour, he would lie down, and then grow stiff and reluctant to get up; while in the snow I was sure I could easily follow his tracks. Therefore I ate my lunch, and then swallowed some mouthfuls of snow in lieu of drinking.

An hour afterward I took the trail. It was evident the bull was hard hit, but even after he had changed his plunging gallop for a trot he showed no signs of stopping; fortunately his trail did not cross any other. The blood signs grew infrequent, and two or three times he went up places which made it difficult for me to believe he was much hurt. At last, however, I came to where he had lain down; but he had risen again and gone forward. For a moment I feared that my approach had

TROPHIES IN THE WHITE HOUSE DINING-ROOM

alarmed him, but this was evidently not the case, for he was now walking. I left the trail, and turning to one side below the wind I took a long circle and again struck back to the bottom of the valley down which the wapiti had been travelling. The timber here was quite thick, and I moved very cautiously, continually halting and listening for five or ten minutes. Not a sound did I hear, and I crossed the valley bottom and began to ascend the other side without finding the trail. Unless he had turned off up the mountains I knew that this meant he must have lain down; so I retraced my steps and with extreme caution began to make my way up the valley. Finally I came to a little opening, and after peering about for five minutes I stepped forward, and instantly heard a struggling and crashing in a clump of young spruce on the other side. It was the wapiti trying to get on his feet. I ran forward at my best pace, and as he was stiff and slow in his movements I was within seventy yards before he got fairly under way. Dropping on one knee, I fired and hit him in the flank. At the moment I could not tell whether or not I had missed him, for he gave no sign; but, running forward very fast, I speedily saw him standing with his head down. He heard me and again started, but at the third bullet down he went in his tracks, the antlers clattering loudly on the branches of a dead tree.

The snow was melting fast, and for fear it might go off entirely, so that I could not follow my back track, I went up the hillside upon which the wapiti lay, and taking a dead tree dragged it down to the bottom, leaving a long furrow. I then repeated the operation on the opposite hillside, thus making a trace which it was impossible for any one coming up or down the valley to overlook; and having conned certain landmarks by which the valley itself could be identified, I struck toward camp at a round trot; for I knew that if I did not get into the valley where the tent lay before dark, I should have to pass the night out. However, the last uncertain light of dusk just enabled me to get over a spur from which I could catch a glimpse of the camp-fire, and as I stumbled toward it through the forest I heard a couple of shots, which showed that the cook and packer were getting anxious as to my whereabouts.

CHAPTER IX

THE most striking and melancholy feature in connection with American big game is the rapidity with which it has vanished. When, just before the outbreak of the Revolutionary War, the rifle-bearing hunters of the backwoods first penetrated the great forests west of the Alleghanies, deer, elk, black bear, and even buffalo, swarmed in what are now the States of Kentucky and Tennessee, and the country north of the Ohio was a great and almost virgin hunting-ground. From that day to this the shrinkage has gone on, only partially checked here and there, and never arrested as a whole. As a matter of historical accuracy, however, it is well to bear in mind that many writers, in lamenting this extinction of the game, have from time to time anticipated or overstated the facts. Thus as good an author as Colonel Richard Irving Dodge spoke of the buffalo as practically extinct, while the great Northern herd still existed in countless thousands. As early as 1880 sporting authorities spoke not only of the buffalo, but of the elk, deer, and antelope as no longer to be found in plenty; and recently one of the greatest of living hunters has stated that it is no longer possible to find any American wapiti bearing heads comparable with the red deer of Hungary. As a matter of fact, in the

early eighties there were still large regions where every
species of game that had ever been known within historic
times on our continent was still to be found as plentifully
as ever.   In the early nineties there were still big tracts
of wilderness in which this was true of all game except
the buffalo; for instance, it was true of the elk in portions
of northwestern Wyoming, of the blacktail in northwestern Colorado, of the whitetail here and there in the
Indian Territory, and of the antelope in parts of New
Mexico.   Even at the present day there are smaller, but
still considerable, regions where these four animals are
yet found in abundance; and I have seen antlers of wapiti
shot since 1900 far surpassing any of which there is record
from Hungary.   In New England and New York, as
well as New Brunswick and Nova Scotia, the whitetail
deer is more plentiful than it was thirty years ago, and
in Maine (and to an even greater extent in New Brunswick) the moose, and here and there the caribou, have, on
the whole, increased during the same period.   There is
yet ample opportunity for the big game hunter in the
United States, Canada and Alaska.

While it is necessary to give this word of warning to
those who, in praising time past, always forget the opportunities of the present, it is a thousandfold more necessary to remember that these opportunities are, nevertheless, vanishing; and if we are a sensible people, we will
make it our business to see that the process of extinction
is arrested.   At the present moment the great herds of
caribou are being butchered, as in the past the great herds
of bison and wapiti have been butchered.   Every be-

liever in manliness, and therefore in manly sport, and every lover of nature, every man who appreciates the majesty and beauty of the wilderness and of wild life, should strike hands with the far-sighted men who wish to preserve our material resources, in the effort to keep our forests and our game beasts, game birds, and game fish—indeed, all the living creatures of prairie, and woodland, and seashore—from wanton destruction.

Above all, we should realize that the effort toward this end is essentially a democratic movement. It is entirely in our power as a nation to preserve large tracts of wilderness, which are valueless for agricultural purposes and unfit for settlement, as playgrounds for rich and poor alike, and to preserve the game so that it shall continue to exist for the benefit of all lovers of nature, and to give reasonable opportunities for the exercise of the skill of the hunter, whether he is or is not a man of means. But this end can only be achieved by wise laws and by a resolute enforcement of the laws. Lack of such legislation and administration will result in harm to all of us, but most of all in harm to the nature lover who does not possess vast wealth. Already there have sprung up here and there through the country, as in New Hampshire and the Adirondacks, large private preserves. These preserves often serve a useful purpose, and should be encouraged within reasonable limits; but it would be a misfortune if they increased beyond a certain extent or if they took the place of great tracts of wild land, which continue as such either because of their very nature, or because of the protection of the State exerted in the form of making them State or national parks or reserves. It is foolish to regard proper game laws as undemocratic, unrepublican. On the contrary, they are essentially in the interests of the people as a whole, because it is only through their enactment and enforcement that the people as a whole can preserve the game and can prevent its becoming purely the property of the rich, who are able to create and maintain extensive private preserves. The wealthy man can get hunting anyhow, but the man of small means is dependent solely upon wise and well-executed game laws for his enjoyment of the sturdy pleasure of the chase. In Maine, in Vermont, in the Adirondacks, even in parts of Massachusetts and on Long Island, people have waked up to this fact, particularly so far as the common white-tail deer is concerned, and in Maine also as regards the moose and caribou. The effect is shown in the increase in these animals. Such game protection results, in the first place, in securing to the people who live in the neighborhood permanent opportunities for hunting; and in the next place, it provides no small source of wealth to the locality because of the visitors which it attracts. A deer wild in the woods is worth to the people of the neighborhood many times the value of its carcass, because of the way it attracts sportsmen, who give employment and leave money behind them.

True sportsmen, worthy of the name, men who shoot only in season and in moderation, do no harm whatever to game. The most objectionable of all game destroyers is, of course, the kind of game butcher who simply kills for the sake of the record of slaughter, who leaves deer and ducks and prairie-chickens to rot after he has slain them. Such a man is wholly obnoxious; and, indeed, so is any man who shoots for the purpose of establishing a record of the amount of game killed. To my mind this is one very unfortunate feature of what is otherwise the admirably sportsmanlike English spirit in these matters. The custom of shooting great bags of deer, grouse, partridges, and pheasants, the keen rivalry in making such bags, and their publication in sporting journals, are symptoms of a spirit which is most unhealthy from every standpoint. It is to be earnestly hoped that every American hunting or fishing club will strive to inculcate among its own members, and in the minds of the general public, that anything like an excessive bag, any destruction for the sake of making a record, is to be severely reprobated.

But after all, this kind of perverted sportsman, unworthy though he be, is not the chief actor in the destruction of our game. The professional skin or market hunter is the real offender. Yet he is of all others the man who would ultimately be most benefited by the preservation of the game. The frontier settler, in a thoroughly wild country, is certain to kill game for his own use. As long as he does no more than this, it is hard to blame him; although if he is awake to his own interests he will soon realize that to him, too, the live deer is worth far more than the dead deer, because of the way in which it brings money into the wilderness. The professional market hunter who kills game for the hide, or for the feathers, or for the meat, or to sell antlers and other trophies; the market men who put game in cold storage; and the rich people, who are content to buy what they have not the skill to get by their own exertions—these are the men who are the real enemies of game. Where there is no law which checks the market hunters, the inevitable result of their butchery is that the game is completely destroyed, and with it their own means of livelihood. If, on the other hand, they were willing to preserve it, they could make much more money by acting as guides. In northwestern Colorado, at the present moment, there are still blacktail deer in abundance, and some elk are left. Colorado has fairly good game laws, but they are indifferently enforced. The country in which the game is found can probably never support any but a very sparse population, and a large portion of the summer range is practically useless for settlement. If the people of Colorado generally, and above all the people of the counties in which the game is located, would resolutely cooperate with those of their own number who are already alive to the importance of preserving the game, it could, without difficulty, be kept always as abundant as it now is, and this beautiful region would be a permanent health resort and playground for the people of a large part of the Union. Such action would be a benefit to every one, but it would be a benefit most of all to the people of the immediate locality.

The practical common sense of the American people has been in no way made more evident during the last few years than by the creation and use of a series of large land reserves—situated for the most part on the great plains and among the mountains of the West—intended to keep the forests from destruction, and therefore to conserve the water supply. These reserves are, and should be, created primarily for economic purposes. The semi-arid regions can only support a reasonable population under conditions of the strictest economy and wisdom in the use of the water supply, and in addition to their other economic uses the forests are indispensably necessary for the preservation of the water supply and for rendering possible its useful distribution throughout the proper seasons. In addition, however, to this economic use of the wilderness, selected portions of it have been kept here and there in a state of nature, not merely for the sake of preserving the forests and the water, but for the sake of preserving all its beauties and wonders unspoiled by greedy and short-sighted vandalism. What has been actually accomplished in the Yellowstone Park affords the best possible object-lesson as to the desirability and practicability of establishing such wilderness reserves. This reserve is a natural breeding-ground and nursery for those stately and beautiful haunters of the wilds which have now vanished from so many of the great forests, the vast lonely plains, and the high mountain ranges, where they once abounded.

On April 8, 1903, John Burroughs and I reached the Yellowstone Park, and were met by Major John Pitcher of the Regular Army, the Superintendent of the Park. The Major and I forthwith took horses; he telling me that he could show me a good deal of game while riding up to his house at the Mammoth Hot Springs. Hardly had we left the little town of Gardiner and gotten within the limits of the Park before we saw prongbuck. There was a band of at least a hundred feeding some distance from the road. We rode leisurely toward them. They were tame compared to their kindred in unprotected places; that is, it was easy to ride within fair rifle range of them; and though they were not familiar in the sense that we afterwards found the bighorn and the deer to be familiar, it was extraordinary to find them showing such familiarity almost literally in the streets of a frontier town. It spoke volumes for the good sense and law-abiding spirit of the people of the town. During the two hours following my entry into the Park we rode around the plains and lower slopes of the foothills in the neighborhood of the mouth of the Gardiner and we saw several hundred—probably a thousand all told —of these antelopes. Major Pitcher informed me that all the pronghorns in the Park wintered in this neighborhood. Toward the end of April or the first of May they migrate back to their summering homes in the open valleys along the Yellowstone and in the plains south of the Golden Gate. While migrating they go over the mountains and through forests if occasion demands. Although there are plenty of coyotes in the Park, there are no big wolves, and save for very infrequent poachers the only enemy of the antelope, as indeed the only enemy of all the game, is the cougar.

Cougars, known in the Park, as elsewhere through the West, as "mountain lions," are plentiful, having increased in numbers of recent years. Except in the neighborhood

ANTELOPE IN THE STREETS OF GARDINER

of the Gardiner River, that is within a few miles of Mammoth Hot Springs, I found them feeding on elk, which in the Park far outnumber all other game put together, being so numerous that the ravages of the cougars are of no real damage to the herds. But in the neighborhood of the Mammoth Hot Springs the cougars are noxious because of the antelope, mountain sheep, and deer which they kill; and the Superintendent has imported some hounds with which to hunt them. These hounds are managed by Buffalo Jones, a famous old plainsman, who is now in the Park taking care of the buffalo. On this first day of my visit to the Park I came across the carcasses of a deer and of an antelope which the cougars had killed. On the great plains cougars rarely get antelope, but here the country is broken so that the big cats can make their stalks under favorable circumstances. To deer and mountain sheep the cougar is a most dangerous enemy—much more so than the wolf.

The antelope we saw were usually in bands of from twenty to one hundred and fifty, and they travelled strung out almost in single file, though those in the rear would sometimes bunch up. I did not try to stalk them, but got as near them as I could on horseback. The closest approach I was able to make was to within about eighty yards of two which were by themselves—I think a doe and a last year's fawn. As I was riding up to them, although they looked suspiciously at me, one actually lay down. When I was passing them at about eighty yards' distance the big one became nervous, gave a sudden jump, and away the two went at full speed.

Why the prongbucks were so comparatively shy I do not know, for right on the ground with them we came upon deer, and, in the immediate neighborhood, mountain sheep, which were absurdly tame. The mountain sheep were nineteen in number, for the most part does and yearlings with a couple of three-year-old rams, but not a single big fellow—for the big fellows at this season are off by themselves, singly or in little bunches, high up in the mountains. The band I saw was tame to a degree matched by but few domestic animals.

They were feeding on the brink of a steep washout at the upper edge of one of the benches on the mountain-side just below where the abrupt slope began. They were alongside a little gully with sheer walls. I rode my horse to within forty yards of them, one of them occasionally looking up and at once continuing to feed. Then they moved slowly off and leisurely crossed the gully to the other side. I dismounted, walked around the head of the gully, and moving cautiously, but in plain sight, came closer and closer until I was within twenty yards, when I sat down on a stone and spent certainly twenty minutes looking at them. They paid hardly any attention to my presence—certainly no more than well-treated domestic creatures would pay. One of the rams rose on his hind legs, leaning his fore-hoofs against a little pine tree, and browsed the ends of the budding branches. The others grazed on the short grass and herbage or lay down and rested—two of the yearlings several times playfully butting at one another. Now and then one would glance in my direction without the slightest sign of fear—barely

even of curiosity. I have no question whatever but that
with a little patience this particular band could be made
to feed out of a man's hand. Major Pitcher intends
during the coming winter to feed them alfalfa—for game
animals of several kinds have become so plentiful in the
neighborhood of the Hot Springs, and the Major has
grown so interested in them, that he wishes to do something toward feeding them during the severe weather.
After I had looked at the sheep to my heart's content,
I walked back to my horse, my departure arousing as
little interest as my advent.

Soon after leaving them we began to come across
blacktail deer, singly, in twos and threes, and in small
bunches of a dozen or so. They were almost as tame
as the mountain sheep, but not quite. That is, they always looked alertly at me, and though if I stayed still
they would graze, they kept a watch over my movements
and usually moved slowly off when I got within less than
forty yards of them. Up to that distance, whether on
foot or on horseback, they paid but little heed to me, and
on several occasions they allowed me to come much
closer. Like the bighorn, the blacktails at this time were
grazing, not browsing; but I occasionally saw them nib-
ble some willow buds. During the winter they had been
browsing. As we got close to the Hot Springs we came
across several whitetail in an open, marshy meadow.
They were not quite as tame as the blacktail, although
without any difficulty I walked up to within fifty yards
of them. Handsome though the blacktail is, the whitetail is the most beautiful of all deer when in motion,

because of the springy, bounding grace of its trot and canter, and the way it carries its head and white flag aloft.

Before reaching the Mammoth Hot Springs we also saw a number of ducks in the little pools and on the Gardiner. Some of them were rather shy. Others— probably those which, as Major Pitcher informed me, had spent the winter there—were as tame as barn-yard fowls.

Just before reaching the post the Major took me into the big field where Buffalo Jones had some Texas and Flathead Lake buffalo—bulls and cows—which he was tending with solicitous care. The original stock of buffalo in the Park have now been reduced to fifteen or twenty individuals, and their blood is being recruited by the addition of buffalo purchased out of the Flathead Lake and Texas Panhandle herds. The buffalo were at first put within a wire fence, which, when it was built, was found to have included both blacktail and whitetail deer. A bull elk was also put in with them at one time, he having met with some accident which made the Major and Buffalo Jones bring him in to doctor him. When he recovered his health he became very cross. Not only would he attack men, but also buffalo, even the old and surly master bull, thumping them savagely with his antlers if they did anything to which he objected. The buffalo are now breeding well.

When I reached the post and dismounted at the Major's house, I supposed my experiences with wild beasts were ended for the day; but this was an error. The

BLACKTAIL DEER ON PARADE GROUND

quarters of the officers and men and the various hotel buildings, stables, residences of the civilian officials, etc., almost completely surround the big parade-ground at the post, near the middle of which stands the flag-pole, while the gun used for morning and evening salutes is well off to one side. There are large gaps between some of the buildings, and Major Pitcher informed me that throughout the winter he had been leaving alfalfa on the parade-grounds, and that numbers of blacktail deer had been in the habit of visiting it every day, sometimes as many as seventy being on the parade-ground at once. As spring-time came on the numbers diminished. However, in mid-afternoon, while I was writing in my room in Major Pitcher's house, on looking out of the window I saw five deer on the parade-ground. They were as tame as so many Alderney cows, and when I walked out I got within twenty yards of them without any difficulty. It was most amusing to see them as the time approached for the sunset gun to be fired. The notes of the trumpeter attracted their attention at once. They all looked at him eagerly. One of them resumed feeding, and paid no attention whatever either to the bugle, the gun or the flag. The other four, however, watched the preparations for firing the gun with an intent gaze, and at the sound of the report gave two or three jumps; then instantly wheeling, looked up at the flag as it came down. This they seemed to regard as something rather more suspicious than the gun, and they remained very much on the alert until the ceremony was over. Once it was finished, they resumed feeding as if nothing had happened.

Before it was dark they trotted away from the parade-ground back to the mountains.

The next day we rode off to the Yellowstone River, camping some miles below Cottonwood Creek. It was a very pleasant camp. Major Pitcher, an old friend, had a first-class pack-train, so that we were as comfortable as possible, and on such a trip there could be no pleasanter or more interesting companion than John Burroughs—"Oom John," as we soon grew to call him. Where our tents were pitched the bottom of the valley was narrow, the mountains rising steep and cliff-broken on either side. There were quite a number of blacktail in the valley, which were tame and unsuspicious, although not nearly as much so as those in the immediate neighborhood of the Mammoth Hot Springs. One mid-afternoon three of them swam across the river a hundred yards above our camp. But the characteristic animals of the region were the elk—the wapiti. They were certainly more numerous than when I was last through the Park twelve years before.

In the summer the elk spread all over the interior of the Park. As winter approaches they divide, some going north and others south. The southern bands, which, at a guess, may possibly include ten thousand individuals, winter out of the Park, for the most part in Jackson's Hole—though of course here and there within the limits of the Park a few elk may spend both winter and summer in an unusually favorable location. It was the members of the northern band that I met. During the winter time they are nearly stationary, each band staying within a very few miles of the same place, and from their size and the open nature of their habitat it is almost as easy to count them as if they were cattle. From a spur of Bison Peak one day, Major Pitcher, the guide Elwood Hofer, John Burroughs and I spent about four hours with the glasses counting and estimating the different herds within sight. After most careful work and cautious reduction of estimates in each case to the minimum the truth would permit, we reckoned three thousand head of elk, all lying or feeding and all in sight at the same time. An estimate of some fifteen thousand for the number of elk in these Northern bands cannot be far wrong. These bands do not go out of the Park at all, but winter just within its northern boundary. At the time when we saw them, the snow had vanished from the bottoms of the valleys and the lower slopes of the mountains, but remained as continuous sheets farther up their sides. The elk were for the most part found up on the snow slopes, occasionally singly or in small gangs—more often in bands of from fifty to a couple of hundred. The larger bulls were highest up the mountains and generally in small troops by themselves, although occasionally one or two would be found associating with a big herd of cows, yearlings, and two-year-olds. Many of the bulls had shed their antlers; many had not. During the winter the elk had evidently done much browsing, but at this time they were grazing almost exclusively, and seemed by preference to seek out the patches of old grass which were last left bare by the retreating snow. The bands moved about very little, and if one were seen one day it was generally possible to find

it within a few hundred yards of the same spot the next
day, and certainly not more than a mile or two off. There
were severe frosts at night, and occasionally light flurries
of snow; but the hardy beasts evidently cared nothing for
any but heavy storms, and seemed to prefer to lie in the
snow rather than upon the open ground. They fed at
irregular hours throughout the day, just like cattle; one
band might be lying down while another was feeding.
While travelling they usually went almost in single file.
Evidently the winter had weakened them, and they were
not in condition for running; for on the one or two occasions when I wanted to see them close up I ran right into
them on horseback, both on level plains and going up
hill along the sides of rather steep mountains. One band
in particular I practically rounded up for John Burroughs, finally getting them to stand in a huddle while
he and I sat on our horses less than fifty yards off. After
they had run a little distance they opened their mouths
wide and showed evident signs of distress.

We came across a good many carcasses. Two, a bull
and a cow, had died from scab. Over half the remainder
had evidently perished from cold or starvation. The
others, including a bull, three cows and a score of yearlings, had been killed by cougars. In the Park the cougar is at present their only animal foe. The cougars
were preying on nothing but elk in the Yellowstone Valley, and kept hanging about the neighborhood of the big
bands. Evidently they usually selected some outlying
yearling, stalked it as it lay or as it fed, and seized it
by the head and throat. The bull which they killed was

in a little open valley by himself, many miles from any other elk. The cougar which killed it, judging from its tracks, was a big male. As the elk were evidently rather too numerous for the feed, I do not think the cougars were doing any damage.

Coyotes are plentiful, but the elk evidently have no dread of them. One day I crawled up to within fifty yards of a band of elk lying down. A coyote was walking about among them, and beyond an occasional look they paid no heed to him. He did not venture to go within fifteen or twenty paces of any one of them. In fact, except the cougar, I saw but one living thing attempt to molest the elk. This was a golden eagle. We saw several of these great birds. On one occasion we had ridden out to the foot of a sloping mountain side, dotted over with bands and strings of elk amounting in the aggregate probably to a thousand head. Most of the bands were above the snow-line—some appearing away back toward the ridge crests, and looking as small as mice. There was one band well below the snow-line, and toward this we rode. While the elk were not shy or wary, in the sense that a hunter would use the words, they were by no means as familiar as the deer; and this particular band of elk, some twenty or thirty in all, watched us with interest as we approached. When we were still half a mile off they suddenly started to run toward us, evidently frightened by something. They ran quartering, and when about four hundred yards away we saw that an eagle was after them. Soon it swooped, and a yearling in the rear, weakly, and probably frightened by the swoop, turned a complete somersault, and when it recovered its feet stood still. The great bird followed the rest of the band across a little ridge, beyond which they disappeared. Then it returned, soaring high in the heavens, and after two or three wide circles, swooped down at the solitary yearling, its legs hanging down. We halted at two hundred yards to see the end. But the eagle could not quite make up its mind to attack. Twice it hovered within a foot or two of the yearling's head, again flew off and again returned. Finally the yearling trotted off after the rest of the band, and the eagle returned to the upper air. Later we found the carcass of a yearling, with two eagles, not to mention ravens and magpies, feeding on it; but I could not tell whether they had themselves killed the yearling or not.

Here and there in the region where the elk were abundant we came upon horses, which for some reason had been left out through the winter. They were much wilder than the elk. Evidently the Yellowstone Park is a natural nursery and breeding-ground of the elk, which here, as said above, far outnumber all the other game put together. In the winter, if they cannot get to open water, they eat snow; but in several places where there had been springs which kept open all winter, we could see by the tracks that they had been regularly used by bands of elk. The men working at the new road along the face of the cliffs beside the Yellowstone River near Tower Falls informed me that in October enormous droves of elk coming from the interior of the Park and travelling northward to the lower lands had crossed the Yellow-

ELK IN SNOW

stone just above Tower Falls. Judging by their description, the elk had crossed by thousands in an uninter-
rupted stream, the passage taking many hours. In fact
nowadays these Yellowstone elk are, with the exception
of the Arctic caribou, the only American game which
at times travel in immense droves like the buffalo of the
old days.

A couple of days after leaving Cottonwood Creek—
where we had spent several days—we camped at the Yellowstone Canyon below Tower Falls. Here we saw a
second band of mountain sheep, numbering only eight—
none of them old rams. We were camped on the west
side of the canyon; the sheep had their abode on the opposite side, where they had spent the winter. It has
recently been customary among some authorities, especially the English hunters and naturalists who have
written of the Asiatic sheep, to speak as if sheep were
naturally creatures of the plains rather than mountain
climbers. I know nothing of the Old World sheep, but
the Rocky Mountain bighorn is to the full as characteristic a mountain animal, in every sense of the word, as
the chamois, and, I think, as the ibex. These sheep
were well known to the road builders, who had spent the
winter in the locality. They told me they never went
back on the plains, but throughout the winter had spent
their days and nights on the top of the cliff and along
its face. This cliff was an alternation of sheer precipices
and very steep inclines. When coated with ice it would
be difficult to imagine an uglier bit of climbing; but
throughout the winter, and even in the wildest storms,

the sheep had habitually gone down it to drink at the water below. When we first saw them they were lying sunning themselves on the edge of the canyon, where the rolling grassy country behind it broke off into the sheer descent. It was mid-afternoon and they were under some pines. After a while they got up and began to graze, and soon hopped unconcernedly down the side of the cliff until they were half-way to the bottom. They then grazed along the sides, and spent some time licking at a place where there was evidently a mineral deposit. Before dark they all lay down again on a steeply inclined jutting spur midway between the top and bottom of the canyon.

Next morning I thought I would like to see them close up, so I walked down three or four miles below where the canyon ended, crossed the stream, and came up the other side until I got on what was literally the stamping-ground of the sheep. Their tracks showed that they had spent their time for many weeks, and probably for all the winter, within a very narrow radius. For perhaps a mile and a half, or two miles at the very outside, they had wandered to and fro on the summit of the canyon, making what was almost a well-beaten path; always very near and usually on the edge of the cliff, and hardly ever going more than a few yards back into the grassy plain-and-hill country. Their tracks and dung covered the ground. They had also evidently descended into the depths of the canyon wherever there was the slightest break or even lowering in the upper line of the basalt cliffs. Although mountain sheep often browse in winter,

I saw but few traces of browsing here; probably on the sheer cliff side they always get some grazing.

When I spied the band they were lying not far from the spot in which they had lain the day before, and in the same position on the brink of the canyon. They saw me and watched me with interest when I was two hundred yards off, but they let me get up within forty yards and sit down on a large stone to look at them, without running off. Most of them were lying down, but a couple were feeding steadily throughout the time I watched them. Suddenly one took the alarm and dashed straight over the cliff, the others all following at once. I ran after them to the edge in time to see the last yearling drop off the edge of the basalt cliff and stop short on the sheer slope below, while the stones dislodged by his hoofs rattled down the canyon. They all looked up at me with great interest, and then strolled off to the edge of a jutting spur and lay down almost directly underneath me and some fifty yards off. That evening on my return to camp we watched the band make its way right down to the river bed, going over places where it did not seem possible a four-footed creature could pass. They halted to graze here and there, and down the worst places they went very fast with great bounds. It was a marvellous exhibition of climbing.

After we had finished this horseback trip we went on sleds and skis to the upper Geyser Basin and the Falls of the Yellowstone. Although it was the third week in April, the snow was still several feet deep, and only thoroughly trained snow horses could have taken the sleighs along, while around the Yellowstone Falls it was possible to move only on snowshoes. There was little life in those woods. In the upper basin I caught a meadow mouse on the snow; I afterwards sent it to Hart Merriam, who told me it was of a species he had described from Idaho, *Microtus nanus;* it had not been previously found in the Yellowstone region. We saw an occasional pine squirrel, snowshoe rabbit or marten; and in the open meadows around the hot waters there were Canada geese and ducks of several species, and now and then a coyote. Around camp Clark's crows and Stellar's jays, and occasionally magpies, came to pick at the refuse; and of course they were accompanied by the whiskey jacks, which behaved with their usual astounding familiarity. At Norris Geyser Basin there was a perfect chorus of bird music from robins, western purple finches, juncos and mountain bluebirds. In the woods there were mountain chickadees and pygmy nuthatches, together with an occasional woodpecker. In the northern country we had come across a very few blue grouse and ruffed grouse, both as tame as possible. We had seen a pygmy owl no larger than a robin sitting on the top of a pine in broad daylight, and uttering at short intervals a queer un-owl-like cry.

The birds that interested us most were the solitaires, and especially the dippers or water-ousels. We were fortunate enough to hear the solitaires sing not only when perched on trees, but on the wing, soaring over a great canyon. They are striking birds in every way, and their habit of singing while soaring, and their song, are alike

OOM JOHN

noteworthy. Once I heard a solitaire singing at the top of a canyon, and an ousel also singing but a thousand feet below him; and in this case I thought the ousel sang better than his unconscious rival. The ousels are to my mind wellnigh the most attractive of all our birds, because of their song, their extraordinary habits, their whole personality. They stay through the winter in the Yellowstone because the waters are in many places open. We heard them singing cheerfully, their ringing melody having a certain suggestion of the winter wren's. Usually they sang while perched on some rock on the edge or in the middle of the stream; but sometimes on the wing; and often just before dipping under the torrent, or just after slipping out from it onto some ledge of rock or ice. In the open places the Western meadow lark was uttering its beautiful song; a real song as compared to the plaintive notes of its Eastern brother, and though short, yet with continuity and tune as well as melody. I love to hear the Eastern meadow lark in the early spring; but I love still more the song of the Western meadow lark. No bird escaped John Burroughs' eye; no bird note escaped his ear.

I cannot understand why the Old World ousel should have received such comparatively scant attention in the books, whether from nature writers or poets; whereas our ousel has greatly impressed all who know him. John Muir's description comes nearest doing him justice. To me he seems a more striking bird than for instance the skylark; though of course I not only admire but am very fond of the skylark. There are various pipits and larks in our own country which sing in highest air, as does the skylark, and their songs, though not as loud, are almost as sustained; and though they lack the finer kind of melody, so does his. The ousel, on the contrary, is a really brilliant singer, and in his habits he is even farther removed from the commonplace and the uninteresting than the lark himself. Some birds, such as the ousel, the mocking-bird, the solitaire, show marked originality, marked distinction; others do not; the chipping sparrow, for instance, while in no way objectionable (like the imported house sparrow), is yet a hopelessly commonplace little bird alike in looks, habits and voice.

On the last day of my stay it was arranged that I should ride down from Mammoth Hot Springs to the town of Gardiner, just outside the Park limits, and there make an address at the laying of the corner-stone of the arch by which the main road is to enter the Park. Some three thousand people had gathered to attend the ceremonies. A little over a mile from Gardiner we came down out of the hills to the flat plain; from the hills we could see the crowd gathered around the arch waiting for me to come. We put spurs to our horses and cantered rapidly toward the appointed place, and on the way we passed within forty yards of a score of blacktails, which merely moved to one side and looked at us, and within almost as short a distance of half a dozen antelope. To any lover of nature it could not help being a delightful thing to see the wild and timid creatures of the wilderness rendered so tame; and their tameness in the immediate neighborhood of Gardiner, on the very edge of the Park,

BEARS AND TOURISTS

spoke volumes for the patriotic good sense of the citizens
of Montana. At times the antelope actually cross the
Park line to Gardiner, which is just outside, and feed
unmolested in the very streets of the town; a fact which
shows how very far advanced the citizens of Gardiner
are in right feeling on this subject; for of course the
Federal laws cease to protect the antelope as soon as they
are out of the Park. Major Pitcher informed me that
both the Montana and Wyoming people were cooperat-
ing with him in zealous fashion to preserve the game
and put a stop to poaching. For their attitude in this
regard they deserve the cordial thanks of all Americans
interested in these great popular playgrounds, where
bits of the old wilderness scenery and the old wilderness
life are to be kept unspoiled for the benefit of our children's children. Eastern people, and especially Eastern
sportsmen, need to keep steadily in mind the fact that the
westerners who live in the neighborhood. of the forest
preserves are the men who in the last resort will determine whether or not these preserves are to be permanent.
They cannot in the long run be kept as forest and game
reservations unless the settlers roundabout believe in
them and heartily support them; and the rights of these
settlers must be carefully safeguarded, and they must be
shown that the movement is really in their interest. The
Eastern sportsman who fails to recognize these facts can
do little but harm by advocacy of forest reserves.

It was in the interior of the Park, at the hotels beside
the lake, the falls, and the various geyser basins, that
we would have seen the bears had the season been late

enough; but unfortunately the bears were still for the most part hibernating. We saw two or three tracks, but the animals themselves had not yet begun to come about the hotels. Nor were the hotels open. No visitors had previously entered the Park in the winter or early spring, the scouts and other employees being the only ones who occasionally traverse it. I was sorry not to see the bears, for the effect of protection upon bear life in the Yellowstone has been one of the phenomena of natural history. Not only have they grown to realize that they are safe, but, being natural scavengers and foul feeders, they have come to recognize the garbage heaps of the hotels as their special sources of food supply. Throughout the summer months they come to all the hotels in numbers, usually appearing in the late afternoon or evening, and they have become as indifferent to the presence of men as the deer themselves—some of them very much more indifferent. They have now taken their place among the recognized sights of the Park, and the tourists are nearly as much interested in them as in the geysers. In mussing over the garbage heaps they sometimes get tin cans stuck on their paws, and the result is painful. Buffalo Jones and some of the other scouts in extreme cases rope the bear, tie him up, cut the tin can off his paw, and let him go again. It is not an easy feat, but the astonishing thing is that it should be performed at all.

It was amusing to read the proclamations addressed to the tourists by the Park management, in which they were solemnly warned that the bears were really wild animals, and that they must on no account be either fed or teased. It is curious to think that the descendants of the great grizzlies which were the dread of the early explorers and hunters should now be semi-domesticated creatures, boldly hanging around crowded hotels for the sake of what they can pick up, and quite harmless so long as any reasonable precaution is exercised. They are much safer, for instance, than any ordinary bull or stallion, or even ram, and, in fact, there is no danger from them at all unless they are encouraged to grow too familiar or are in some way molested. Of course among the thousands of tourists there is a percentage of fools; and when fools go out in the afternoon to look at the bears feeding they occasionally bring themselves into jeopardy by some senseless act. The black bears and the cubs of the bigger bears can readily be driven up trees, and some of the tourists occasionally do this. Most of the animals never think of resenting it; but now and then one is run across which has its feelings ruffled by the performance. In the summer of 1902 the result proved disastrous to a too inquisitive tourist. He was travelling with his wife, and at one of the hotels they went out toward the garbage pile to see the bears feeding. The only bear in sight was a large she, which, as it turned out, was in a bad temper because another party of tourists a few minutes before had been chasing her cubs up a tree. The man left his wife and walked toward the bear to see how close he could get. When he was some distance off she charged him, whereupon he bolted back toward his wife. The bear overtook him, knocked him down and bit him severely. But the man's wife, without hesitation, attacked the bear with that thoroughly feminine weapon, an umbrella, and frightened her off. The man spent several weeks in the Park hospital before he recovered. Perhaps the following telegram sent by the manager of the Lake Hotel to Major Pitcher illustrates with sufficient clearness the mutual relations of the bears, the tourists, and the guardians of the public weal in the Park. The original was sent me by Major Pitcher. It runs:

" Lake. 7-27-'03. Major Pitcher, Yellowstone: As many as seventeen bears in an evening appear on my garbage dump. To-night eight or ten. Campers and people not of my hotel throw things at them to make them run away. I cannot, unless there personally, control this. Do you think you could detail a trooper to be there every evening from say six o'clock until dark and make people remain behind danger line laid out by Warden Jones? Otherwise I fear some accident. The arrest of one or two of these campers might help. My own guests do pretty well as they are told. James Barton Key. 9 A. M."

Major Pitcher issued the order as requested.

At times the bears get so bold that they take to making inroads on the kitchen. One completely terrorized a Chinese cook. It would drive him off and then feast upon whatever was left behind. When a bear begins to act in this way or to show surliness it is sometimes necessary to shoot it. Other bears are tamed until they will feed out of the hand, and will come at once if called. Not only have some of the soldiers and scouts tamed bears in this fashion, but occasionally a chambermaid or waiter

GRIZZLY BEAR AND COOK

girl at one of the hotels has thus developed a bear as a pet.

The accompanying photographs not only show bears very close up, with men standing by within a few yards of them, but they also show one bear being fed from the piazza by a cook, and another standing beside a particular friend, a chambermaid in one of the hotels. In these photographs it will be seen that some are grizzlies and some black bears.

This whole episode of bear life in the Yellowstone is so extraordinary that it will be well worth while for any man who has the right powers and enough time, to make a complete study of the life and history of the Yellowstone bears. Indeed, nothing better could be done by some of our out-door faunal naturalists than to spend at least a year in the Yellowstone, and to study the life habits of all the wild creatures therein. A man able to do this, and to write down accurately and interestingly what he had seen, would make a contribution of permanent value to our nature literature.

In May, after leaving the Yellowstone, I visited the Grand Canyon of the Colorado, and then went through the Yosemite Park with John Muir—the companion above all others for such a trip. It is hard to make comparisons among different kinds of scenery, all of them very grand and very beautiful; but nothing that I have ever seen has impressed me quite as much as the desolate and awful sublimity of the Grand Canyon of the Colorado. I earnestly wish that Congress would make it a national park, and I am sure that such course would meet the approbation of the people of Arizona. The people of California with wise and generous forethought have given the Yosemite Valley to the National Government to be kept as a national park, just as the surrounding country, including some of the groves of giant trees, has been kept. The flower-clad slopes of the Sierras—golden with the blazing poppy, brilliant with lilies and tulips and red-stemmed Manzinita bush—are unlike anything else in this country. As for the giant trees, no words can describe their majesty and beauty.

John Muir and I, with two packers and three pack mules, spent a delightful three days in the Yosemite. The first night was clear, and we lay in the open, on beds of soft fir boughs, among the huge, cinnamon-colored trunks of the sequoias. It was like lying in a great solemn cathedral, far vaster and more beautiful than any built by hand of man. Just at nightfall I heard, among other birds, thrushes which I think were Rocky Mountain hermits—the appropriate choir for such a place of worship. Next day we went by trail through the woods, seeing some deer—which were not wild—as well as mountain quail and blue grouse. Among the birds which we saw was a white-headed woodpecker; the interesting carpenter woodpeckers were less numerous than lower down. In the afternoon we struck snow, and had considerable difficulty in breaking our trails. A snow-storm came on toward evening, but we kept warm and comfortable in a grove of splendid silver firs—rightly named " magnificent "—near the brink of the wonderful Yosemite Valley. Next day we clambered down into it and

THE BEAR AND THE CHAMBERMAID

at nightfall camped in its bottom, facing the giant cliffs over which the waterfalls thundered.

Surely our people do not understand even yet the rich heritage that is theirs. There can be nothing in the world more beautiful than the Yosemite, the groves of giant sequoias and redwoods, the Canyon of the Colorado, the Canyon of the Yellowstone, the Three Tetons; and our people should see to it that they are preserved for their children and their children's children forever, with their majestic beauty all unmarred.

CHAPTER X

BOOKS ON BIG GAME

THE nineteenth century was, beyond all others, the century of big game hunters, and of books about big game. From the days of Nimrod to our own there have been mighty hunters before the Lord, and most warlike and masterful races have taken kindly to the chase, as chief among those rough pastimes which appeal naturally to men with plenty of red blood in their veins. But until the nineteenth century the difficulties of travel were so great that men of our race with a taste for sport could rarely gratify this taste except in their own neighborhood. The earlier among the great conquering kings of Egypt and Assyria, when they made their forays into Syria and the region of the Upper Euphrates, hunted the elephant and the wild bull, as well as the lions with which the country swarmed; and Tiglath-Pileser the First, as over-lord of Phœnicia, embarked on the Mediterranean, and there killed a " sea-monster," presumably a whale—a feat which has been paralleled by no sport-loving sovereign of modern times, save by that stout hunter, the German Kaiser; though I believe the present English King, like several members of his family, has slain both elephants and tigers before he came to the throne. But the elephant disappeared from Eastern Asia a thousand years before our era; and the lion had become rare or unknown in lands where the dwellers were of European stock, long before the days of written records.

There was good hunting in Macedonia in the days of Alexander the Great; there was good hunting in the Hercynian Forest when Frank and Bergund were turning Gaul into France; there was good hunting in Lithuania and Poland as late as the days of Sobiéski; but the most famous kings and nobles of Europe, within historic times, though they might kill the aurochs and the bison, the bear and the boar, had no chance to test their prowess against the mightier and more terrible beasts of the tropics.

No modern man could be more devoted to the chase than were the territorial lords of the Middle Ages. Two of the most famous books of the chase ever written were the *Livre de Chasse* of Count Gaston de Foix— Gaston Phœbus, well known to all readers of Froissart —and the translation or adaptation and continuation of the same, the " Master of Game," by that Duke of York who " died victorious " at Agincourt. Mr. Baillie-Grohman, himself a hunter and mountaineer of wide experience, a trained writer and observer, and a close student of the hunting lore of the past, has edited and reproduced the " Master of Game," in form which makes it a delight to every true lover of books no less than to every true lover of sport. A very interesting little book is Clamorgan's *Chasse du Loup*, dedicated to Charles the Ninth of France; my copy is of the edition of 1566. The text and the illustrations are almost equally attractive.

As the centuries passed it became more and more difficult to obtain sport in the thickly settled parts of Europe
save in the vast game preserves of the Kings and great
lords. These magnates of Continental Europe, down to
the beginning of the last century, followed the chase
with all the ardor of Gaston Phœbus; indeed, they erred
generally on the side of fantastic extravagance and exag-
geration in their favorite pursuit, turning it into a solemn
and rather ridiculous business instead of a healthy and
vigorous pastime; but they could hunt only the beasts of
their own forests. The men who went on long voyages
usually had quite enough to do simply as travellers; the
occupation of getting into unknown lands, and of keeping
alive when once in them, was in itself sufficiently absorbing and hazardous to exclude any chance of combining
with it the rôle of sportsman.

With the last century all this had changed. Even in
the eighteenth century it began to change. The Dutch
settlers at the Cape of Good Hope, and the English settlers on the Atlantic coast of North America, found themselves thrown back into a stage of life where hunting was
one of the main means of livelihood, as well as the most
exciting and adventurous of pastimes. These men knew
the chase as men of their race had not known it since the
days before history dawned; and until the closing decades
of the last century the Americans and the Afrikanders of
the frontier largely led the lives of professional hunters.
Oom Paul and Buffalo Bill led very different careers
after they reached middle age; but in their youth warfare
against wild beasts and wild men was the most serious

part of the life-work of both. They and their fellows did the rough pioneer work of civilization, under conditions which have now vanished for ever, and their type will perish with the passing of the forces that called it into being. But the big game hunter, whose campaigns against big game are not simply incidents in his career as a pioneer settler, will remain with us for some time longer; and it is of him and his writings that we wish to treat.

Toward the end of the eighteenth century this big game hunter had already appeared, although, like all early types, he was not yet thoroughly specialized. Le Vaillant hunted in South Africa, and his volumes are excellent reading now. A still better book is that of Bruce, the Abyssinian explorer, who was a kind of Burton of his days, with a marvellous faculty for getting into quarrels, but an even more marvellous faculty for doing work which no other man could do. He really opened a new world to European men of letters and science; who thereupon promptly united in disbelieving all he said, though they were credulous enough toward people who really should have been distrusted. But his tales have been proved true by many an explorer since then, and his book will always possess interest for big game hunters, because of his experiences in the chase. Sometimes he shot merely in self-defense or for food, but he also made regular hunting trips in company with the wild lords of the shifting frontier between dusky Christian and dusky infidel. He feasted in their cane palaces, where the walls were hung with the trophies of giant game, and in their company, with horse and spear, he attacked and overcame the buffalo and the rhinoceros.

By the beginning of the nineteenth century the hunting book proper became differentiated, as it were, from the book of the explorer. One of the earliest was Williamson's " Oriental Field Sports." This is to the present day a most satisfactory book, especially to sporting parents with large families of small children. The pictures are all in colors, and the foliage is so very green, and the tigers are so very red, and the boars so very black, and the tragedies so uncommonly vivid and startling, that for the youthful mind the book really has no formidable rival outside of the charmed circle where Slovenly Peter stands first.

Since then multitudes of books have been written about big game hunting. Most of them are bad, of course, just as most novels and most poems are bad; but some of them are very good indeed, while a few are entitled to rank high in literature—though it cannot be said that as yet big game hunters as a whole have produced such writers as those who dwell on the homelier and less grandiose side of nature. They have not produced a White or Burroughs, for instance. What could not Burroughs have done if only he had cared for adventure and for the rifle, and had roamed across the Great Plains and the Rockies, and through the dim forests, as he has wandered along the banks of the Hudson and the Potomac! Thoreau, it is true, did go to the Maine Woods; but then Thoreau was a transcendentalist and slightly anæmic. A man must feel the beat of hardy life in his veins before he can be a good big game hunter. Fortunately, Richard Jeffries has written an altogether charming little volume on the Red Deer, so that there is at least one game animal which has been fully described by a man of letters, who was also both a naturalist and a sportsman; but it is irritating to think that no one has done as much for the lordlier game of the wilderness. Not only should the hunter be able to describe vividly the chase, and the life habits of the quarry, but he should also draw the wilderness itself, and the life of those who dwell or sojourn therein. We wish to see before us the cautious stalk and the headlong gallop; the great beasts as they feed or rest or run or make love or fight; the wild hunting camps; the endless plains shimmering in the sunlight; the vast, solemn forests; the desert and the marsh and the mountain chain; and all that lies hidden in the lonely lands through which the wilderness wanderer roams and hunts game.

But there remain a goodly number of books which are not merely filled with truthful information of importance, but which are also absorbingly interesting; and if a book is both truthful and interesting it is surely entitled to a place somewhere in general literature. Unfortunately, the first requisite bars out a great many hunting books. There are not a few mighty hunters who have left long records of their achievements, and who undoubtedly did achieve a great deal, but who contrive to leave in the mind of the reader the uncomfortable suspicion, that besides their prowess with the rifle they were skilled in the use of that more archaic weapon, the long bow.

" The Old Shekarry," who wrote of Indian and African
sport, was one of these. Gerard was a great lion-killer,
but some of his accounts of the lives, deaths, and especially the courtships, of lions, bear much less relation to
actual facts than do the novels of Dumas. Not a few
of the productions of hunters of this type should be
grouped under the head-lines used by the newspapers of
our native land in describing something which they are
perfectly sure hasn't happened—" Important, if True."
The exactly opposite type is presented in another French-
man, M. Foa, a really great hunter who also knows how
to observe and to put down what he has observed.   His
two books on big game hunting in Africa have permanent
value.

If we were limited to the choice of one big game
writer, who was merely such, and not in addition a scientific observer, we should have to choose Sir Samuel Baker,
for his experiences are very wide, and we can accept without question all that he says in his books. He hunted
in India, in Africa, and in North America; he killed all
the chief kinds of heavy and dangerous game; and he
followed them on foot and on horseback, with the rifle
and the knife, and with hounds. For the same reason, if
we could choose but one work, it would have to be the
volumes of " Big Game Shooting," in the Badminton
Library, edited by Mr. Phillipps Wolley—himself a man
who has written well of big game hunting in out-of-the-
way places, from the Caucasus to the Cascades. These
volumes contain pieces by many different authors; but
they differ from most volumes of the kind in that all the

THE NORTH ROOM AT SAGAMORE HILL

writers are trustworthy and interesting; though the palm must be given to Oswell's delightful account of his South African hunting. The book on the game beasts of Africa edited by Mr. Bryden is admirable in every way.

In all these books the one point to be insisted on is that a big game hunter has nothing in common with so many of the men who delight to call themselves sportsmen. Sir Samuel Baker has left a very amusing record of the horror he felt for the Ceylon sportsmen who, by the term "sport," meant horse-racing instead of elephant shooting. Half a century ago, Gordon-Cumming wrote of "the life of the wild hunter, so far preferable to that of the mere sportsman"; and his justification for this somewhat sneering reference to the man who takes his sport in too artificial a manner, may be found in the pages of a then noted authority on such sports as horse-racing and fox-hunting; for in Apperly's "Nimrod Abroad," in the course of an article on the game of the American wilderness, there occurs this delicious sentence: "A damper, however, is thrown over all systems of deer-stalking in Canada by the necessity, which is said to be unavoidable, of bivouacking in the woods instead of in well-aired sheets!" Verily, there was a great gulf between the two men.

In the present century the world has known three great hunting-grounds: Africa, from the equator to the southernmost point; India, both farther and hither; and North America west of the Mississippi, from the Rio Grande to the Arctic Circle. The latter never approached either of the former in the wealth and variety of the species, or in the size and terror of the chief beasts

of the chase; but it surpassed India in the countless numbers of the individual animals, and in the wild and unknown nature of the hunting-grounds, while the climate
and surroundings made the conditions under which the
hunter worked pleasanter and healthier than those in
any other land.

South Africa was the true hunter's paradise. If the
happy hunting-grounds were to be found anywhere in
this world, they lay between the Orange and the Zambesi,
and extended northward here and there to the Nile countries and Somaliland. Nowhere else were there such
multitudes of game, representing so many and such widely
different kinds of animals, of such size, such beauty, such
infinite variety. We should have to go back to the fauna
of the Pleistocene to find its equal. Never before did
men enjoy such hunting as fell to the lot of those roving
adventurers, who first penetrated its hidden fastnesses,
camped by its shrunken rivers, and galloped over its sun-
scorched wastes; and, alas that it should be written, no
man will ever see the like again. Fortunately, its mem-
ory will forever be kept alive in some of the books that
the great hunters have written about it, such as Cornwallis
Harris' "Wild Sports of South Africa," Gordon-Cumming's "Hunter's Life in South Africa," Baldwin's
"African Hunting," Drummond's "Large Game and
Natural History of South Africa," and, best of all,
Selous' two books, "A Hunter's Wanderings in South
Africa" and "Travel and Adventure in Southeast
Africa." Selous was the last of the great hunters of
South Africa, and no other has left books of such value

as his. In central Africa the game has lasted to our own time; the hunting described by Alfred Neumann and Vaughn Kirby in the closing years of the nineteenth century was almost as good as any enjoyed by their brothers who fifty years before steered their ox-drawn wagons across the " high veldt " of the south land.

Moreover, the pencil has done its part as well as the pen. Harris, who was the pioneer of all the hunters, published an admirable illustrated folio entitled " The Game and Wild Animals of South Africa." It is perhaps of more value than any other single work of the kind. J. G. Millais, in "A Breath from the Veldt," has rendered a unique service, not only by his charming descriptions, but by his really extraordinary sketches of the South African antelopes, both at rest, and in every imaginable form of motion. Nearly at the other end of the continent there is an admirable book on lion-hunting in Somaliland, by Captain C. J. Melliss. Much information about big game can be taken from the books of various missionaries and explorers; Livingstone and Du Chaillu doing for Africa in this respect what Catlin did for North America.

As we have said before, one great merit of these books is that they are interesting. Quite a number of men who are good sportsmen, as well as men of means, have written books about their experiences in Africa; but the trouble with too many of these short and simple annals of the rich is, that they are very dull. They are not literature, any more than treatises on farriery and cooking are literature. To read a mere itinerary is like reading a guide-book.

No great enthusiasm in the reader can be roused by such a statement as " this day walked twenty-three miles, shot one giraffe and two zebras; porter deserted with the load containing the spare boots "; and the most exciting events, if chronicled simply as " shot three rhinos and two buffalo; the first rhino and both buffalo charged," become about as thrilling as a paragraph in Baedeker. There is no need of additional literature of the guide-book and cookery-book kind. " Fine writing " is, of course, abhorrent in a way that is not possible for mere baldness of statement, and would-be " funny " writing is even worse, as it almost invariably denotes an underbred quality of mind; but there is need of a certain amount of detail, and of vivid and graphic, though simple, description. In other words, the writer on big game should avoid equally Carlyle's theory and Carlyle's practice in the matter of verbosity. Really good game books are sure to contain descriptions which linger in the mind just like one's pet passages in any other good book. One example is Selous' account of his night watch close to the wagon, when in the pitchy darkness he killed three of the five lions which had attacked his oxen; or his extraordinary experience while hunting elephants on a stallion which turned sulky, and declined to gallop out of danger. The same is true of Drummond's descriptions of the camps of native hunting parties, of tracking wounded buffalo through the reeds, and of waiting for rhinos by a desert pool under the brilliancy of the South African moon; descriptions, by the way, which show that the power of writing interestingly is not dependent upon even approximate correctness in style, for some of Mr. Drummond's sentences, in point of length and involution, would compare not unfavorably with those of a Populist Senator discussing bimetallism. Drummond is not as trustworthy an observer as Selous.

The experiences of a hunter in Africa, with its teeming wealth of strange and uncouth beasts, must have been, and in places must still be, about what one's experience would be if one could suddenly go back a few hundred thousand years for a hunting trip in the Pliocene or Pleistocene. In Mr. Astor Chanler's book, "Through Jungle and Desert," the record of his trip through the melancholy reed beds of the Guaso Nyiro, and of his return journey, carrying his wounded companion, through regions where the caravan was perpetually charged by rhinoceros, reads like a bit out of the unreckoned ages of the past, before the huge and fierce monsters of old had vanished from the earth, or acknowledged man as their master. An excellent book of mixed hunting and scientific exploration is Mr. Donaldson Smith's "Through Unknown African Countries." If anything, the hunting part is unduly sacrificed to some of the minor scientific work. Full knowledge of a new breed of rhinoceros, or a full description of the life history and chase of almost any kind of big game, is worth more than any quantity of matter about new spiders and scorpions. Small birds and insects remain in the land, and can always be described by the shoal of scientific investigators who follow the first adventurous explorers; but it is only the pioneer hunter who can tell us all about the far more interesting and important beasts of the chase, the different kinds of big game, and especially dangerous big game; and it is a mistake in any way to subordinate the greater work to the lesser.

Books on big game hunting in India are as plentiful, and as good, as those about Africa. Forsyth's " Highlands of Central India," Sanderson's " Thirteen Years Among the Wild Beasts of India," Shakespeare's " Wild Sports of India," and Kinloch's " Large Game Shooting," are perhaps the best; but there are many other writers, like Markham, Baldwin, Rice, Macintyre, and Stone, who are also very good. Indeed, to give even a mere list of the titles of the good books on Indian shooting would read too much like the Homeric catalogue of ships, or the biblical generations of the Jewish patriarchs. The four books singled out for special reference are interesting reading for anyone; particularly the accounts of the deaths of man-eating tigers at the hands of Forsyth, Shakespeare, and Sanderson, and some of Kinloch's Himalayan stalks. It is indeed royal sport which the hunter has among the stupendous mountain masses of the Himalayas, and in the rank jungles and steamy tropical forests of India.

Hunting should go hand in hand with the love of natural history, as well as with descriptive and narrative power. Hornaday's " Two Years in the Jungle " is especially interesting to the naturalist; but he adds not a little to our knowledge of big game. It is earnestly to be wished that some hunter will do for the gorilla what Hornaday has done for the great East Indian ape, the mias or orang.

There are many good books on American big game, but, rather curiously, they are for the most part modern. Until within the present generation Americans only hunted big game if they were frontier settlers, professional trappers, Southern planters, army officers, or explorers. The people of the cities of the old States were bred in the pleasing faith that anything unconcerned with business was both a waste of time and presumably immoral. Those who travelled went to Europe instead of to the Rocky Mountains.

Throughout the pioneer stages of American history, big game hunting was not merely a pleasure, but a business, and often a very important and in fact vital business. At different times many of the men who rose to great distinction in our after history took part in it as such: men like Andrew Jackson and Sam Houston, for instance. Moreover, aside from these pioneers who afterward won distinction purely as statesmen or soldiers, there were other members of the class of professional hunters—men who never became eminent in the complex life of the old civilized regions, who always remained hunters, and gloried in the title—who, nevertheless, through and because of their life in the wilderness, rose to national fame and left their mark on our history. The three most famous men of this class were Daniel Boone, David Crockett, and Kit Carson, who were renowned in every quarter of the Union for their skill as game-killers, Indian-fighters, and wilderness explorers, and whose deeds are still stock themes in the floating legendary lore of the border. They stand for all time as types of the pioneer settlers who won our land; the bridge-builders, the road-makers, the forest-fellers, the explorers, the land-tillers, the mighty men of their hands, who laid the foundations of this great commonwealth.

There are good descriptions of big game hunting in the books of writers like Catlin, but they come in incidentally. Elliott's " South Carolina Field Sports " is a very interesting and entirely trustworthy record of the sporting side of existence on the old Southern plantations, and not only commemorates how the planters hunted bear, deer, fox, and wildcat on the uplands and in the cane-brakes, but also gives a unique description of harpooning the great devil-fish in the warm Southern waters. John Palliser, an Englishman, in his " Solitary Hunter," has given us the best descriptions of hunting in the far West, when it was still an untrodden wilderness. Another Englishman, Ruxton, in two volumes, has left us a most vivid picture of the old hunters and trappers themselves. Unfortunately, these old hunters and trappers, the men who had most experience in the life of the wilderness, were utterly unable to write about it; they could not tell what they had seen or done. Occasional attempts have been made to get noted hunters to write books, either personally or by proxy, but these attempts have not as a rule been successful. Perhaps the best of the books thus produced is Hittell's " Adventures of James Capen Adams, Mountaineer and Grizzly Bear Hunter."

The first effort to get men of means and cultivation in the Northern and Eastern States of the Union to look at field sports in the right light was made by an Englishman who wrote over the signature of Frank Forrester. He did much for the shotgun men; but, unfortunately, he was a true cockney, who cared little for really wild sports, and he was afflicted with that dreadful pedantry which pays more heed to ceremonial and terminology than to the thing itself. He was sincerely distressed because the male of the ordinary American deer was called a buck instead of a stag; and it seemed to him to be a matter of moment whether one spoke of a " gang " or a " herd " of elk.

There are plenty of excellent books nowadays, however. The best book upon the old plains country was Colonel Richard Irving Dodge's " Hunting-Grounds of the Great West," which dealt with the chase of most kinds of plains game proper. Judge Caton, in his " Antelope and Deer of America," gave a full account of not only the habits and appearance, but the methods of chase and life histories of the prongbuck, and of all the different kinds of deer found in the United States. Dr. Allen, in his memoir on the bisons of America, and Hornaday, in his book upon their extermination, have rendered similar service for the vast herds of shaggy-maned wild cattle which have vanished with such melancholy rapidity during the lifetime of the present generation. Mr. Van Dyke's " Still-Hunter " is a noteworthy book, which, for the first time, approaches the still-hunter and his favorite game, the deer, from what may be called the standpoint of the scientific sportsman. It is one of the few hunting-books which should really be studied by the beginner because of what he can learn therefrom in reference to the hunter's craft. The Century Co.'s volume " Sport With Gun and Rod " contains accounts of the chase of most of the kinds of American big game, although there are two or three notable omissions, such as the elk, the grizzly bear, and the white goat. Warburton Pike, Caspar Whitney, and Frederick Schwatka have given fairly full and very interesting accounts of boreal sport; and Pendarves Vivian and Baillie-Grohman of hunting trips in the Rockies. A new and most important departure, that of photographing wild animals in their homes, was marked by Mr. Wallihan's " Camera Shots at Big Game." This is a noteworthy volume. Mr. Wallihan was the pioneer in a work which is of the utmost importance to the naturalist, the man of science; and what he accomplished was far more creditable to himself, and of far more importance to others, than any amount of game-killing. Finally, in Parkman's " Oregon Trail " and Irving's " Trip on the Prairie," two great writers have left us a lasting record of the free life of the rifle-bearing wanderers who first hunted in the wild Western lands.

Though not hunting-books, John Burroughs' writings and John Muir's volumes on the Sierras should be in the hands of every lover of outdoor life, and therefore in the hands of every hunter who is a nature lover, and not a mere game-butcher.

Of course, there are plenty of books on European game. Scrope's "Art of Deerstalking," Bromley Davenport's " Sport," and all the books of Charles St. John, are classic. The chase of the wolf and boar is excellently described by an unnamed writer in " Wolf-Hunting and Wild Sports of Brittany." Baillie-Grohman's " Sport in the Alps " is devoted to the mountain game of Central Europe, and is, moreover, a mine of curious hunting lore, most of which is entirely new to men unacquainted with the history of the chase in Continental Europe during the last few centuries. An entirely novel type of adventure was set forth in Lamont's " Seasons with the Sea Horses," wherein he described his hunting in arctic waters with rifle and harpoon. Lloyd's " Scandinavian Adventures " and " Northern Field Sports," and Whishaw's " Out of Doors in Tsar Land," tell of the life and game of the snowy northern forests. Chapman has done excellent work for both Norway and Spain. It would be impossible even to allude to the German and French books on the chase, such as the admirable but rather technical treatises of Le Couteulx de Canteleu. Moreover, these books for the most part belong rather in the category which includes English fox-hunting literature, not in that which deals with big game and the life of the wilderness. This is merely to state a difference—not to draw a comparison; for the artificial sports of highly civilized countries are strongly to be commended for their effect on national character in making good the loss of certain of the rougher virtues which tend to disappear with the rougher conditions.

In Mr. Edward North Buxton's two volumes of " Short Stalks " we find the books of a man who is a hardy lover of nature, a skilled hunter, but not a game-butcher; a man who has too much serious work on hand ever to let himself become a mere globe-trotting rifleman. His volumes teach us just what a big game hunter, a true sportsman, should be. But the best recent book on the wilderness is Herr C. G. Schilling's " Mit Blitzlicht und Büchse," giving the writer's hunting adventures, and above all his acute scientific observations and his extraordinary photographic work among the teeming wild creatures of German East Africa. Mr. Schilling is a great field naturalist, a trained scientific observer, as well as a mighty hunter; and no mere hunter can ever do work even remotely approaching in value that which he has done. His book should be translated into English at once. Every effort should be made to turn the modern big game hunter into the Schilling type of adventure-loving field naturalist and observer.

I am not disposed to undervalue manly outdoor sports, or to fail to appreciate the advantage to a nation, as well as to an individual, of such pastimes; but they must be pastimes, and not business, and they must not be carried to excess. There is much to be said for the life of a professional hunter in lonely lands; but the man able to be something more, should be that something more —an explorer, a naturalist, or else a man who makes his hunting trips merely delightful interludes in his life work. As for excessive game butchery, it amounts to a repulsive debauch. The man whose chief title to glory is that, during an industrious career of destruction, he has slaughtered 200,000 head of deer and partridges, stands unpleasantly near those continental kings and nobles who, during the centuries before the French Revolution, deified the chase of the stag, and made it into a highly artificial cult, which they followed to the exclusion of State-craft and war-craft and everything else. James, the founder of the ignoble English branch of the Stuart kings, as unkingly a man as ever sat on a throne, was fanatical in his devotion to the artificial kind of chase which then absorbed the souls of the magnates of continental Europe.

There is no need to exercise much patience with men who protest against field sports, unless, indeed, they are logical vegetarians of the flabbiest Hindoo type. If no deer or rabbits were killed, no crops could be cultivated. If it is morally right to kill an animal to eat its body, then it is morally right to kill it to preserve its head. A good sportsman will not hesitate as to the relative value he puts upon the two, and to get the one he will go a long time without eating the other. No nation facing the unhealthy softening and relaxation of fibre which tend to accompany civilization can afford to neglect anything that will develop hardihood, resolution, and the scorn of discomfort and danger. But if sport is made an end instead of a means, it is better to avoid it altogether. The greatest stag-hunter of the seventeenth century was the Elector of Saxony. During the Thirty Years' War he killed some 80,000 deer and boar. Now, if there ever was a time when a ruler needed to apply himself to serious matters, it was during the Thirty Years' War in Germany, and if the Elector in question had eschewed hunting he might have compared more favorably with Gustavus Adolphus in his own generation, or the Great

Elector of Brandenburg in the next generation. The kings of the House of Savoy have shown that the love of hardy field sports in no way interferes with the exercise of the highest kind of governmental ability.

Wellington was fond of fox-hunting, but he did very little of it during the period of the Peninsular War. Grant cared much for fine horses, but he devoted his attention to other matters when facing Lee before Richmond. Perhaps as good an illustration as could be wished of the effects of the opposite course is furnished by poor Louis XVI. He took his sport more seriously than he did his position as ruler of his people. On the day when the revolutionary mob came to Versailles, he merely recorded in his diary that he had " gone out shooting, and had killed eighty-one head when he was interrupted by events." The particular event to which this " interruption " led up was the guillotine. Not many sportsmen have to face such a possibility; but they do run the risk of becoming a curse to themselves and to everyone else, if they once get into the frame of mind which can look on the business of life as merely an interruption to sport.

CHAPTER XI

AT HOME

ONLY a few men, comparatively speaking, lead their lives in the wilderness; only a few others, again speaking comparatively, are able to take their holidays in the shape of hunting trips in the wilderness. But all who live in the country, or who even spend a month now and then in the country, can enjoy outdoor life themselves, and can see that their children enjoy it in the hardy fashion which will do them good. Camping out, and therefore the cultivation of the capacity to live in the open, and the education of the faculties which teach observation, resourcefulness, self-reliance, are within the reach of all who really care for the life of the woods, the fields, and the waters. Marksmanship with the rifle can be cultivated with small cost or trouble; and if any one passes much time in the country he can, if only he chooses, learn much about horsemanship.

But aside from any such benefit, it is an incalculable added pleasure to any one's sum of happiness if he or she grows to know, even slightly and imperfectly, how to read and enjoy the wonder-book of nature. All hunters should be nature lovers. It is to be hoped that the days of mere wasteful, boastful slaughter, are past, and that from now on the hunter will stand foremost in working

339

for the preservation and perpetuation of the wild life, whether big or little.

The Audubon Society and kindred organizations have done much for the proper protection of birds and of wild creatures generally; they have taken the lead in putting a stop to wanton or short-sighted destruction, and in giving effective utterance to the desires of those who wish to cultivate a spirit as far removed as possible from that which brings about such destruction. Sometimes, however, in endeavoring to impress upon a not easily aroused public the need for action, they in their zeal over-state this need. This is a very venial error compared to the good they have done; but in the interest of scientific accuracy it is to be desired that their cause should not be buttressed in such manner. Many of our birds have diminished lamentably in numbers, and there is every reason for taking steps to preserve them. There are wa-ter birds, shore birds, game birds, and an occasional con-spicuous bird of some other kind, which can only be preserved by such agitation. It is also most desirable to prevent the slaughter of small birds in the neighbor-hood of towns. But I question very much whether there has been any diminution of small-bird life throughout the country at large. Certainly no such diminution has taken place during the past thirty years in any region of considerable size with which I am personally acquainted. Take Long Island, for instance. During this period there has been a lamentable decrease in the waders—the shore-birds—which used to flock along its southern shore. But in northern Long Island, in the neighborhood of my

RENOWN

From a photograph by Arthur Hewitt

Theodore, Jr. (Ted)

own home, birds, taken as a whole, are quite as plentiful
as they were when I was a boy. There are one or two
species which have decreased in numbers, notably the
woodcock; while the passenger pigeon, which was then
a rarely seen straggler, does not now appear at all. Bob-
whites are less plentiful. On the other hand, some birds
have certainly increased in numbers. This is true, for
instance, of the conspicuously beautiful and showy scarlet tanager. I think meadow larks are rather more
plentiful than they were, and wrens less so. Bluebirds
have never been common with us, but are now rather
more common than formerly. It seems to me as if the
chickadees were more numerous than formerly. Purple
grakles are more plentiful than when I was a boy, and
the far more attractive redwing blackbirds less so. But
these may all be, and doubtless some must be, purely
local changes, which apply only to our immediate neighborhood. As regards most of the birds, it would be hard
to say that there has been any change. Of course, obvious local causes will now and then account for a partial
change. Thus, while the little green herons are quite
as plentiful as formerly in our immediate neighborhood,
the white-crowned night herons are not as plentiful, because they abandoned their big heronry on Lloyd's Neck
upon the erection of a sandmill close by. The only ducks
which are now, or at any time during the last thirty years
have been, abundant in our neighborhood are the surf-
ducks or scoters, and the old-squaws, sometimes known
as long-tailed or sou'-sou'-southerly ducks. From late
fall until early spring the continuous musical clangor of

the great flocks of sou'-sou'-southerlies, sounding across the steel-gray, wintry waves, is well known to all who sail the waters of the Sound.

Neither the birds nor the flowers are as numerous on Long Island, or at any rate in my neighborhood, as they are, for instance, along the Hudson and near Washington. It is hard to say exactly why flowers and birds are at times so local in their distribution. For instance, the bobolinks hardly ever come around us at Sagamore Hill. Within a radius of three or four miles of the house I do not remember to have ever seen more than two or three couples breeding. Sharp-tailed finches are common in the marsh which lies back of our beach; but the closely allied seaside finches and the interesting and attractive little marsh wrens, both of which are common in various parts of Long Island, are not found near our home. Similarly, I know of but one place near our house where the bloodroot grows; the may-flowers are plentiful, but among hillsides to all appearance equally favored, are found on some, and not on others. For wealth of bloom, aside from the orchards, we must rely chiefly upon the great masses of laurel and the many groves of locusts. The bloom of the locust is as evanescent as it is fragrant. During the short time that the trees are in flower the whole air is heavy with the sweet scent. In the fall, in the days of the aster and the golden-rod, there is no such brilliant coloring on Long Island as farther north, for we miss from among the forest hues the flaming crimsons and scarlets of the northern maples.

Among Long Island singers the wood-thrushes are

HIS FIRST BUCK
Ted

the sweetest; they nest right around our house, and also
in the more open woods of oak, hickory, and chestnut,
where their serene, leisurely songs ring through the leafy
arches all day long, but especially at daybreak and in
the afternoons. Baltimore orioles, beautiful of voice
and plumage, hang their nests in a young elm near a
corner of the porch; robins, catbirds, valiant kingbirds,
song-sparrows, chippies, bright colored thistle-finches,
nest within a stone's throw of the house, in the shrubbery or among the birches and maples; grasshopper
sparrows, humble little creatures with insect-like voices,
nest almost as close, in the open field, just beyond the
line where the grass is kept cut; humming-birds visit
the honeysuckles and trumpet-flowers; chimney swallows
build in the chimneys; barn swallows nest in the stable
and old barn, wrens in the bushes near by. Downy
woodpeckers and many other birds make their homes
in the old orchard; during the migrations it is alive
with warblers. Towhees, thrashers, and Maryland yel-
low-throats build and sing in the hedges by the garden;
bush sparrows and dainty little prairie warblers in the
cedar-grown field beyond. Red-wing blackbirds haunt
the wet places. Chickadees wander everywhere; the
wood-pewees, red-eyed vireos, and black and white creepers keep to the tall timber, where the wary, thievish
jays chatter, and the great-crested fly-catchers flit and
scream. In the early spring, when the woods are still
bare, when the hen-hawks cry as they soar high in the
upper air, and the flickers call and drum on the dead
trees, the strong, plaintive note of the meadow lark is

one of the most noticeable and most attractive sounds. On the other hand, the cooing of the mourning doves is most noticeable in the still, hot summer days. In the thick tangles chats creep and flutter and jerk, and chuckle and whoop as they sing; I have heard them sing by night. The cedar birds offer the most absolute contrast to the chats, in voice, manner, and habits. They never hide, they are never fussy or noisy; they always behave as if they were so well-bred that it is impossible to resent the inroads the soft, quiet, pretty creatures make among the cherries. One flicker became possessed of a mania to dig its hole in one corner of the house, just under the roof. It hammered lustily at boards and shingles, and returned whenever driven away; until at last we were reluctantly forced to decree its death. Ovenbirds are very plentiful, and it seems to me that their flight song is more frequently given after dusk than in daylight. It is sometimes given when the whippoorwills are calling. In late June evenings, especially by moonlight, but occasionally even when the night is dark, we hear this song from the foot of the hill where the woods begin. There seems to be one particular corner where year after year one or more oven-birds dwell which possess an especial fondness for this night-singing in the air. It is a pity the little eared owl is called screech-owl. Its tremulous, quavering cry is not a screech at all, and has an attraction of its own. These little owls come up to the house after dark, and are fond of sitting on the elk antlers over the gable. When the moon is up, by choosing one's position, the little owl

ALGONQUIN AND SKIP

Archibald (Archie)

appears in sharp outline against the bright disk, seated on his many-tined perch.

The neighborhood of Washington abounds in birds no less than in flowers. There have been one or two rather curious changes among its birds since John Burroughs wrote of them forty years ago. He speaks of the red-headed woodpecker as being then one of the most abundant of all birds—even more so than the robin. It is not uncommon now, and a pair have for three years nested in the White House grounds; but it is at present by no means an abundant bird. On the other hand, John Burroughs never saw any mocking-birds, whereas during the last few years these have been increasing in numbers, and there are now several places within easy walking or riding distance where we are almost sure to find them. The mocking-bird is as conspicuous as it is attractive, and when at its best it is the sweetest singer of all birds; though its talent for mimicry, and a certain odd perversity in its nature, often combine to mar its performances. The way it flutters and dances in the air when settling in a tree-top, its alert intelligence, its good looks, and the comparative ease with which it can be made friendly and familiar, all add to its charm. I am sorry to say that it does not nest in the White House grounds. Neither does the wood-thrush, which is so abundant in Rock Creek Park, within the city limits. Numbers of robins, song-sparrows, sputtering, creaking purple grakles— crow blackbirds—and catbirds nest in the grounds. So, I regret to say, do crows, the sworn foes of all small birds, and as such entitled to no mercy. The hearty, wholesome, vigorous songs of the robins, and the sweet, home-like strains of the song-sparrows are the first to be regularly heard in the grounds, and they lead the chorus. The catbirds chime in later; they are queer, familiar, strongly individual birds, and are really good singers; but they persist in interrupting their songs with cat-like squalling. Two or three pairs of flickers nest with us, as well as the red-headed woodpeckers above mentioned; and a pair of furtive cuckoos. A pair of orchard orioles nested with us one spring, but not again; the redstarts, warbling vireos, and summer warblers have been more faithful. Baltimore orioles frequently visit us, as do the scarlet tanagers and tufted titmice, but for some reason they have not nested here. This spring a cardinal bird took up his abode in the neighborhood of the White House, and now and then waked us in the morning by his vigorous whistling in a magnolia tree just outside our windows. A Carolina wren also spent the winter with us, and sang freely. In both spring and fall the white-throated sparrows sing while stopping over in the course of their migrations. Their delicate, plaintive, musical notes are among the most attractive of bird sounds. In the early spring we sometimes hear the fox-sparrows and tree-sparrows, and of course the twittering snow-birds. Later warblers of many kinds throng the trees around the house. Rabbits breed in the grounds, and every now and then possums wander into them. Gray squirrels are numerous, and some of them so tame that they will eat out of our hands. In spring they cut the flowers from the stately

PETER RABBIT

From a photograph, copyright, 1904, by E. S. Curtis

Quentin

tulip trees. In the hot June days the indigo birds are especially in evidence among the singers around Washington; they do not mind the heat at all, but perch in the tops of little trees in the full glare of the sun, and chant their not very musical, but to my ears rather pleasing, song throughout the long afternoons. This June two new guests came to the White House in the shape of two little saw-whet owls; little bits of fellows, with round heads, and no head tufts, or " ears." I think they were the young of the year; they never uttered the saw-whet sound, but made soft snoring noises. They always appeared after nightfall, when we were sitting on the south porch, in the warm, starlit darkness. They were fearless and unsuspicious. Sometimes they flew noiselessly to and fro, and seemingly caught big insects on the wing. At other times they would perch on the iron awningbars, directly overhead. Once one of them perched over one of the windows, and sat motionless, looking exactly like an owl of Pallas Athene.

At Sagamore Hill we like to have the wood-folk and field-folk familiar; but there are necessary bounds to such familiarity where chickens are kept for use and where the dogs are valued family friends. The rabbits and gray squirrels are as plenty as ever. The flying squirrels and chipmunks still hold their own; so do the muskrats in the marshes. The woodchucks, which we used to watch as we sat in rocking-chairs on the broad veranda, have disappeared; but recently one has made himself a home under the old barn, where we are doing our best to protect him. A mink which lived by the edge of the bay under a great pile of lumber had to be killed; its lair showed the remains not only of chickens and ducks, but of two muskrats, and, what was rather curious, of two skates or flatfish. A fox which lived in the big wood lot evidently disliked our companionship and abandoned his home. Of recent years I have actually seen but one fox near Sagamore Hill. This was early one morning, when I had spent the night camping on the wooded shores near the mouth of Huntington Harbor. The younger children were with me, this being one of the camping-out trips, in rowboats, on the Sound, taken especially for their benefit. We had camped the previous evening in a glade by the edge of a low sea-bluff, far away from any house; and while the children were intently watching me as I fried strips of beefsteak and thin slices of potatoes in bacon fat, we heard a fox barking in the woods. This gave them a delightfully wild feeling, and with refreshing confidence they discussed the likelihood of seeing it next morning; and to my astonishment see it we did, on the shore, soon after we started to row home.

One pleasant fall morning in 1892 I was writing in the gun-room, on the top floor of the house, from the windows of which one can see far over the Sound. Suddenly my small boy of five bustled up in great excitement to tell me that the hired-man had come back from the wood-pile pond—a muddy pool in a beech and hickory grove a few hundred yards from the house—to say that he had seen a coon and that I should come down at once with my rifle; for Davis, the colored gar-

THE GUINEA-PIGS
Kermit, Ethel, Ted

dener, had been complaining much about the loss of his chickens and did not know whether the malefactor was a coon or a mink. Accordingly, I picked up a rifle and trotted down to the pond holding it in one hand, while the little boy trotted after me, affectionately clasping the butt. Sure enough, in a big blasted chestnut close to the pond was the coon, asleep in a shallow hollow of the trunk, some forty feet from the ground. It was a very exposed place for a coon to lie during the daytime, but this was a bold fellow and seemed entirely undisturbed by our voices. He was altogether too near the house, or rather the chicken-coops, to be permitted to stay where he was—especially as but a short time before I had, with mistaken soft-heartedness, spared a possum I found on the place—and accordingly I raised my rifle; then I remembered for the first time that the rear sight was off, as I had taken it out for some reason; and in consequence I underwent the humiliation of firing two or three shots in vain before I got the coon. As he fell out of the tree the little boy pounced gleefully on him; fortunately he was dead, and we walked back to the house in triumph, each holding a hind leg of the quarry.

The possum spoken of above was found in a dogwood tree not more than eighty yards from the house, one afternoon when we were returning from a walk in the woods. As something had been killing the hens, I felt that it was at least under suspicion and that I ought to kill it, but a possum is such an absurd creature that I could not resist playing with it for some time; after that I felt that to kill it in cold-blood would be too much like murder, and let it go. This tender-heartedness was regarded as much misplaced both by farmer and gardener; hence the coon suffered.

A couple of years later, on a clear, cold Thanksgiving Day, we had walked off some five miles to chop out a bridle-path which had become choked with down-timber; the two elder of our little boys were with us. The sun had set long ere our return; we were walking home on a road through our own woods and were near the house. We had with us a stanch friend, a large yellow dog, which one of the children, with fine disregard for considerations of sex, had named Susan. Suddenly Susan gave tongue off in the woods to one side and we found he had treed a possum. This time I was hard-hearted and the possum fell a victim; the five-year-old boy explaining to the seven-year-old that " it was the first time he had ever seen a fellow killed."

Susan was one of many dogs whose lives were a joy and whose deaths were a real grief to the family; among them and their successors are or have been Sailor Boy, the Chesapeake Bay dog, who not only loves guns, but also fireworks and rockets, and who exercises a close and delighted supervision over every detail of each Fourth of July celebration; Alan and Jessie, the Scotch terriers; and Jack, the most loved of all, a black smooth-haired Manchester terrier. Jack lived in the house; the others outside, ever on the lookout to join the family in rambles through the woods. Jack was human in his intelligence and affection; he learned all kinds of tricks,

FAMILY FRIENDS

was a high-bred gentleman, never brawled, and was a dauntless fighter. Besides the family, his especial friend, playfellow, and teacher was colored Charles, the footman at Washington. Skip, the little black-and-tan terrier that I brought back from the Colorado bear hunt, changed at once into a real little-boy's dog. He never lets his small master out of his sight, and rides on every horse that will let him—by preference on Algonquin the sheltie, whose nerves are of iron.

The first night possum hunt in which I ever took part was at Quantico, on the Virginia side of the Potomac, some twenty miles below Washington. It was a number of years ago, and several of us were guests of a loved friend, Hallett Phillips, since dead. Although no hunter, Phillips was devoted to outdoor life. I think it was at this time that Rudyard Kipling had sent him the manuscript of " The Feet of the Young Men," which he read aloud to us.

Quantico is an island, a quaint, delightful place, with a club-house. We started immediately after dark, going across to the mainland, accompanied by a dozen hounds, with three or four negroes to manage them and serve as axemen. Each member of the party carried a torch, as without one it was impossible to go at any speed through the woods. The dogs, of course, have to be specially trained not to follow either fox or rabbit. It was dawn before we got back, wet, muddy, and weary, carrying eleven possums. All night long we rambled through the woods and across the fields, the dogs working about us as we followed in single file. After a while some dog would strike a trail. It might take some time to puzzle it out; then the whole pack would be away, and all the men ran helter-skelter after them, plunging over logs and through swamps, and now and then taking headers in the darkness. We were never fortunate enough to strike a coon, which would have given a good run and a fight at the end of it. When the unfortunate possum was over-taken on the ground he was killed before we got up. Otherwise he was popped alive into one of the big bags carried by the axemen. Two or three times he got into a hollow log or hole and we dug or chopped him out. Gen-erally, however, he went up a tree. It was a picturesque sight, in the flickering glare of the torches, to see the dogs leaping up around the trunk of a tree and finally to make out the possum clinging to the trunk or perched on some slender branch, his eyes shining brightly through the darkness; or to watch the muscular grace with which the darky axemen, ragged and sinewy, chopped into any tree if it had too large and smooth a trunk to climb. A pos-sum is a queer, sluggish creature, whose brain seems to work more like that of some reptile than like a mam-mal's. When one is found in a tree there is no difficulty whatever in picking it off with the naked hand. Two or three times during the night I climbed the tree myself, either going from branch to branch or swarming up some tangle of grape-vines. The possum opened his mouth as I approached and looked as menacing as he knew how; but if I pulled him by the tail he forgot everything ex-cept trying to grab with all four feet, and then I could take him by the back of the neck and lift him off—either carrying him down, held gingerly at arm's length, or dropping him into the open mouth of a bag if I felt sufficiently sure of my aim.

In the spring of 1903, while in western Kansas, a little girl gave me a baby badger, captured by her brother, and named after him, Josiah. I took Josiah home to Sagamore Hill, where the children received him literally with open arms, while even the dogs finally came to tolerate him. He grew apace, and was a quaint and on the whole a friendly—though occasionally short-tempered—pet. He played tag with us with inexhaustible energy, looking much like a small mattress with a leg at each corner; he dug holes with marvellous rapidity; and when he grew snappish we lifted him up by the back of the neck, which rendered him harmless. He ate bread and milk, dead mice and birds, and eggs; he would take a hen's egg in his mouth, break it, and avoid spilling any of the contents. When angered, he hissed, and at other times he made low guttural sounds. The nine-year-old boy became his especial friend. Now and then he nipped the little boy's legs, but this never seemed to interrupt the amicable relations between the two; as the little boy normally wore neither shoes nor stockings, and his blue overalls were thin, Josiah probably found the temptation at times irresistible. If on such occasions the boy was in Josiah's wire-fenced enclosure, he sat on a box with his legs tucked under him; if the play was taking place outside, he usually climbed into the hammock, while Josiah pranced and capered clumsily beneath, tail up and head thrown back. But Josiah never bit when picked up; although he hissed like a teakettle as the little boy carried him about, usually tightly clasped round where his waist would have been if he had had one.

At different times I have been given a fairly appalling number of animals, from known and unknown friends; in one year the list included—besides a lion, a hyena, and a zebra from the Emperor of Ethiopia—five bears, a wildcat, a coyote, two macaws, an eagle, a barn owl, and several snakes and lizards. Most of these went to the Zoo, but a few were kept by the children. Those thus kept numbered at one end of the scale gentle, trustful, pretty things, like kangaroo rats and flying squirrels; and at the other end a queer-tempered young black bear, which the children named Jonathan Edwards, partly because of certain well-marked Calvinistic tendencies in his disposition, partly out of compliment to their mother, whose ancestors included that Puritan divine. The kangaroo rats and flying squirrels slept in their pockets and blouses, went to school with them, and sometimes unexpectedly appeared at breakfast or dinner. The bear added zest to life in more ways than one. When we took him to walk, it was always with a chain and club; and when at last he went to the Zoo, the entire household breathed a sigh of relief, although I think the dogs missed him, as he had occasionally yielded them the pleasure of the chase in its strongest form.

As a steady thing, the children found rabbits and guinea pigs the most satisfactory pets. The guinea pigs usually rejoiced in the names of the local or national celebrities of the moment; at one time there were five,

JOSIAH
Archie

which were named after naval heroes and friendly ecclesi-astical dignitaries—an Episcopalian Bishop, a Catholic Priest, and my own Dutch Reformed Pastor—Bishop Doane, Father O'Grady, Dr. Johnson, Fighting Bob Evans, and Admiral Dewey. Father O'Grady, by the way, proved to be of the softer sex; a fact definitely established when two of his joint owners, rushing breathless into the room, announced to a mixed company, " Oh, oh, Father O'Grady has had some children!"

Of course there are no pets like horses; and horse-manship is a test of prowess. The best among vigorous out-of-door sports should be more than pastimes. Play is good for play's sake, within moderate limits, especially if it is athletic play; and, again within moderate limits, it is good because a healthy body helps toward healthi-ness of mind. But if play serves only either of these ends, it does not deserve the serious consideration which rightly attaches to play which in itself fits a man to do things worth doing; and there exists no creature much more contemptible than a man past his first youth who leads a life devoted to mere sport, without thought of the serious work of life. In a free Government the average citizen should be able to do his duty in war as well as in peace; otherwise he falls short. Cavalrymen and infan-trymen, who do not need special technical knowledge, are easily developed out of men who are already soldiers in the rough, that is, who, in addition to the essential quali-ties of manliness and character, the qualities of resolution, daring and intelligence, which go to make up the " fight-ing edge," also possess physical hardihood; who can live

in the open, walk long distances, ride, shoot, and endure
fatigue, hardship, and exposure. But if all these traits
must be painfully acquired, then it takes a long time indeed before the man can be turned into a good soldier.
Now, there is little tendency to develop these traits in our
highly complex, rather over-civilized, modern industrial
life, and therefore the sports which produce them serve
a useful purpose. Hence, when able to afford a horse,
or to practise on a rifle range, one can feel that the enjoyment is warranted by what may be called considerations
of national ethics.

As with everything else, so with riding; some take to
it naturally, others never can become even fairly good
horsemen. All the children ride, with varying skill.
While young, a Shetland pony serves; the present pony,
Algonquin, a calico or pinto, being as knowing and
friendly as possible. His first small owner simply adored
him, treating him as a twin brother, and having implicit
faith in his mental powers. On one occasion, when a
naval officer of whom the children were fond came to
call, in full dress, Algonquin's master, who was much
impressed by the sight, led up Algonquin to enjoy it too,
and was shocked by the entire indifference with which the
greedy pony persisted in eating grass. One favorite polo
pony, old Diamond, long after he became a pensioner,
served for whichever child had just graduated from the
sheltie. Next in order was a little mare named Yagenka,
after the heroine of one of Sienkewicz's blood-curdling
romances of mediæval Poland. When every rideable
animal is impressed, all the children sometimes go out

BLEISTEIN JUMPING

From a photograph, copyright, 1902, by Clinedinst, Washington, D. C.

with their mother and me; looking much like the Cumberbatch family in Caldecott's pictures.

Of recent years I have not been able to ride to hounds; but when opportunity has offered I have kept as saddle horses one or two hunters, so that instead of riding the road I could strike off across country; the hunter scrambling handily through rough places, and jumping an occasional fence if necessary. While in Washington this is often, except for an occasional long walk down Rock Creek or along the Virginia side of the Potomac, the only exercise I can get. Among the various horses I have owned in recent years Bleistein was the one I liked best, because of his good nature and courage. He was a fair, although in no way a remarkable, jumper. One day, May 3, 1902, I took him out to Chevy Chase and had him photographed while jumping various fences and brush hurdles; the accompanying picture is from one of these photos. Another hunter, Renown, was a much higher, but an uncertain, jumper. He was a beautiful horse, and very good-tempered, but excessively timid.

We have been able to fix a rifle range at Sagamore, though only up to 200 yards. Some of the children take to shooting naturally, others can only with difficulty be made to learn the rudiments of what they regard as a tiresome business. Many friends have shot on this range. We use only sporting rifles; my own is one of the new model Government Springfields, stocked and sighted to suit myself. For American game the modern small calibre, high power, smokeless powder rifle, of any one among several makes, is superseding the others; although for some purposes an old 45–70 or 45–90, even with black powder, is as good as any modern weapon, and for very heavy game the calibre should be larger than that of the typical modern arm, with a heavier ball and more powder. But after all, any good modern rifle is good enough; when a certain pitch of excellence in the weapon has been attained, then the determining factor in achieving success is the quality of the man behind the gun.

My eldest boy killed his first buck just before he was fourteen, and his first moose—a big bull with horns which spread 56 inches—just before he was seventeen. Both were killed in the wilderness, in the great north woods, on trips sufficiently hard to afford some test of endurance and skill. Such a hunting trip is even more than a delightful holiday, provided the work is hard as well as enjoyable; and therefore it must be taken in the wilderness. Big private preserves may serve a useful purpose if managed with such judgment and kindliness that the good will of the neighborhood is secured; but the sport in them somehow seems to have lost its savor, even though they may be large enough to give the chance of testing a man's woodcraft no less than his marksmanship. I have but once hunted in one of them. That was in the fall of 1902, when Senator Proctor took me into the Corbin Park game preserve in New Hampshire. The Senator is not merely a good shot; he is a good hunter, with the eye, the knowledge of the game, and the ability to take advantage of cover and walk silently, which are even more important than straight powder.

He took me out alone for the afternoon, and, besides the tame buffalo, he showed me one elk and over twenty deer. We were only after the wild boar, which have flourished wonderfully. Just at dusk we saw a three-year-old boar making his way toward an old deserted orchard; and creeping up, I shot him as he munched apples under one of the trees.

APPENDIX

APPENDIX

THE following letters explain themselves. It would seem that not only when wild but when in a menagerie the cougar is a much less dangerous animal than the jaguar or leopard; and it also looks as if it were more mild-tempered, and indeed playful, than either of the big spotted cats. In the wild state, I personally have not happened to come across instances of full-grown pumas frolicking or playing, except when two were mating; but I have known young pumas to play.

"OYSTER BAY, N. Y., *July* 18, 1905.
" MY DEAR MR. BOSTOCK :

" In connection with your book on the training of wild animals, in which I was greatly interested, I would like to ask whether you find that the puma or cougar shows a different kind of temper from the leopard or old world panther, and from the jaguar? I ask this, because in hunting it I have found it to be, compared to the big bear, a cowardly animal, and if what I read of the danger of hunting the Indian and African leopard is true, then the puma is not nearly as formidable as the leopard or the jaguar—in short, is not nearly so formidable as the big spotted cats, though it is as big and as formidably armed. Have you noticed any difference in your work among these species, taking the average of one and comparing it, as to temper, ferocity, etc., with the average of the other? Of course there are wide individual differences; but that is not what I am after at present. I notice that you say there is little or no difference as among the tiger, lion, leopard, and jaguar, comparing species with species.

"With regard, sincerely yours,
"THEODORE ROOSEVELT.
"FRANK C. BOSTOCK, ESQ., NEW YORK, N. Y."

"RIDGEFIELD, CONN., *July* 17, 1905.
"THEODORE ROOSEVELT, ESQ.

"DEAR SIR: I see by the papers that you have written to Mr. Bostock asking a question about the puma. As I wrote the entire book, 'The Training of Wild Animals,' from facts given me by Mr. Bostock and his trainers, added to my own personal knowledge and study, I think I can answer your question, which may be useful in addition to any information Mr. Bostock may send you, which cannot reach you for some little time.

"In my own opinion, the puma is not *nearly* so formidable as either the tiger, jaguar, lion, or leopard—it is, as a rule, a timid and, unless unexpectedly surprised, cowardly creature.

"I spent many weeks in Mr. Bostock's animal show before writing the book, studying the animals from every point of view.   Yours very truly,
"ELLEN VELVIN, F.Z.S."

"RIDGEFIELD, CONN., *July* 31, 1905.
"THEODORE ROOSEVELT, ESQ.

"DEAR SIR: Very many thanks for your kind letter. My own personal experiences with pumas in captivity (I know nothing personally about them in their wild state) confirms my impression that they are not in any way as formidable as either the tiger, jaguar, lion, or leopard, as I said in my last letter. I have often watched for hours at a time wild animals being trained, and in nearly all cases of the big carnivora there is rage, resentment, and finally enforced submission. Habit, constant insistence, and the superior will of a strong-minded man or woman generally gain the day after endless trouble, patience, and what at times appears like useless repetitions. This applies to lions, tigers, leopards, jaguars, bears, hyenas, sloth bears, elephants, and chimpanzees. With the puma it is different.

"When studying in the show, I found that it was next to impossible to get even a look from a lion, tiger, cheetah, leopard, or jaguar, no matter what cries, movements, or methods I employed, unless I touched the bars or doors of their cages. Then there would be an instant transformation. With a vicious growl or snarl, and with tail straight and stiff, the lion would spring forward with such a sudden bound that I would draw back unconsciously. The tiger would swing his tail in a gentle manner, but the growl and gleam of eyes and teeth would tell what he would do if he were only able. The leopards and jaguars would behave in the same manner; the bears would move forward heavily, but with deadly intention, but in all cases I found the puma playful and ready for any little bit of fun like a young kitten. Even when being taught tricks—pumas are not easily taught anything—they generally seemed to have the idea that the trainer was playing with them. There would occasionally be a snarl and a hiss, but these always ended in a playful pat and a stolid indifference. I used to shake my muff—it had tails of fur on either side— at two pumas, and they would roll over on the floor with delight, pat the tip of it through the bars, and purr their loudest.

"It is the same with four fine pumas in the New York Zoological Park. By waving something at them and talking in a gentle manner, one or the other, sometimes all four, will come forward, play like kittens, and purr loudly. I have often put my hands through the bars and stroked them over the head and ears, seemingly to their great pleasure, but to do this to any of the other carnivora is a dangerous and fool-hardy thing, as I have seen many a time.

" I asked a trainer's opinion of pumas, and his answer was that ' there was nothing to be feared with them, but they would never do much—a jump through a ring being about the most they would ever do, except sit on a pedestal and swear.' Another trainer told me it was an easy thing to train a puma, while a third told me it was almost impossible. The fact is, that with these trainers, as with other men, some can accomplish what others cannot, and so in many cases, after hearing five or six versions, I had to draw my own conclusions from personal observations, and sift out the truth from the many little embellishments which trainers are so apt to put in.

" It happened one morning that a puma got out. I met it walking calmly round the show (this was before the public was admitted) and sniffing at all that came in its way, includ-ing myself. It seemed nervous and uneasy, but when its keeper called it, went straight back into its cage and began purring at once. My opinion is that it would have allowed me to stroke it had not the keeper called it at that moment.

" Trusting that these few facts about the puma may be of some use to you, Yours very truly,

" ELLEN VELVIN."

" PARIS, *August* 4, 1905.
" TO THE PRESIDENT OF THE UNITED STATES,
" WASHINGTON, D. C.

" MY DEAR MR. PRESIDENT :

" I have the honor to acknowledge receipt of your letter, July 18th, forwarded to me here from New York.

" My experience with *pumas* fully justifies my calling them *cowardly*. Comparing them with the leopard and panther of India and Africa I might say that out of 20 of the former we might be able to train *8 or 10 at most*, whereas with

20 pumas I feel safe in saying that we should *handle* nearly if not quite *all* of them; true they are very similar in size and are equally as well armed with teeth and claws, but they have not for a moment the *courage* or *audacity* of the leopard and panther.

"Bears vary *much* and there are but few animals more dangerous. Several of the worst accidents that have happened in our establishment which dates back exactly 100 years, 1805–1905, have been occasioned by bears.

"Assuring you of my kindly appreciation of your honorable inquiry and holding myself at all times at your service, I am, dear Mr. President,

"Very sincerely yours,
"FRANK C. BOSTOCK."

From this it looks as if there were a curious psychic difference between the cougar and the other big cats. I do not believe a leopard or jaguar would go up a tree for one rather small dog, as a cougar will often (although by no means always) do. Yet the cougar often preys on animals as big and as formidable as those preyed on by the jaguar or leopard. The biggest male which I killed was, in point of size, of muscular power, and of development of claws and teeth, more formidable by far than the average leopard or jaguar, nor do I believe that the ordinary individual of either of these species could have opposed it in fight; it had been killing full-grown steers and horses; yet it made no offer to charge me, though killed under circumstances which would probably have earned a charge from a big spotted cat; and we got it at all only because it finally went up a tree before a single hound which it could have caught and killed without the slightest difficulty.

How fortunate we should be if only a sufficient number of big-game hunters would train themselves, as the best field naturalists do, to habits of close and accurate observation! It is fairly astonishing to see how often the professional hunter—not only the white man, but the Indian—is either ignorant or utterly misinformed as to all the habits of the game except those which he must know in order to kill it. This was eminently true of the sport-loving nobles of the middle ages. They constantly repeated the same baseless fables about the very animals which they spent their lives in hunting. Thus, for instance, Gaston Phœbus writes much that is sheer fantastic nonsense about the wolf; his account of the wolf does not begin to compare in interest and value with that of a modern French hunter and close observer, Le Couteulx.

I wish, for example, that I could get trustworthy information of any instance in which the male wolf or coyote has remained with his mate and joined in the care of the cubs. In the cases of breeding wolves which have come to my personal knowledge, the mother has been alone, and no male has had anything to do with the care of the family. Some " nature writers," whose writings are mere agreeable fiction, describe the father and mother wolves as living together and caring jointly for the family; but they also describe this arrangement as existing among cougars, with which animal, as I know, it does not obtain at all, the male having no share whatever in caring for the young, and not associating with the female while she is herself caring for the litter. My own observations tend to show that the same is true of wolves; but these observations are not numerous enough for me to be sure on this point.